Dance and Ethics

Dance and Ethics

Moving Towards a More
Humane Dance Culture

Naomi M. Jackson

Bristol, UK / Chicago, USA

First published in the UK in 2022 by
Intellect, The Mill, Parnall Road, Fishponds, Bristol, BS16 3JG, UK

First published in the USA in 2022 by
Intellect, The University of Chicago Press, 1427 E. 60th Street,
Chicago, IL 60637, USA

A catalogue record for this book is available from
the British Library.

Copy editor: MPS Limited
Cover designer: Tanya Montefusco
Cover image: from 'Human-Elm-Sky' series, copyright 2022 by Jody Sperling
Choreographer/Dancer/Artist: Jody Sperling; costume constructed by Mary Jo
Mecca; textile painting by Gina Nagy Burns; cinematography by Benjamin Wolf.
Production manager: Laura Christopher
Typesetter: MPS Limited

Print ISBN 978-1-78938-613-4
ePDF ISBN 978-1-78938-614-1
ePUB ISBN 978-1-78938-615-8

To find out about all our publications, please visit our website.
There you can subscribe to our e-newsletter, browse or download our current
catalogue and buy any titles that are in print.

www.intellectbooks.com

This is a peer-reviewed publication.

To André and Damon,
for making me want to be the best human I can be.

Contents

Acknowledgements

I would like to first and foremost thank Dena Davida for her unwavering support for this work and her encouragement for seeing it through to its completion, and to Jennifer Quincey who assisted in getting the book to publishable form.

I would also like to acknowledge Jennifer Fisher, Andy Horwitz, Anthony Shay, Ellen Bromberg and Douglas Rosenberg, who all provided valuable feedback at various stages of the long birthing process of the manuscript, and to other colleagues such as Julie Van Camp, Lynn Garafola and Deborah Jowitt, who provided valuable insights along the way. This also includes the many choreographers, critics, educators and presenters who graciously agreed to be interviewed for the book. A special recognition for Robin Lakes, whose critical examinations of traditional pedagogical practices have been so important to the dance field and to my own understanding – my deepest respect for her pioneering work in this area.

I would also like to thank the Lincoln Center for Applied Ethics, at Arizona State University, and Margaret Urban Walker, for introducing me to the field of ethics in all its wonder and complexity. And last, but not least, to numerous incredible students who assisted with different aspects of the research, including (but not limited to) Audi Miller, Faith Markovetz, Ashley Cole, Shannon Smith, Austen Tackett and Hannah Cooper.

Generous funding for this project was made possible from ASU's Institute for Humanities Research and the Herberger Institute for Design and the Arts. Financial support is also provided in part by ASU Jewish Studies. Special thanks to Hava Tirosh-Samuelson, Director and the dedicated staff of ASU Jewish Studies for their support of this project.

1

Why Study Ethical Issues in Dance?

When it appears so obvious that dance can either enhance or diminish our humanness, [why] do we seem to use it so frequently for the latter and so infrequently for the former?

(Stinson 1984: 17)

At its most profound, ethics asks how we should live. Where is the line between right and wrong? What does it mean to be a good human being and create a good society? The question is one of *ought* versus *is*. Just because something has been a certain way for hundreds, even thousands, of years is not a justification for its continuance.

In the case of the dance field, this is especially relevant. While dance is an exciting and vast domain with many different facets that offers a means of entertainment, exercise, solace, personal expression, cultural connection, insight and spiritual fulfilment, among other benefits, the field writ large has not always grown from a deep consideration of the ethical dimensions of its prevailing practices and values. This book aims to address this disparity by applying central questions of the philosophical discipline of ethics to the arc of a dance artist's career, where a dance artist is broadly defined as anyone who pursues a future in dance as a performer, creator, educator, writer, presenter, administrator or some combination of such roles. Topics include the ethical implications of becoming a dance artist and ethical issues involved in the student/teacher and dancer/choreographer relationships. I also consider how ethical concerns relate to the creation and reception of actual dances, ethical aspects of the critical assessment of dance and dancers, and ethical issues related to presenting systems and changing paradigms and institutional infrastructures in the dance field.

This book focuses on concert dance forms that students in North America and Europe typically encounter, such as ballet, modern/postmodern dance and theatrical jazz. These are the dance styles that many students study at a young age and then engage in the pursuit of their professional as well as recreational lives in dance. At the same time, the book also references social/vernacular dance, hip hop/urban dance, dance on the internet (through blogs and other social networks), competition dance and commercial dance. The line between non-profit and for-profit dance is difficult to draw; for the purposes of this book, 'commercial dance' refers to for-profit dance activities related to Broadway shows, Hollywood films, music videos, live music concerts and mainstream television commercials and programmes.

These diverse forms of dance will be useful for drawing interesting connections, challenging traditional high/low art distinctions and indicating creative new ways people are finding to support humane values. For instance, the 2012 YouTube sensation 'Where the Hell Is Matt?' – in which an ordinary young man does an awkward jig-like dance at different locations around the world – continues a series of videos that first went viral in 2005. It is one of the most life-affirming examples of dance to emerge in the last two decades. Matt Harding, the computer programmer turned 'dancer' behind the video, has stated, 'Some people will probably accuse me of spreading humanist propaganda [...] Everybody knows that we can all be small-minded and petty. But we also like to be reminded once and a while about what we can be at our best' (Sandoval 2008: n.pag.).

The goal is to explore issues that appear across the full spectrum of the dance experience: from shaping oneself as an artist to performing, teaching, making, critiquing and presenting work. In so doing, I will consider how power and meaning-making work in the dance world through structures such as institutions (studios, universities, companies) and wide-reaching presenting networks. Some of these topics have garnered more attention, such as the treatment of dancers and, to some extent, ethical issues related to dance criticism. Other topics have little written on them, like the presenting of particular choreographers over others or how major aesthetic and ideological shifts impact institutions. Still, other subjects are well covered in other art forms yet remain underrepresented in the dance literature.[1] These include the nature of the artistic temperament and the concept of 'genius', how the final dance work connects to artists' lives and how morality relates to aesthetics in experiencing individual dance works.

Ethical basics: Providing perspectives and possibilities

As a dance historian educated in the fundamentals of ethical theory and writing a book for the dance field and general public, I am sensitive to the need to make ethical concepts accessible and easy to relate to readers' own experiences. This introduction to ethics provides basic categories and processes that can be helpful in working through moral issues – rather than speaking in generalities or ignoring or dismissing such issues as irrelevant. In Western philosophy, the specific area of normative ethics is the study of what is good and bad, right and wrong. Or, put another way, normative ethics attempts to derive standards of right and wrong. Normative ethics divides different ethical theories into three main categories: these are known as virtue, deontological and consequentialist theories.[2] Each is revealing when looking at dance. The first, virtue ethics, focuses more on the character of a person; the second, deontological ethics, concentrates on rules, laws and rights; the third, consequentialist ethics, centres on results or consequences of behaviour. By considering the central features of these categories, one quickly comes to recognize both serious limitations in the dance world and ways to improve conditions.

This book illuminates the strong tendency in Western theatrical dance – as practiced initially in Europe and Russia and then the United States, especially since the dawn of the twentieth century – to present honourable-sounding statements as rationalizations (often poorly conceived) for how the field actually functions. Whether intentionally or not, moral-sounding (versus morally sound) perspectives have come to mask a broad spectrum of questionable behaviours. These include everything from an irate choreographer dragging a dancer by the hair across the floor in rehearsal to a performer verbally attacking an audience member, a critic enlisting favours from the choreographer whose work they are going to review, an agent working with one of their presenter friends to ensure a company they represent is in a coveted festival showcase and an atmosphere of fear dominating an entire dance institution.

The claim that a great dance work leads to profound, uplifting insights into humanity lies at the core of what may be considered a predominantly *consequentialist* paradigm of the dance field; i.e., where results are what are most valued. Charles Reinhart, the wonderfully charismatic director for the American Dance Festival for over forty years, put it this way. He argued that everything comes down to 'the work', because when you experience great dance, it provides 'a deep spirituality'. He asserted:

> Audiences get the message of dance not through the traditional ways of gaining information. We're talking about a non-verbal art form. In essence, it's nothing you can put down on paper. The audiences get that. It's like waves entering them. It's something you can feel. It's such a spiritual lift, a pleasure unto itself when it moves you […] It can send my spirit soaring. It's my spirituality. My religion. It's a high. The best kind of high.
>
> (quoted in Alexander 2011: n.pag.)

For many in the dance world, this belief leads to the following conclusion: one should do all one can to get the work made and seen. Everything taken together – choreographers, dancers, contracts, funding, etc. – contributes to the manifestation of something outstandingly good: the uplift experienced by viewing great dance, 'the best kind of high'.

These statements and beliefs seem harmless enough, if not positively inspirational. They motivate participants towards achieving a positive outcome that is said to be, and certainly is, of great benefit to society. Indeed, this book will demonstrate that the predominant narrative justifying the value of dance to society has been, and continues to be, that of revering the perceived masterwork and its impact on audiences. Within the dance field, the experience a masterpiece evokes has been used to instil unquestioning reverence for choreographic geniuses and the pedagogical practices they employ.

When analysed in relation to the discipline of ethics, the perspective that dance's value resides in its great works' uplifting outcomes sounds like a moral theory called utilitarianism, a version of consequentialism, the third of the class of theories outlined here. With classical utilitarianism, right actions are basically those that produce the greatest overall happiness and the least suffering for all involved. In *The Elements of Moral Philosophy*, philosopher James Rachels explains it as requiring us to always choose whatever 'action or social policy would have the best consequences for everyone concerned' (2007: 90). As will be shown, many examples of similar-sounding claims exist in the dance field. These form a pattern that, even though not systematically articulated, embraces the further idea that an artwork's or performance's production yields so great a total benefit to civilization (itself impossible to accurately predict or assess) that the outcome not only makes the actions necessary to bring it about tolerable: it morally and aesthetically justifies them. In other words, it is morally permissible to be an oppressive choreographer, for example, in order to produce great art/dance, because the good of providing a superior aesthetic experience outweighs the bad that might arise from being a choreographic bully. I will return to this point with further examples throughout the book.

My claim here is that attempted justifications of many traditional attitudes and behaviours in the dance world tend to be framed in pseudo-consequentialist terms, even though they need not be and even though actual consequentialism is not adhered to but only referenced in a vague and inaccurate manner. Responsible advocates of consequentialism recognize the need to consider the well-being of *all* those involved in assessing the rightness of an act and would not tolerate the kind of injustices that have historically existed, for instance, in dancer treatment.

This book illuminates the serious problems with these 'justifications' and with what has become a collectively passed-down cluster of proclamations and largely unspoken assumptions. Many examples will be offered of this quasi-consequentialism's placing of inappropriate and ultimately damaging value on mutually supportive, sacrosanct products (rather than processes) – namely, genius choreographers, virtuosic dancers, choreographic masterpieces, major presenting venues and elite institutions. I will also illustrate how these valued 'ends' can involve some form of abusive behaviours causing suffering, severely limiting individuals' rights and compromising decent, humane conduct. This flawed perspective, then, is not actually 'consequentialist', as ethicists commonly apply the term today, since it fails to take into account the well-being of each and every individual involved in making and presenting dances.

Venerating 'the dance', in other words, can mask inhumane practices that exist beyond the image of angelic ballerinas, the smiling faces of the Rockettes and even the democratic values that certain modern/postmodern dance choreography espouse.[3] To be sure, especially in relation to what is often framed as 'contemporary' concert dance in the United States – with its frequently strong emphasis on social justice concerns – these claims have led to mistaken and damaging suppositions, not only within the field but by members of the general public. We may erroneously infer that it is more or less decent human beings who bring about 'dance masterworks', that they behave in humane ways and engage in ethical educational and creative processes, socially beneficial aesthetic ideologies and equitable presenting approaches. In short, when it comes to the art dance world, that which we deem aesthetically superior we too often assume to be morally sound. But that may be far from the case. A famous choreographer who received a standing ovation one night might have thrown hot coffee at his dancers that morning for not meeting his expectations.

The problem of genius and allowing the ends to justify the means

To better understand the problem, let us briefly consider choreographic genius, a topic I will discuss in more detail in the book. A belief in genius closely accompanies worship of the choreographic work. This is because of the commonly held belief that it takes someone of exceptional talent, someone apart from the everyday person, to generate a masterpiece. Again, we can turn to Reinhart as an example of someone who has expressed this perspective. He viewed great choreographers as 'huge vacuum cleaners who exert a superhuman effort in generating work' (Reinhart 2012: n.pag.). Such a perspective supports and simultaneously downplays the extremely egocentric attitude of many choreographers, which Reinhart seemed to recognize, for example when he joked with me that 'I used to say, I would never want to live with an artist for more than twelve hours; now I say six' (Reinhart 2012: n.pag.). For dance makers, striving to create excellent work is certainly a, if not *the*, major focus of their efforts. However, contrary to the assertions of a theory like utilitarianism, they are not usually interested in having any kind of constraints on the messages emerging from their art, such as specifically those evoking happiness or joy. Rather, choreographers connected with the theatrical context are more often interested in the complete freedom to express whatever they wish to – as when choreographer Bill T. Jones observes, 'The artist should be the freest person in this society, running naked, literally or metaphorically, through the streets, thumbing their nose at all dogma, at all teachers, at all authority' (2000: n.pag.).

Choreographers in this tradition are also generally more interested in receiving recognition from a small respected group they trust, rather than evoking the greatest amount of happiness (as, for instance, utilitarianism would conceive it: a sum total of well-being that a course of action will produce once the happiness outcomes for all are considered). In fact, certain choreographers (and critics, presenters, etc.) would regard concern for the net well-being of 'all' – catering to 'the masses' – as both crass and leading to poor or at best mediocre art. This sentiment runs through the following statement; although made by Oscar Wilde, many a choreographer has echoed it:

> A work of art is the unique result of a unique temperament. Its beauty comes from the fact that the author is what he is. It has nothing to do with the fact that other people want what they want. Indeed, the moment that an artist takes notice of what other people want, and tries to supply the demand, he ceases to be an artist, and becomes a dull or an amusing craftsman, an honest or dishonest tradesman.
>
> (1891: n.pag.)

Such a view resonates in statements quoted in an article offering advice to young choreographers in *Dance Spirit* magazine from 2018: 'Don't create what you think someone else wants to see. Be true to your vision. Be bold in your choices' (Beard 2018: n.pag.).

That many artists conceive of their efforts in such a way powerfully indicates just how inappropriate it is to engage classical utilitarianism as an ethical doctrine underlying dance practice, since, as Jeremy Bentham stated in *A Fragment on Government*, in utilitarianism, 'it is the greatest happiness of the greatest number that is the measure of right and wrong' (quoted in Crimmins 2021: n.pag.). At the same time, it is important to note that despite the popularity of this phrase, utilitarianism has been critiqued for not caring about particular individuals and for the minority perspective. Philosopher John Rawls, for instance, argues that utilitarianism fails to respect the 'separateness' of individuals with their unique situations, and others have said that it treats individuals and their happiness as merely a means to the greatest sum of happiness, irrespective of who has it or how it is distributed. People often gloss over this when they talk about the 'common good' or 'the benefit of humanity', a move I aim to avoid by drawing out the complexities involved. Those phrases do not tell you whether the welfare of each and every individual must be respected. This is another reason that utilitarianism might be said to be lacking, both in general and in the dance context specifically.

It is certainly true that some supporters of the dance tradition might try to fold these choreographers' attitudes into an alternative moral theory. One might assume, for instance, a perspective falling under the designation of 'ethical egoism'. The egoist thinks that people are permitted to do anything that promotes their self-interests and survival. One could argue this is the fulfilment of a person's desires: getting what one wants, regardless of whether it is good or bad, virtuous or vicious.[4] Such a position might allow the various kinds of problematic behaviour exhibited by choreographers I discuss in this book.

However, certain conditions in the dance world ultimately diffuse such an argument's validity and reveal it as a misguided attempt to bring moral credibility to what is, at root, simply mean and cruel behaviour. Sadly, long-standing abuses of power by so-called master teachers and genius choreographers – and the structures that support them – do exist. Emotional and physical abuse have coursed through actions leading to, and allowing for, the production of dance works, namely the educating of dancers and the making and performing of dances. During my correspondence with celebrated director and choreographer Vincent Paterson, who has worked in art and commercial contexts with the likes of Michael Jackson and Madonna, he summed up the realities traditionally encountered in both these contexts by recalling that:

> When I was a dancer, often the choreographer had 'GOD' status. Dancers could be verbally abused; we could work for long hours without breaks and often on surfaces that were injurious to the body. The music video industry was chronic in this regard. Films, commercials and TV were usually better. If we complained, we were reminded that we were replaceable. Our voices were too often left unheard even by Union representatives.
>
> (Paterson 2021: n.pag.)

Such a situation illustrates that teachers and choreographers (and again, critics and presenters, etc.) who work in this manner are not ethical in any true philosophical sense, since it is not morally sound to claim that overall goodness (happiness, well-being, etc.) should come with the cost of such obvious ill-treatment. Rather, as I will argue in the following chapters, in many cases, the choreographer has been – and (a crucial point) *has been allowed to be, amoral*, to act as if morality did not apply to them or as if they are 'beyond' morality because of their 'genius' status. This certainly seems to have been the case with individuals like Jerome Robbins, choreographer of *West Side Story* and of ballets for New York City Ballet. Robbins could be extremely vicious in rehearsals and was known to quite deliberately, consciously and pleasurably terrorize dancers. His stated justification? 'You know, when I'm working, all I can see is *the work*, for everything else I have blinders on' (quoted in Lawrence 2001: 264, emphasis added).

Marion Kant observes the danger of idealizing 'the dance' as 'a higher form of living, as a higher artistic principle – above and beyond social and political reality' (2008: 12). In her article 'Practical imperative: German dance, dancers, and Nazi politics', she observes, 'If the idea is proclaimed more important than the human being, who expresses it, then the foundations for totalitarian thought and power structures are laid. Totalitarianism begins with the obliteration of the balance between idea and its enacted practice' (2008: 12).

Indeed, one could suggest that in certain cases (and the line that separates them is pretty thin) a kind of aestheticism reigns, in which art is the highest value, transcending even ethics. This certainly may allow some in the dance world to tolerate excessive sacrifices or bad actions because they contribute to the art, and artistic value is deemed higher than morality. Morality then does not even have to enter the picture as a matter to be addressed. But is this really a tenable position? One would have to prove, for one thing, that artists are part of some special group, like the clinically insane, who cannot function as moral beings in any context. Such is clearly not the case, except in rare situations like that of the famous dancer Vaslav Nijinsky, who suffered from schizophrenia. Outside the studio walls, choreographers have the same capacity as other members of society to make moral decisions, and it is valuable for us all to keep this in mind in our encounters with the dance world.

The importance of deontological theories, virtue ethics and social contract theory

This book uses approaches influenced by the field of ethics to challenge such problematic assumptions and assertions. It calls for more extensively valuing kindness, fairness, humility, generosity, patience, forgiveness, hope, trust, equity and mutual respect (Smith 2011: 419). These 'moral goods' provide greater opportunities for more individuals to be valued and flourish in the dance world and for the dance field as a whole to operate in a more compassionate manner. We should not consider them expendable. They encourage the field to be more humane, in a manner keeping with similar changes taking place in other professions, such as gymnastics, which has many similarities with dance and has witnessed a strong push for greater oversight in relation to ethical issues (USA Gymnastics 2021: n.pag.).[5] They also specifically counteract the varying degrees of objectification, disrespect, domination, humiliation, degradation, coercion, deception, betrayal, exploitation, manipulation, discrimination, negligence, aggression and cruelty that are part of a long tradition that persists – overtly and sometimes tacitly – in some dance studios, educational contexts, companies, presenting networks and other dance institutions.

One set of arguments draws inspiration from the deontological realm, which asserts that certain acts are in themselves good or bad largely regardless of circumstances. The word 'deontological' comes from 'deon', or 'duty', and is founded on the belief that we have a duty to follow certain principles. Such rules may be expressed negatively, as in 'do not lie', 'do not steal', 'do not harm the innocent' or they may be expressed positively, such as 'keep your promises', 'treat all persons as beings with rights' and 'tell the truth'. Kantian ethics falls under this category, since philosopher Immanuel Kant determined that certain categorical imperatives exist that should never be broken. While Kant took a few of his ideas to questionable extremes, followers have nonetheless upheld his emphasis on fundamental moral ideals identifiable through reason as important for the good of humankind. An example is Kant's assertion that all human beings should be treated with dignity and respect – as ends in themselves and never solely as a means to an end. Recognizing certain human rights as fundamental would also fit in this realm.[6] As the *Universal Declaration of Human Rights* proclaims, 'equal and inalienable rights of all members of the human family is the foundation of freedom, justice and peace in the world.'[7]

In dance, a more deontological approach might translate into a situation in which a company or school runs according to a set of clearly stated principles, with the desire to create a constructive and caring environment. Such principles would disallow shaming techniques and uphold the respect of all persons without regard to status, gender, sexuality, ethnicity, race, religion or physical ability. The same could be true of a class in which a discussion at the beginning of the semester provides students with the standing principles by which the course operates to bring about the greatest benefit. A dancer who stood their ground in a class or rehearsal and claimed being treated with respect and dignity as an inherent right would also be demonstrating a deontological approach. Each of these examples finds expression in the coming chapters.

At the same time, this book draws upon virtue ethics and especially an ethics of care in acknowledging an individual's character as highly significant in making a better and more humane life. Deontological thinking in the dance context stresses mainly what *not* to do (do not use people merely as a means, do not humiliate people, do not deny the voice and subjectivity of the other). But it is also important to consider assets that would change entrenched habits arising from the power differential, creativity and extreme intimacy of dance training and discipline. Rather than focusing so much on specific acts or consequences of actions, virtue theory considers the nature of the individual involved and the degree to which they continuously and consciously cultivate various traits such as compassion, patience, generosity, fairness, sensitivity, etc. While 'virtue' may sound like an old-fashioned word and concept, it speaks to what people do and their motivations for doing it. To have moral virtues is to have the consistent desire to value good things and to have developed good judgement about how to value those things in particular contexts.

Feminist approaches to virtue ethics, in particular, centralize care and compassion as action-driving values and guide this book. Known also as 'relational ethics', 'ethics of care' or 'care ethics', this approach acknowledges the place of care, traditionally though not necessarily associated with women, as morally appropriate in guiding good action. It recognizes, furthermore, that context matters and that our relationships with those around us affect our moral decision-making. This perspective, promoted by such theorists as Carol Gilligan and Nel Noddings, foregrounds empathy for others, especially those close to you and to those who are more vulnerable. It sees it as one's responsibility to attend to the perceived needs of these individuals in a mindful, respectful and responsive manner that strives to avoid harm and helps to improve the cared-for's position.[8]

Finally, social contract theory, or contractarianism more generally, is useful for its openness and for grounding ethical decision-making in everyday contexts, where it is usually to our benefit to collaborate with others on deciding what we are willing to accept as ethical behaviour. According to this approach, our moral obligations arise out of, and depend on, shared understanding and agreement. Morality within this view is not dependent on an external source, such as a higher metaphysical power; nor is it awaiting discovery by reason, or reliant on individual character or preferences. Rather, it is a set of rules or guidelines governing behaviour that a group of independent, rational people freely choose to abide by, on the condition that the others in the group accept them too. To agree, the members must be better off overall in the system that the contract makes possible than they would be outside of it.

From a dance perspective, considering rights and virtues along with insights from social contract theory means looking at those participating in the dance field in a very different light from the norm. Everyone from administrators to choreographers/teachers, students/dancers and parents would be encouraged to follow the deontological requirements and strive to cultivate qualities such as care and compassion. Working collaboratively to determine shared values, principles, rights and responsibilities of those directly affected by any particular studio, school, programme or company would also help to provide greater clarity and a sense of shared responsibility. The virtues discussed in this book allow us to act consistently with the dignity of others and permit those under others' power to maintain their self-respect. In this way, dignity and virtues harmonize; they add different elements to the picture of good persons pursuing good practices and beliefs in dance, as in many other fields. For instance, dance company directors influenced by this way of thinking might construe success as caring for their individual members and attending closely to their needs along with creating new work; a choreographer operating along these lines might discuss their budget with their dancers and use funds to provide their performers with healthcare for a year rather than pay the expenses related to presenting a season of new work in New York.

This overview establishes the important concepts, inspired by the field of ethics, that I engage throughout the chapters that follow. The next sections of this chapter provide insight into just how close dance has always been to ethical concerns. In particular, I outline the increasing challenges to the dance field that so clearly demonstrate the limitations of institutions and individuals sometimes driven by outdated and problematic thinking and the reasons needed for continued transformation and alternative approaches. In doing so, I reveal the issues, problems and alternatives – personal, professional, scholarly – forming the background against which this book is written and to which it contributes.

The story of Lucretzia Crum: A personal perspective

The children's book *Bad Habits!* tells the story of cute Lucretzia Crum. She is an 'uncivilized little monster' (Cole 1999) who spits, farts, burps, yells at her parents, steals babies' toys and pulls girls' pigtails. Worst of all, the other kids at school begin to copy her. Their parents complain and demand Lucretzia's mother and father bring her under control. They try but are unsuccessful. So instead, all the parents get together and arrange for a surprise at Lucretzia's birthday party. Dressed up as really big, disgusting monsters, they scare the children and tell them that this is what they will turn into if they continue their bad behaviour. Well, none of the kids want this to happen, so they all reform. What is the last image in the book? It is Lucretzia in a tutu, poised in an endearing arabesque, with a halo over her head. The author pronounces: 'And Lucretzia Crum became a civilized little angel!' (1999: n.pag.).

When I first read this to my two boys, ages 6 and 4 at the time, I burst out laughing. My initial thought was that perhaps I laughed because ballet is not usually held up as the epitome of civilized society. However, this is clearly not the case. Since King Louis XIV of France and the courts of Europe in the seventeenth century, society has made sure that ballet often represents Western civilization at its greatest. Then, was it because little girls and their parents do not think of ballet as beautiful and reflecting good values? Again, that cannot be the case. If one thing is clear about dance in North America, it is that many little girls are enamoured by ballet and the sweetness, discipline, obedience and beauty it represents to them.

As I reflected more deeply, what came crowding into my mind were the experiences and theories acquired over forty years of thinking about the nature and role of art in society, and dancing and studying dance, that raised questions or outright challenged certain norms in the theatrical dance realm. My upbringing undoubtedly influenced my ideas. My parents were secular Jews from extremely poor, working-class families in the United States and the United Kingdom. They were strong defenders of excellence in terms of mastering the skills or craft of any activity, be it writing or woodworking. They were also committed to democratic practices such as including community members in making art or contributing to the creative process. My mother was a visual artist originally from Detroit, Michigan who attended to every detail of her creations and found an early patron in Joseph Hirshhorn, who purchased many of her sculptures. At the same time, she was an innovator in the creation of 'mail art', organizing exhibitions, documenting the work and defending the notion that art should be fully available to everyone. My father, an architectural historian and theorist born in London, England, admired the creations of celebrated architects but consistently called for the involvement of communities in the creation of their built environments.[9]

It is against this backdrop that I encountered the dance world – initially excited by the euphoria of expressive physicality and then increasingly more critical of certain aspects of the profession due to a strong sense of justice. Take, for instance, one of my first ballet teachers in Nova Scotia, Canada, where I grew up. As we lay on our stomachs, she sat on our legs turned out in triangles in the 'frog' position, sometimes until we cried. She frequently created erotic duets for her young female students with the one much older male in the class. Somehow her professional experience with companies in Europe and the United States gave her the authority to start a school and convince parents that she was the best teacher in the area. Undoubtedly, she believed passionately in her mission to train professional dancers, but she also gave us excessive three-hour barres, was overly possessive and played the diva. When the father of her most talented male student once gently said, 'knock it off' during one of her backstage outbursts, that was pretty much the last we saw of that family. I too left shortly after for another studio, after asking a simple question that she interpreted as an act of insurrection and a lack of unquestionable devotion. Being a 'good girl', I was devastated for being misunderstood and having my character questioned. Something struck me as not quite right, but I was only a teenager, and my family had little experience with the inner workings of the dance field.

There was a clear difference between this teacher's behaviour and that of many others I experienced as a child and teenager, which indicates the complex nature of this topic. My very first ballet teacher was from the United Kingdom and provided a solid introduction to the Royal Academy of Dance (RAD). While having a rather cool disposition, she did not display exaggerated signs of authoritarian behaviour. Other teachers in the realms of jazz, modern dance as well as ballet were warm and supportive as well as technically challenging. The most telling difference between this one teacher and the others was her perceived status as the most accomplished and best teacher of ballet in the area. It is this trait that makes her stand out as an example of the pervasiveness of this kind of approach in the professional dance field, especially at the elite levels.

Then later in graduate school at New York University (NYU), I was introduced to feminist theory, which launched a stinging critique of some of ballet's norms and conventions. Writers like Ann Daly, Ann Cooper Albright, Susan Foster and Brenda Dixon-Gottschild convincingly revealed from the early 1990s onward various patriarchal and discriminatory aspects of traditional ballet culture, in which, as Evan Alderson put it in his revelatory article 'Ballet as ideology: Giselle, Act 2', we are so devastatingly hooked by our own desire (1997: 123). By this he meant that the image of ideal beauty and modesty that the floating, pale, graceful ballerina embodies has become so embedded in the Western imagination that we can forget about the potentially tragic existence of the real woman behind that image – the real person possibly caught in a pre-pubescent, childlike state, experiencing either bulimia and/or anorexia.[10] Moreover, she is forever sacrificing herself (i.e., dying) in male patriarchal narratives that seem to maintain the existing social order. Alderson argues this in his analysis of the ballet *Giselle*, in which a peasant girl dies of heartbreak over a nobleman's errant ways (he pretended he was a peasant and seduced Giselle, while in reality he was of noble rank and already betrothed to another woman). While there are many other compelling ways to interpret this ballet, Alderson's reading illuminates a particular story about how feminine beauty is presented in ballet that veils a dark underside of the profession.

As I pursued research as a professor into the relationship between dance, human rights and social justice, from 2001 onward, concerns with the ballet world crossed the footlights into the real lives of dancers. Initially, what stood out was the exploitation of young women. In the nineteenth and early twentieth centuries, members of the *corps de ballet* in France and Russia, for instance, were undeniably fodder for sexual liaisons with members of the upper classes. In France, Dr Véron, director of the Paris Opera in the 1830s, opened the backstage Green Room to gentlemen patrons for the purpose of seeking out mistresses. Arnold Bennett observed in later years that

> [i]f such a one wants an evening's entertainment, or a mistress, or to get rid of a mistress, the Opéra is there, at his disposition. The foyer de la danse is the most wonderful seraglio in the western world, and it is reserved to the Government and to subscribers.
>
> (1913: 67)

This was sometimes an agreeable arrangement for the largely poor dancers, but it still signalled an egregious abuse of power. Later in Russia, Anna Pavlova referred to a system where a Grand Duke could come backstage and order the ballet master to line up the ballet *corps* for his inspection, then point with his cane and state: 'There. That one! Put her in my carriage. I will take that one for tonight' (Money 1982: 140).[11]

The inability of those lower in the hierarchical Western world of dance to refuse such commands is particularly distressing to read about. Choreographers seemed at the mercy of the nobility, dancers at the beck and call of choreographers, and so on down the chain of command. Anyone with authority expected devotion and unquestioned loyalty from those below them. This lack of reciprocal recognition of others' rights, except amongst those at the very top of the hierarchy (such as between famous choreographers and famous dancers, for instance), was later transmitted from Europe and Russia to America. As dance as an art form was cultivated on American soil in the early to mid twentieth century by modern dance pioneers such as Ruth St. Denis, the cult-like culture of guru and disciple continued. Icons like Busby Berkeley, as well as George Balanchine, Jerome Robbins and celebrated modern dancer Martha Graham, expected and often received religious-like devotion from their dancers, male and female alike. These dancer-choreographers did not seem to recognize the contradiction between the messages of democracy or equality embedded in some of their work and the behind-the-scenes authoritarian assumptions that continued largely unchanged. The same cultural narrative of transplanting Old-World values in the New World extended from at least the late 1800s to cases like that of my own ballet teacher's efforts in a small North American city in the 1970s.

We might not consider any of this very significant without the growing recognition of a long record of beliefs and practices that make us question the prevalent ethics of the ballet world specifically, and the dance world in general, especially in modern/postmodern and commercial dance. Events of the last few decades encapsulate the recent snowballing effect, as outlined in more detail in the following section of this introduction. For me, the 1983 publication of Suzanne Gordon's devastating critique of the inner workings of the elite ballet world titled *Off Balance: The Real World of Ballet*, and the 2010 movie *Black Swan*, which brought many of her insights to life for the wider public, mark the trend. Gordon observed in her op-ed piece about the film that it 'accurately conveys the essential misogyny of an art form that idealizes the feminine while leaving many young women in terrible physical and emotional shape' (Gordon 2010: n.pag.). More recently, the #MeToo movement has brought more of these abuses to light for both female and male dancers in the dance field. Without a doubt, it is important to recognize that while often less publicized, male dancers have also been entangled in harmful relations with those holding more power – the 2020 sexual misconduct claims by male students against choreographer Liam Scarlett at the Royal Ballet being just one such example (Marshall 2020: n.pag.).

Which leads back to the question of Lucretzia Crum. Could it be that I laughed because, in the end, in her beguiling arabesque, rather than a little angel, she becomes – rather like Natalie Portman's character Nina in *Black Swan* – a kind of monster in her own right? Portman becomes mentally unhinged as part-victim and part-agent of her own destiny as she strives to attain 'perfection' as the ballet world defines it. This perfection has meant constructing herself as girlish, innocent and obedient. The problem is that she is now being told (indeed, coerced by the artistic director and a fellow dancer through seductive kisses and drugs) that she must also be able to access the opposite, namely the worldly, conniving temptress, to successfully play the lead role in *Swan Lake*. The result is a collision of duelling identities and Nina's implosion as she loses hold of reality. With her growing hallucinations, Nina becomes capable of murder but ultimately takes her own life in the mistaken belief that by mirroring the suicide of the ballet's heroine, Odette, she is attaining the required excellence of her discipline.

As she whispers the word 'perfect', red blood spreads over her snowy white tutu. I am taken back to Alderson's argument and the painful realization that our culture too often defines beauty and goodness in terms that, when taken to their full realization, require the death of the female heroine. That the audience's enthusiasm for her performance (the sounds of 'bravos' filling the background audio) coincides with Nina's demented death immediately behind the stage curtain provides the clue to the shadows lurking behind Lucretzia Crum. I recognize that in peeling back the cute image of Lucretzia, one finds an unsavoury message about individuals and their socialization – that being a good citizen can mean following this distorted vision/embodiment of goodness: naïve, childlike and submissive is the ideal, as opposed to influencing others through freely chosen behaviour. Therein lies the monstrous side of Lucretzia's story. What is so shocking is that we continue to accept this as a mainstream narrative even as we learn that ballet's (and other dance forms') traditional, harsh disciplinary system can lead to serious emotional instability and possible physical harm.

However, I also want to stress that my laughter was neither bitter nor cynical. As I began to seriously study the topic of dance and ethics, it was clear that as much as frustration with certain attitudes and traditions remains, much joy and satisfaction also exists, and constructive alternatives occur and continue to emerge in all sectors of the dance field and in relation to all dance styles, including ballet. These broader professional and scholarly contexts will be briefly examined to understand how this book contributes to existing movements in the field towards sensitivity to ethical concerns.

Dance: Professional and scholarly movements for change

Two clear developments in the professional and academic spheres strongly relate ethics to dance and assist in contextualizing my own study. One consists of a series of initially separate body-oriented practices (like Alexander Technique, Feldenkrais Method®, Rolf, Trager, Bartenieff Fundamentals, etc.), which became associated and were coined as 'somatics' in the l970s and 1980s. Such practices can be related to the late nineteenth and early twentieth-century developments by dancers who were striving to discover a freer, more natural way of moving, and the humanistic and scientifically informed teachings of Margaret H'Doubler, who established the first dance major in the United States. H'Doubler's guiding philosophy for creating the first university dance programme was all about nurturing a better person and citizen, in contrast to the conservatory training approach that later evolved (see Chapter 3 of this book for further discussion of this issue). In the 1960s and 1970s especially, various activities created an environment that favoured the growth of these forms. Anna Halprin's radical experiments on the West Coast explored inner experience, intimate relationships to nature and healing of the self and whole communities. In New York the Judson Dance Theatre valued everyday movement and non-hierarchical relationships and believed that anybody could be a dancer. The egalitarian philosophy of contact improvisation as it evolved through the work of Steve Paxton from 1972 onward also contributed to an ethos that supported the dissemination of somatics.[12]

These emerging body practices 'guided [people] to pay attention to bodily sensations emerging from within and move slowly and gently in order to gain deeper awareness of 'the self that moves' (Eddy 2009: 6). Martha Myers in particular was seminal in introducing somatics to the dance world by sponsoring body therapy workshops at the American Dance Festival in the late 1970s. She believed that somatics allowed dancers to move with greater efficiency and less injury. This concept evolved into a strong conviction among many postmodern and ballet dance practitioners that somatics, in partnership with dance science, is critical to dancers' physical, emotional and spiritual health and wellness.

The focus on the 'soma', or the individual's internal experience that connected movement with inner feeling, and individual anatomical structure, increasingly became part of a teaching ideology that validated the uniqueness of individuals and their movement abilities as well as their distinctive creative voices. In this way, some technique teachers shifted the emphasis away from notions of one ideal body or dance style and encouraged dancers to use somatics as a basis for an internally driven understanding of their bodies and of creative enquiry (Bales and Nettl-Fiol 2008). They also stressed a humane approach that emphasized gentleness, pleasure, respect and choice-making. As scholar Martha Eddy notes, 'Perhaps the most striking feature of the historical emergence of each of these somatic movement disciplines is that they defined, and now share, a theme that there are many possibilities, no one truth, and always the option to make choices if one chooses to take responsibility for one's body and living process' (2009: 18).

The second and related development was an initially small but powerful scholarly movement in the specialized area of dance education that accelerated in the late 1970s and has evolved until the present day. Dance education addresses how to teach specific dance styles and other approaches to the movement (such as improvisation) in K–12 and higher-educational settings. It is inclusive of various practices and content, depending on the institution teaching dance and the institution's values. Dance pedagogy refers to the art/science of teaching. It refers more specifically to the method of instruction, including the theories and approaches a teacher uses to educate their students. Dance education specialists like Susan Stinson, Sherry Shapiro, Doug Risner, Karen Schupp, Nyama McCarthy-Brown and Julie Kerr-Berry have developed a more sustained and sophisticated analysis of traditional attitudes and practices in the dance field.[13] Stinson's ground-breaking 1984 dissertation, titled 'Reflections and visions: A hermeneutic study of dangers and possibilities in dance education', brought overt attention to the ethical implications of what was happening in the dance field. In this work she observed:

> Why do we not choose what and how we teach based upon what will make us more fully human? Why are the most popular approaches to dance education those which do not attempt to disturb the status quo, those in which we are either obediently adapting to or else escaping from a very problematic world, instead of trying to make it better?
>
> (1984: 1718)

In this and following articles, Stinson and her colleagues exposed and challenged many of the traditional methods found in dance education and provided an alternative vision intent on stressing dance educators' responsibility to create a 'better world'. Looking back later in her career, Stinson noted that Maxine Greene's writings:

> helped me see that arts education and social justice work can support each other, depending on specific content and methodology. Particularly appealing to me has been Greene's belief that arts education should not be 'linked entirely to the life of the senses or the emotions, or [...] subsumed under rubrics like "literacy".'
>
> (Risner and Stinson 2010: 17)

As Stinson observes, for Greene, arts education should emphasize moving people 'to critical awareness, to a sense of moral agency, and to a conscious engagement with the world' (quoted in Risner and Stinson 2010: 17).[14]

In her article 'An argument for social and moral arts curricula', for instance, Stinson argues for an experiential view of art rather than a product-oriented perspective. She advocates that the art *experience* will

> contribute to a particular way of living in and responding to the world – a way characterized by vision, consciousness, and sensitivity. If we focus on the experience of

doing art, we may see that its essential nature includes not just transformation of art materials, but transformation of persons.

(1985: 78)

She continues to assert:

[W]e can and should become aware of our own values, and not allow those most significant dimensions of the arts experience to be buried or ignored [...] Questions about the nature of the arts experience are not disassociated from questions regarding its social and moral context. Both rest on common ground – on our vision of what it is to be human, and how we might live in the world. [...] It is not that arts education should lead to moral behavior, but that the root of both ought to be the same. If such a root – the search for what it is to be a person in the world – were central in education, we might well expect a flowering of both moral action and meaningful artistic expression.

(1985: 79)

This highly reflexive line of enquiry, linking dance education to the moral evolution of persons, institutions, the dance field and society as a whole, soon involved detailed studies advocating greater gender and racial equity, curricular equity between different dance forms, and equity across arts professions. Sherry Shapiro's (1998) edited collection *Dance, Power, and Difference: Critical and Feminist Perspectives on Dance Education*, Nyama McCarthy-Brown's collection *Dance Pedagogy for a Diverse World: Culturally Relevant Teaching in Theory, Research and Practice* (2017) and Doug Risner and Karen Schupp's *Ethical Dilemmas in Dance Education: Case Studies on Humanizing Dance Pedagogy* (2020), are just three of the important landmarks in the literature. The authors in these anthologies draw on a tradition of critical pedagogy to critique traditional approaches for emphasizing obedience and silent conformity, in which dancers reproduce what they receive without any kind of critical reflection. Such reflection could lead to greater recognition of both the social construction of learning and the potential for transformation, in which students and teachers acknowledge and validate diversity (e.g., physical ability, body shape, race, ethnicity, class, nationality, religion, sexuality and gender), collaborate in meaning-making and take responsibility for making dance classrooms, studios, the field and society fairer and more just spaces of interaction.

Jill Green, starting with her dissertation in 1993, integrated somatics theory with this work in dance education, thereby enriching these critiques. Her studies have addressed areas such as embodiment, health and wellness and emphasized the rights of the dance student to prevent violation of their person through practices of humiliation and physical manipulation. Green in particular has been ground-breaking, with her reflexive manner of looking at somatics and her engagement of contemporary cultural studies to critique its use. As she has observed, rather than seeing somatics as a 'panacea' for the problems in dance training, it is an important tool that requires just as much scrutiny as other aspects of the dance experience. Drawing on the influential work of Michel Foucault, Green considers how forces of power in dance classrooms mould 'docile bodies' through constant surveillance and techniques that involve repetition and habituated movement patterning.[15] She states:

> If bodily experience is socially constructed any experience that moves toward a universal truth is impossible. That is why I attempted to present somatics, not as a[n] [...] answer to 'bad' dance training or education, but as a tool to explore body perceptions. Yet, I acknowledge that any attention to inner experience begs us to ask how real somatic experiences are for students.
>
> (2001: 59)

Much of her work has actually proceeded along these lines, which has not only examined students' experiences of embodiment but also how she herself strives to reconcile somatic insights with postmodern concepts of constructed identities. Green has also pointed out that somatics is often confused with dance science, when in fact they are distinct. While dance science focuses more on anatomy and dancing based on an understanding of the body's functional abilities, somatics considers the mind/body as an integrated system to which individual dancers can qualitatively attend through internal sensing. Green notes that somatics practitioners may be unfamiliar with the scholarly literature on the topic; there are also self-proclaimed practitioners who are not certified in a particular technique.

All of this work, and more, is reflected in a 2002 report on abysmal conditions at the Paris Opera's ballet school. The scandalizing report determined that a culture of 'moral harassment' reigned at the school. The dancers were said to lead 'secret lives of terror' in which they 'regularly bear humiliation' and the staff refused to recognize or treat injuries (Webster 2002: n.pag.). Aurélie Dupont, one of the most famous stars of the professional company associated with the school, publicly supported the findings and observed:

> What upset me more than the pain of exercising during six years at the school was the nastiness [...] The adults were so cold. We were children all alone at a boarding school. A little kindness and sweetness wouldn't have made us worse dancers.
>
> (Webster 2002: n.pag.)

Similar concerns also resonate through a series of conferences in the last few decades. These include the National Association of Schools of Dance conference in 1995, the *Not Just Any Body* global conference in 1999 and the *Millennium* conference of 2000, which brought together many different organizations from the dance field. Gatherings that have focused specifically on moral issues include the *Ethics and Politics Embodied in Dance* conference held in 2004 in Finland and the 2005 *International Congress on Research in Dance Conference on Dance and Human Rights* held in Canada organized by myself and Dena Davida. More recently conferences by grassroots organizations like the German-based Dancersconnect (starting in 2017) have met to empower dancers and educate them in lobbying for greater rights.[16] These conferences have spawned more scholarship critiquing traditional dance practices and revealing their faulty and damaging assumptions.

For instance, in her influential essay 'The messages behind the methods: The authoritarian pedagogical legacy in Western concert dance technique training and rehearsals', Robin Lakes cites certain of these conferences as leading her to trace the roots of authoritarian practices in ballet and modern dance (2005: 4). The problematic behaviours she documents and critiques include shaming, mocking and demeaning dancers; discriminating against dancers based on a range of factors including gender and physical ability; physically assaulting dancers by biting, scratching and throwing chairs at them; encouraging competitive, obsessive and manipulative behaviour in dancers and choreographers and placing perceived authorities above morality by allowing them complete freedom to behave as they wish inside the rehearsal studio (and sometimes outside of it).

During a discussion with feminist ethicist Margaret Walker in 2010, she observed to me that what goes on in the traditional Western dance class or rehearsal space would be considered 'moral bads' because they represent the kind of disrespect, humiliation, coercion and violence denounced by most contemporary moral philosophers. Fortunately, the work of the scholars and practitioners mentioned here, along with others, is clearly leading to positive changes. This is evident in the efforts of many choreographers, dancers, critics, presenters and administrators who uniquely contribute to understanding how humane ideals have been and are transforming dance as a lived experience. Most of these people are not versed in the basics of moral philosophy yet have strong values that are changing the field. Many of these changes are reactions to the training they themselves received. Others have formed these values following developments such as the rise of 'community dance' and interest in making dance education more sensitive to cultural, especially racial and gender, diversity. Still other values have grown out of the somatic realm discussed earlier, which so honours the integrity of the individual embodied subject.

Liz Lerman is one of the most outspoken spokespersons for these shifts. As a choreographer who is also a highly visible public intellectual, she constantly challenges her audiences to rethink the conventional paradigms. A signature gesture memorably captures her ideas. Lerman lifts her two hands into the air, palms facing each other, with one stacked above the other. She then carefully shifts the shape ninety degrees so that now her hands are on the same level in front of her chest. This is what it is, she says, to move from a destructive hierarchical perspective, full of unproductive judgemental assumptions, to one in which all dance exists on a constructive, celebratory continuum of different, yet equally valid, footing (2012: xv–xvi). For Lerman, what has become important is not so much whether one is dancing ballet or ballroom, or is on a stage or in the streets or is a professional or amateur, but: who gets to dance? Where is the dance happening? What is it about? And why does it matter? These questions move dance beyond a formalist or physical exercise to an act that is highly meaningful for the participants and society as a whole. I have witnessed this first-hand as well as in various iterations by those who share Lerman's outlook.

The interviews I have undertaken for this book reveal some of the many innovations taking place in the United States. The statements from sources ranging from students to celebrities are helpful because there is so little published research in the area of dance and ethics; many topics are considered taboo, and individuals often fear retaliation from authority figures. More specifically, the interviews bring awareness to the changing ethos and the increasing number of successful leaders in the dance field who are committed to positive change and are willing to go on record about how moral issues figure in their work. James Fayette, for example, was a principal dancer with New York City Ballet for fifteen years, during which time he witnessed the unfair treatment that led him to become a union representative for the American Guild of Musical Artists. As a contract negotiator for major companies on the East Coast, he consciously brought to each interaction a few basic moral values, including treating everyone equally, refraining from prejudging people, and condemning actions rather than people. He has fought to give dancers more autonomy and shared with me that 'companies are recognizing that mistreating dancers does not work as well as if they treat them with more respect' (Fayette 2010: n.pag.).

The interviews also add an ethnographic dimension to the book. Ethnography in this instance involves fieldwork with specific communities (such as contemporary dance choreographers or presenters who represent universities) to validate multiple embodied perspectives along with my own. My goal in collecting and revealing the insider-practitioners' views is to ground certain philosophical concepts from the realm of ethics in actual lived situations. For instance, the values of joy, happiness, honour and respect of diversity raised in virtue theory find expression in the humour Sean Curran uses in studio classes. Curran, a former dancer with Bill T. Jones/Arnie Zane Company, sometimes, turns to wit as a means to credit past innovators and to bring a quality of lightness to counteract the harsh critiques he experienced in some of his own college dance classes. I experienced his light-hearted spirit during a conversation when he shared that he had developed a 'greatest hits of back warm ups' and 'a *rond de jambe* sequence that had the speed and accuracy of a Balanchine exercise yet sense of release of Trisha Brown' (Curran 2010: n.pag.). (In other words, a sequence that blends ballet with postmodern dance.) For Curran, a lively and talented mimic, humour has a liberating quality for students, audiences and himself. Rigour remains, but alongside a celebration of diverse possibilities versus one ultimate truth.

Recognizing complexity

Meanwhile, I am very conscious of tiptoeing through a minefield in this book. There are a number of serious issues and problems to consider to provide a full picture of the interaction between dance and ethics. Perhaps most obvious is that it would be easy to denounce certain attitudes and behaviours and advo-cate for others in a self-righteous manner. The reality is that the topic is much more multi-layered than it may initially seem. People and situations are complex. Disciplines have their histories and hierarchies. Institutions wield incredible power. Authors are individuals with distinct histories and goals. So how does one balance transparency and self-reflexivity with effective arguments and evidence to genu-inely move readers?

For instance, I recognize the importance of not framing ethics (or dance) in a black-and-white manner of 'bad' versus 'good'. Let us return to the example of a female ballet dancer shifting into an arabesque, leg stretched out high behind her. On the one side, as noted earlier, we can make a strong argument for denouncing it is a 'bad' image embodying the patriarchal state's domination of the ethereal female body. However, as Jennifer Fisher (1998) has argued, and as I will emphasize throughout the book, other perspectives are also possible. For example, her detailed ethnographic research on a *Nutcracker* staged in Leesburg, Virginia indicated that when many girls watch and experience ballet as part of a close-knit, highly community-oriented event, what usually attracts them is the strength of the female dancers (especially the Sugar Plum Fairy) – not her role as a patriarchal puppet. To many of them, and for the female director of the time, Sheila Hoffman-Robertson, the ballerina could be a role model of female power. This is because, amongst other elements, girls perceive the dancer performing incredible feats of strength and control as she stands in her pointe shoes. She dominates the spotlight, leaving the boys in the shadows.

During research for this book, specific issues also quickly surfaced regarding the academic disciplines of dance and ethics. Perhaps most challenging was my growing awareness that while dance studies are dominated by a view common to the humanities generally – that elements of culture are socially constructed according to time and place – normative ethics argues for particular positions largely regardless of these factors. Ethicists might see entering a more historically contextualized realm of conversation as the terrain of metaethics, which strives to understand the nature of ethical statements, attitudes, properties and judgments. Along with this comes the fraught question of whether what is morally acceptable changes or depends on timeless views about what should be morally acceptable. It is difficult for us to not see morality as being just as historically and culturally shaped as any other aspect of society, so I will periodically revisit this point. Nonetheless, my overall aim is to question long-standing myths in the dance field with strong reasoning based on arguments influenced by the realm of normative ethics.

Simultaneously, and perhaps as an ironic counterpoint, the dancers and choreographers I spoke with sometimes seemed to think that ethics is a fairly simple, one-sided entity, rather than a multiple, ever-evolving field of theories and practices. They believed that if they called something 'ethical', it necessarily meant the same thing to everyone and always denoted something like 'fair, decent, principled and just'. In this way, they started to appropriate the term to provide a kind of undisputable rationalization of their own actions, as if calling their behaviour ethical made it automatically and unquestionably 'good'.

Meanwhile, those with a strong moral agenda, within both conservative religious circles and radical leftist contexts, can perceive dance – in its broadest form – in an equally simplistic way. For instance, in its association with sexual intimacy in the popular imagination, dance has a long history of being regarded as the Devil's work. In fact, an entire body of 'anti-dance' literature exists, written mostly by Christian clergy between the seventeenth and nineteenth centuries.[17] These diatribes usually targeted social dancing between members of the opposite sex, during which women's virtue was seen to be gravely at risk. Social dancing, critics declared, would lead to illicit sex, adultery and worse (like death from chills caught at balls). They drew their arguments from the Bible, from contemporary ideas regarding women's delicate constitutions and from perceptions regarding the proper use of time for more appropriate Christian acts of piety and industriousness. These critics also made unflattering references to savages and animals. Such talk did not stop people from waltzing, but the eroticized image of dance has persisted beyond the imagined perspective of a few religious zealots. As of today in the United States, the first amendment protects concert dance but not social dancing, while exotic dance exists in a grey area of constant legal assault (the US Supreme Court removed social dancing from First Amendment protection in the 1989 decision *City of Dallas* v. *Stanglin,* where it was successfully argued that social dancing – unlike music used in such dancing – is not an expressive, communicative act).[18]

Other problems reside in the structure of today's academic dance field. Many still perceive dance education as a marginalized specialization within dance studies. The old adage that 'those who can, do, and those who can't, teach' can become, in the academic setting, 'those who can, either become dancers or choreographers or study dance history and theory and receive a Ph.D., and those who cannot, study dance education and receive an Ed.D.' (with the implicit and often explicit assumption that it is inferior to a Ph.D. or a professional career). Risner has astutely observed that

> it is important to acknowledge the powerful polemic of "artist versus educator" in postsecondary education that positions dance education faculty and future teachers in a distinctly inferior position in which a commitment to teaching is grossly under-valued in dance education faculty and students' work.

> (2008: 75)

Finally, anti-humanist elements exist in certain strands of contemporary theory in performance and dance studies, which are not in alignment with the more humanist tradition in ethics discussed in this book. Drawing on the work of post-structuralist theorists like Jacques Derrida and Michel Foucault, supporters of anti-humanism sometimes deny humans as rationally autonomous and capable of any free choice and therefore as morally responsible for their actions. According to extreme versions of these views, *everything* is socially constructed, or 'text', in which all meaning is based on a play of differences between linguistic signs and there is no objective reality whatsoever.[19] Such views certainly fit with moral theories that share similar kinds of values (such as extreme ethical relativism, for instance) and even what is arguably a form of amorality, but they are anathema to the notion of human rights and moral theories that validate human experience as real and significant, which is an assumption of this book.[20]

Such extremist views do not align with my worldview and experiences, especially after 2000. At that time, I befriended a newly arrived family from Afghanistan and began working with women refugees from war-torn countries. I also edited two books and helped to organize the international conference concerning dance, human rights and social justice in Montreal (see Jackson 2004, 2008). These books and conference papers speak of deeply experienced hurt and suffering and the kinds of behaviours that counter those conditions. I believe, based on ongoing encounters, that care, help, affirmation, integrity and compassion were impactful antidotes, over and over again. Discourses that tried to take an amoral stance, deny the reality of torture or justify cruelty in the name of postmodern freedom, ethical relativism and/or a challenge to generally accepted norms within democratic societies simply did not make sense in those contexts.

Choosing a voice and a path

Ultimately, the heart of this book is a narrative about the tension between long-entrenched norms, a belief in basic human rights and the cultivation of certain caring and empathic values that encourage the development and application of moral reasoning applied in particular contexts. In terms of structure, the book follows the arc of a dance artist's career, considering the kinds of ethical issues faced as you, the reader, may train, teach, choreograph, critique and/or present work and how you navigate large institutions facing major changes. Each of the chapters presents examples and scenarios along with historical context and an analysis of different perspectives that lead to a variety of outcomes. Carefully selected choreographers, teachers, curators and companies sometimes appear as examples of a particular perspective in order to emphasize a particular point.

As much as possible, I provide models and emphasize those approaches and actions that create a more humane and peaceful world. In this sense, I share the views of Carol Becker, whose writings advocate a prominent place for artists in public life as potential transformers of consciousness leading to a utopian society.[21] I also embrace the insights of Richard Shusterman, who regards bodily consciousness and experience, within the context of the arts, as a means to enlarging one's 'cognition and capacities for virtue and happiness' (2008: xii).[22] However, the fundamental value of studying dance and ethics lies less in providing specific answers or asserting dogmatic views than in bringing vibrancy, awareness and sensitivity to the many ethical choices we all face on a daily basis. This means that I strive to signal the complexity of situations and provide resources to encourage readers to form their own conclusions.

The worth of studying dance and ethics also lies in our awareness of the continuum between the individual on the one hand and institutions, organizations and networks on the other. Certainly, power works in such effective ways that it is very hard to critique deeply embedded attitudes and practices on an individual basis. Schools, studios, universities, companies and factions of society all develop distinct discourses that make individual resistance difficult, especially when embodied by the leadership. Similarly, presenters act as powerful gatekeepers, dictating who is seen and who remains invisible. Newspapers and their dance critics do the same. The result is that many people simply accept the established traditions and either stick it out or leave the field completely. Higher-ups who have their own agendas and the ability to humiliate anyone they deem a troublemaker can effectively silence those who know other options are available. At the same time, individuals do make up these larger structures, and this book concludes that those in positions of authority have a moral responsibility to the field and to society to be just as self-reflective as any other persons, if not more so.

I am a trained dancer, dance scholar and a mother, who values connecting with members of the varied communities of which I have been a part. For me, this has meant searching for ways to bridge the personal and scholarly in order to stimulate thought and action in many different kinds of readers, whether they be from the professional, academic or amateur dance worlds or are more general lovers of the arts and humanities. In the spirit of recent creative nonfiction, I sometimes turn to personal narrative and storytelling as well as a more conventional academic style of writing to achieve this.[23] As I searched for a way to think about dance and ethics, the experience of reading Lucretzia's story to my sons ultimately helped lead me to this conclusion. It raised many of the issues that I will explore in this book and offered me a human, playful 'voice' with which to convey them. Such a voice reflects my personality and sense of optimism for the field. In many cases, there may be no simple answers and many difficult decisions, yet the creative act of thinking and moving through possible alternatives, as sketched in the following pages, will hopefully benefit those in the field of dance and beyond.

NOTES

1. Most texts on aesthetics and ethics make references to visual art, literature, drama, poetry and opera. See for instance *Art and Morality*, eds. Jose Bermudez and Sebastian Gardner (London: Routledge, 2006). A couple of exceptions are the following: in *Multiple Intelligences Reconsidered*, edited by Joe L. Kincheloe, Donald Blumenfeld-Jones critiques the traditional notion of genius; also see Beatrice Allegranti, 'Ethics and body politics: interdisciplinary possibilities for embodied psychotherapeutic practice and research' for interesting discussions of how people experience ethics at a bodily level. Canadian philosopher Francis Sparshott has focused on dance, although with a limited reflection on its ethical dimensions. See Francis Sparshott, *Off the Ground: First Steps Towards a Philosophical Consideration of Dance* (Princeton: Princeton University Press, 1988), and Francis Sparshott, *A Measured Pace: Towards a Philosophical Understanding of the Arts of Dance* (Darby: Diane Publishing Company, 1995). Larry Shiner provides an insightful examination of changing perceptions of artists in *The Invention of Art: A Cultural History* (Chicago: University of Chicago Press, 2003). Susan Bennett provides a valuable overview of the changing nature of audience receptions of performance in *Theatre Audiences: A Theory of Production and Reception* (London: Routledge, 1990).

2. For an introduction to normative ethics, see James Rachels and Stuart Rachels, *The Elements of Moral Philosophy* (New York: McGraw-Hill, 2007). Another excellent beginner reference is Steve Wilkens, *Beyond Bumper Sticker Ethics: An Introduction to Theories of Right and Wrong* 2nd ed. (Westmont: InterVarsity Press).

3. This is a point also made by Deirdre Kelly in *Ballerina: Sex, Scandal, and Suffering Behind the Symbol of Perfection* (Douglas and McIntyre/Greystone, 2012).

4. I would like to acknowledge the contribution here of philosopher Douglas Portmore, who explained to me that this view might be termed 'preference egoism'.

5. The first international book on the ethics of sports coaching is from 2011 (see Hardman and Jones).

6. For a fuller discussion of the relation between dance and human rights see *Right to Dance: Dancing for Rights* ed. Naomi Jackson (Banff: Banff Centre for Press, 2004), and *Dance, Human Rights, and Social Justice: Dignity in Motion*, eds. Naomi Jackson and Toni Shapiro-Phim (Lanham: Scarecrow Press, 2008).

7. https://www.un.org/en/udhrbook/pdf/udhr_booklet_en_web.pdf. Accessed 19 July 2022.

8. For more on the ethics of care see Daniel Engster, 'The nature of caring and the obligation to care', in *The Heart of Justice: Care Ethics and Political Theory* (Oxford University Press, 2007), Oxford Scholarship Online, https://www.oxfordscholarship.com/view/10.1093/acpr of:oso/9780199214358.001.0001/acprof-9780199214358-chapter-2. Accessed 28 May 2020. As well as *Performing Care: New Perspectives on Socially Engaged Performance*, ed. James Thompson and Amanda Stuart Fisher (Manchester University Press, 2020).

9. See for instance Anthony Jackson, *Reconstructing Architecture for the Twenty-first Century: An Inquiry into the Architect's World* (University of Toronto Press, 1995).

10. Many studies exist related to body image and the young girls drawn to ballet. See for instance, Paula T. Kelso (2003), 'Behind the curtain: The body, control, and ballet', *Edwardsville Journal of Sociology* 3:2, pp. 1–11.

11. This interesting anecdote derives from an interview with Pavlova in Indiana during an American tour. Note that discussions of exploitation of male dancers is also evident historically and more recently. Doug Risner's work examines this topic in relation to young male students, while Courtney Miller Jr. and Tim Stevenson consider the topic in *The Business of Dance: Everything You Need to Know About the Hollywood Dance Industry* (Miller/Stevenson Publishing, 2010).

12. For more information on these various trends see Ann Daly, *Done into Dance: Isadora Duncan in America*, 2nd ed. (Middletown: Wesleyan University Press, 2002); Janice Ross, *Moving Lessons: Margaret H'Doubler and the Beginning of Dance in American Education* (Madison: University of Wisconsin Press, 2000); Sally Banes, *Democracy's Body: Judson Dance Theatre, 1962–1964*, 2nd ed. (Durham: Duke University Press, 1993) and Cynthia Novack, *Sharing the Dance: Contact Improvisation and American Culture* (Madison: University of Wisconsin Press, 1990).

13. See David Purpel's, *The Moral & Spiritual Crisis in Education* (first published in 1989). Purpel's influence has been extensive in dance education since many of the leading dance education experts pursued graduate studies (at the University of North Carolina, Greensboro) and/or have collaborated with him on publications, including Susan Stinson, Sherry Shapiro and Doug Risner. Sylvie Fortin, based in Montreal, Canada, has also been a major contributor to this field. See her major work, *Danse et Santé* (Quebec City: Presses de l'Université du Québec, 2008).

14. See Maxine Greene, *Landscapes of Learning* (New York: Teachers College Press, 1978), 162 and Maxine Greene, *The Dialectic of Freedom* (New York: Teachers College Press, 1988), 13.

15. For more on Michel Foucault and his concept of 'docile bodies' see Michel Foucault, *Discipline and Punish: The Birth of the Prison* (New York: Random House, 1975).

16. See, for instance Deborah Jowitt et al., *Not Just Any Body: Advancing Health, Well-Being and Excellence in Dance and Dancers* (Owen Sound, Ontario: Ginger Press, 2001); Janice D. LaPointe-Crump and Juliette Willis, eds., *Dancing in the Millennium: An International Conference Proceedings*, 2000. *Proceedings: International Dance Conference Ethics and Politics Embodied in Dance* (2004), http://www.dancethics.com/eng/purpose.html. Accessed 15 June 2021. See information on the second conference of Dancers connect at http://www.dancersconnect.de/fileadmin/pdf/2018–04–09_EN_summary__2nd_conference_2018–02–19.pdf. Accessed 15 June 2021.

17. For more on this literature, see Elizabeth Aldrich, 'Plunge not into the mire of worldly folly: Nineteenth-century and early twentieth-century religious objections to social dance in the United States', *Dance, Human Rights, and Social Justice: Dignity in Motion*, eds. Naomi Jackson and Toni Shapiro-Phim (Lanham: Scarecrow Press, 2008). Aldrich points out the fascinating tension between these views and the evident engagement through the same period of social dancing amongst members of the middle class as an acceptable and pleasurable means of demonstrating one's place in polite society.

18. For a good overview of the issues related to social dancing being portrayed in the United States as a kind of 'conduct' rather than 'speech', see Dawn Springer, 'The right to move: an examination of dance, cabaret laws, and social movements', *Proceedings of the Society of Dance History Scholars*, June 2006, pp. 117–23. For more on attacks on exotic dancing in the USA from the Christian right see Judith Lynn Hanna, *Naked Truth* (2012).

19. For a good overview of anti-humanism see Kieran Durkin, 'Anti-humanism: A radical humanist defense', in *The Radical Humanism of Erich Fromm: Critical Political Theory and Radical Practice* (New York: Palgrave Macmillan, 2014), 129–64.

20. For an excellent analysis of this trend and the association of such a position with Nazism, see David H. Hirsch, *The Deconstruction of Literature: Criticism after Auschwitz* (Providence: Brown University Press, 1991).

21. See Carol Becker, *Social Responsibility and the Place of the Artist in Society* (Chicago, IL: Lake View Press, 1990) and *Surpassing the Spectacle: Global Transformations and the Changing Politics of Art* (Lanham: Rowman & Littlefield Publishers, 2002).

22. Also see Joni Maya Cherbo and Margaret J. Wyszomirski, *The Public Life of the Arts in America* (Piscataway: Rutgers University Press, 2000), and James Bau Graves, *Cultural Democracy: The Arts, Community and the Public Purpose* (Champaign: University of Illinois Press, 2004).

23. Many wonderful examples exist of scholarship that includes the author's voice, literary strategies more common in fiction and stories as a means of introducing material. One of the most vocal advocates of this perspective is anthropologist Ruth Behar, as seen in *The Vulnerable Observer: Anthropology That Breaks Your Heart* (Boston: Beacon Press, 1996).

2

Dance, Decency and a Life Well-Lived

My father told me to 'be good'. I have tried to explore every aspect of that.

(Jamison 2007: n.pag.)

Tap dance artist Michelle Dorrance, in a 2020 fundraiser for Jacob's Pillow, said of her mentor Gene Medler that he instilled in his students '[n]ot just to be honest performers' and 'to be torchbearers of tap dance history' but also 'to be good human beings'. One of the most fundamental questions people face as they mature is how their world view and moral perspective relate to their careers. Do they regard them as separate? As connected? And does it matter? Notably, theatre scholar Nicholas Ridout points out that ethics addresses the central question: 'How shall I act?' (2009: 5). And that this question has a double meaning in the context of theatre and performance more generally, because it not only asks: How should I act on stage, but also how should I act off stage and how are they related?

This book begins by exploring this topic since it is so primary to our lives as individuals and determines how collectively we behave towards each other. More specifically, this chapter asks you to think about the value of striving towards being a decent person, especially a caring person, as you pursue a career in dance. To what extent does it matter for dance artists to work towards, and hone, so-called virtuous habits and live a life of integrity, especially as defined by common decency and outlined by an ethics of care? While Chapter 2 addresses this question by focusing more on dance artists' ethical values and the relation of these values to behaviour primarily outside the theatre or classroom setting, Chapter 3 concerns the specific way ethical choices influence the choreographer/dancer and teacher/dancer relationships and why that is also significant to this question. Together, these first chapters consider some of the historical roots and cultural influences that relate to the topic. I also address the implications of these choices, encouraging readers to reflect more deeply on their own views on the relationship between artistic and ethical ideals and behaviour.

The debate

In 2001, a conference was held at Arizona State University on Ethics and the Arts organized by the Lincoln Center for Applied Ethics. I recall that during one of the panels, a presenter claimed that historical evidence indicates that many artists are basically amoral, as in largely unconcerned with morality. He argued that their main focus is on realizing their artistic vision, and driven by this inner compulsion and their ambition, they will frequently take money and support wherever it comes from, even if it means associating with evil regimes. As evidence, he gave examples of several famous composers and conductors who accepted the patronage of the Nazis, such as Richard Strauss and Wilhelm Furtwängler. The response from his fellow panellists and many of the audience members? Absolute outrage! How dare he make such an assertion! Artists are among the most dedicated members of society, devoted to social improvement through challenging the status quo, and bringing attention to the needs of underprivileged and minority populations.

The question of whether artists 'should' lead virtuous lives, and how and whether it relates to their artwork has a long history and is fascinating in how much emotion it generates for those who assume positions in opposing camps: No, there is absolutely no relation between the artist and their art, nor should there be. Yes, there is a close relation between them and so should there be. What is evident, however, is that regardless of the response to this particular scholar, claims of amorality or immorality are certainly not ill-suited to the dance world. In other words, whether one likes it or not, many famous dance artists appear to have been fairly poor role models when it comes to how they lived, and live, their lives. Examples abound of egocentric, autocratic, histrionic choreographers, with varying degrees of substance abuse, anger management issues and histories of harassment of some form. I think of choreographer Richard Move's affectionate yet honest description, 'alcoholic, post-alcoholic, rage-aholic', to once paint a picture of the aging Martha Graham (Noley 2020). Suzanne Gordon has stated, meanwhile, that elite dancers can be 'obsessive, competitive, and ultimately self-destructive' (Gordon 2010).

Certainly, some of the most high-profile cases are those that can be clearly linked with social and political evils outside the walls of theatres and studios. In other words, choreographers and dancers who have consciously turned their loyalty to regimes or groups that have committed atrocities or ruined people's lives on a large scale. Historians Laure Guilbert, Marion Kant and Lilian Karina have brought to light those choreographers, for instance, who shifted their support to the German National Socialist Party in Germany in the 1930s. These researchers demonstrate in meticulous detail how willingly and even enthusiastically many did so, driven by ambition and preoccupation with the success of their own vocations and ideologies.

As Kant notes, 'The collaborators were rewarded with official recognition, commissions, and advancement in their professional careers' (Kant 2008: 8).

Kant asserts that dancers cleansed their profession as early as 1933 when the Nazis proclaimed the *Law for the Re-Establishment of the Professional Civil Service*. She writes:

> They took the new legislation and turned it against those colleagues whom they conveniently labelled 'Jews' or 'degenerate' or both. The legislation had been put in place by the Nazi state; it was being practiced and realized by dancers and choreographers to their own advantage. By denouncing other dancers to the Gestapo, the secret police, and drawing up black lists, which the Nazi bureaucracy could use [...] German dancers were literally kicked out, threatened, and humiliated by other German dancers.
>
> (2008: 10)

Kant provides the examples of the modern dancers Mary Wigman and Gret Palucca, along with other major German teachers and choreographers, who publicly proclaimed their early support of racial criteria and 'closed their schools to Jewish pupils' (1993: 10). Kant also observes that Wigman protested to the cultural administration about the 'Jewish magazine' *Der Tanz* and its editor Josef Lewitan, who was then forced to resign in 1933, later moving to Paris and eventually settling in New York in 1947. Lewitan was just one of many Jews who had to either stay and face the largely lethal consequences of the Holocaust, or emigrate, if they were lucky enough to escape in time, which for many was the end of their dance careers (Guilbert 2012).

Meanwhile, while the United States may not have the same history of dictatorships as exist in other countries, one can certainly look to oppressive periods to see how individual choreographers responded to pressures to expose and thereby potentially ruin the careers of their peers. Take, for instance, the McCarthy era, during the early 1950s, when a vicious campaign was launched against alleged communists in the government and other institutions and industries. In 1953, the celebrated ballet and Broadway choreographer Jerome Robbins chose to cooperate as a 'friendly witness' with the House Un-American Activities Committee (HUAC) by naming actors and dancers who were believed to be communists. During his testimony, Robbins explained his decision to testify by saying, 'I've examined myself. I think I made a great mistake before in entering the Communist Party, and I feel that I am doing the right thing as an American' (United States 1324).

Lloyd Gough, an actor Robbins named, was blacklisted, effectively terminating his career in Hollywood until the late 1960s. Others that he named include Madeline Lee (Gilford), Elliot Sullivan, Edna Ocko and the playwrights Jerome and Edward Chodorov. Both Lee and her husband Jack Gilford were blacklisted for much of the 1950s. Actor Elliot Sullivan ended up fleeing with his family to

London to escape the heavy toll of the experience and subsequent legal proceedings. Playwright and director Arthur Laurents later argued that Robbins became an informant because he wanted to further his career, especially in Hollywood. 'Jerry's ambition made him what he was and was the reason he did what he did' (quoted in Lawrence 2001: n.pag,).

These are just two well-documented examples of choreographers whose actions, arguably motivated by a desire for personal gain, might be considered 'evil' in the sense that they knowingly devastated the lives of others. There are many others that remain part of the undocumented, hidden and overlooked legacy of discriminatory practices by individuals and institutions against minorities in the United States, and elsewhere, including against Native and Aboriginal peoples, Jews, Blacks, Asians and people of Latin and African descent (among others). Does this matter in terms of how we approach these choreographers' dance careers and body of artwork? *Should* it matter? The next sections consider some of the different arguments both against and for a close association between artists and notions of decency and integrity, in order to more carefully outline what is at stake for a dance artist considering the goal of 'being good' in their lives.

Separating the artist from their art

There are those who would, and certainly do, jump to people like Wigman's and Robbins's defence, rationalizing their behaviour in a variety of ways – which we now would recognize as mostly consequentialist in orientation – that ultimately see these actions as secondary or irrelevant to their artistic genius and the masterworks they create. Among their arguments is the claim that how artists live their lives and the artwork they produce should be perceived as two largely separate entities. According to this view, one's appreciation and assessment of art should not be influenced by what one knows of the maker's life. As I will show in the coming pages, it is an assertion a lot of artists themselves repeatedly made. In my personal experience, such a perspective often finds expression by at least one student in my classes discussing this topic. In other words, the view is so prevalent, you do not need to look only to the famous and successful for its articulation – it is voiced by many emerging young dance artists along with members of the general public.

So, how is this position justified and what are its various components? The basic argument goes something as follows: a dance is something that literally stands on its own – it tours, it outlives its creator, it is its own, separate entity that is self-contained. Audience members encounter the artwork on its own terms, aside from the conditions of its creation. Its impact is what is ultimately important – the experience and effect of the artwork on the viewer. The dance work can, is, and should be, therefore, viewed on its aesthetic merits irrespective of its creator's character. In addition, they may well argue, everyone knows that artists are strong personalities who are difficult, egoistic, rebellious, temperamental, unreliable, obsessed by their work, etc. and so information about their character is beside the point to an appreciation and evaluation of their work and their careers. It is just the way things are and is consequently insignificant when considering their artistic legacy. Again, what is most significant in all of this is 'the work' and its impact on the viewer, i.e., the result or 'consequence', is what is important in assessing the overall morality of the situation.

This perspective combines the two most popular arguments for maintaining a separation between art and artist. The first derives most closely from the proponents of the 'art for art's sake' movement that gained popularity at the turn of the twentieth century. For supporters of this movement, most famously Oscar Wilde, art needs no justification for its existence other than itself and its own intrinsic nature. One should not have to rationalize or connect its presence with anything outside of itself, including the life of the artist, or any related social context that may have initially informed its creation or resulted from it. Nor should the artwork be reduced to, or assessed on, its subject matter or its didactic potential to convey a specific (including moral) message. In this view, to do so is to cheapen the nature of art and take away its essence as a unique means of human expression. As Wilde articulated it, 'Art never expresses anything but itself' (quoted in Thomas 1969: 15).

In the dance field, a similar sentiment came to be known as 'movement for movement's sake'. It is closely linked to the outlook of Merce Cunningham and his followers in the postmodern dance movement, who favoured dancing on its own terms. For Cunningham, and his collaborator composer John Cage, dance was about the 'play of bodies in space-and time' (Cunningham 1955: n.pag.). Proponents of this movement eschewed their predecessors' preoccupation with telling a story or intentionally expressing specific emotions; for them, dance was the focus, and the dancing itself was enough. Cunningham is famous for saying, 'I'm not expressing anything. I'm presenting people moving', which captures this sensibility (quoted in Forsyth 2018: n.pag.). For him, the idea that 'A thing is just that thing' is a way to say that dancing in and of itself is sufficient – 'if the dancer *dances*, everything is there' (1955: n.pag., original emphasis). In fact, in their desire to disengage dance and music from its creator's ego, personal taste and preferences, Cunningham and Cage engaged chance methods such as rolling dice to determine the sequence of movements and sounds. I will say more about this view when I revisit it later and elsewhere in this book.

The second argument is one that I will take up in more detail in the next chapter. For now, suffice it to say that the idea that artists are widely known to be egocentric, ambitious and disinterested in customary notions of morality (and even proudly so) and hence that aspect should be considered as an irrelevant condition of their creative ability is closely tied in the arts to the rise of a particular concept of genius in the nineteenth century, although its roots can be traced earlier. In terms of dance as an art form, interestingly, this perspective seems to have arisen very late, namely not until the beginning of the twentieth century. However, it has clearly come to hold a great deal of cultural currency and for that reason is in need of closer perusal, as will occur in chapter three. Suffice to say it is well captured in the free-spirited, egoistic Isadora Duncan, who, as her biographer Ann Daly observes, 'never, ever doubted that she would revolutionize the world' (2014: 4). Isadora, states Daly, 'deployed ambition like a religion. She was a zealot, refusing any setback or obstacle. Her motto: "sans limites"' (2014: 4). And Duncan, like Wilde, perceived morality as setting limits that were to be resisted. She famously wrote, 'Virtuous people are simply those who have not been tempted sufficiently, because they live in a vegetative state, or because their purposes are so concentrated in one direction that they have not had the leisure to glance around them' (Duncan 2013: xxxiv).

Perhaps more significantly, it is important to recognize that this argument also takes another more insidious form that actually leads to a direct connection between vice and creativity. Here, the unprincipled nature of the artist and the community of which he or she is apart are not at all irrelevant but rather, as I mentioned in the introduction, are argued as the *necessary* grounds for making great art. In this case, rather than seen as separate, artist and art and society are closely linked, even if it is in a way that seems highly unflattering to the artists. This view, again made popular with nineteenth-century Romanticism, is famously taken to its extreme in a statement from the 1949 film *The Third Man*:

> in Italy, for thirty years under the Borgias, they had warfare, terror, murder and bloodshed, but they produced Michelangelo, Leonardo da Vinci and the Renaissance. In Switzerland, they had brotherly love, they had five hundred years of democracy and peace – and what did that produce? The cuckoo clock.
>
> (quoted in Gray 2012: n.pag.)

In this perspective, then, so-called virtuous behaviour is anathema to creativity, and engagement in various forms of vices and conflict are what drive artistic productivity and excellence.

This view finds expression in the words and behaviours of various choreographers, artistic directors and dancers. As an example, take Bob Fosse, who is famous for saying, 'I drink too much, I smoke too much, I take pills too much, I work too much, I girl around too much, I *everything* too much'

(Wasson 2013: 327, original emphasis). This statement connects the excesses of alcohol, drugs, and sexual promiscuity with hard work and perfectionism – as if the tendency to take all of these to the extreme is also what drives his 'genius'. Those who write about his work also make this connection as when a critic refers to, 'Fosse's manic workaholic drive, and the many vices he tended to all his adult life in order to keep it up' (Zoladz 2019: n.pag.). Observers perceive a synergy between the dissipations in his everyday lifestyle and the workaholism leading to artistic brilliance. Fosse's biographer, Sam Wasson, reinforces this view when he remarks, 'What he cared about was work. Death scared him, but not as much as the thought of not being a genius scared him. That was the most important thing' (Scott 2013: n.pag.).

The close connection between immorality in everyday life and artistic excellence is well captured and reinforced in popular media about the elite dance world. As mentioned in the book's introduction, in the film *Black Swan*, the main character is encouraged by a choreographer and fellow dancer to take drugs and be promiscuous to be a better performer. A similar narrative plays out in the 2015 television miniseries *Flesh and Bone*, about the dark underbelly of a professional ballet company. In it, the main character, Claire Robbins, is mistakenly perceived as naïve by some of her peers, who derisively call her 'Bambi', and as being too innocent by a guest choreographer, who initially complains about her to artistic director Paul Grayson: 'I need warriors […] I need actual sexual human adults. I can't do anything with some frigid, small-town virgin.' While Grayson defends Claire in that scene, he later encourages her to have sex with the wealthy director of the board (basically pimping her out) so that they can produce the ballet Grayson wants. He justifies it as 'good business', and he says 'Live a little. Have an adventure. It's what being young and beautiful is all about.' (Note the underlying consequentialist argument that whatever it takes to produce the ballet is what is good, so just accept it and go along for the ride.)

As the miniseries evolves, the clear message is that a life of depravity is the way to achieve self-actualization and success as a performer. Claire's deep insecurities about her abilities and desire to excel as a ballerina take her down a path of deceit, self-harm, substance abuse, stripping and an ongoing incestual relationship with her brother. At the culmination of the series, as she ingests a piece of bloodied glass from the bottom of her pointe shoe, it is implied that the grittiness and sordid nature of her life is what drives her outstanding performance in the ballet. In other words, through funnelling all that pain, Claire achieves what the artistic director insists is the only thing of true importance – 'transcendence'. Thus, once again revealing the larger ethical frame as consequentialist – the ends justify the means. (The final image of a somewhat demonic looking Claire gazing towards us, as if looking in a mirror, with the artistic director standing directly behind her, evokes Frankenstein and the idea that she has become a monstrous creation.)

An alternative view: Linking life and art through virtue ethics and ethics of care

But let us pause for a moment, and see if there are other ways to think about the relationship between dance and ethics and consider the value of striving towards being a decent person, especially a caring person, as one pursues a career in dance. This time let us take a different path and try to understand more fully what a 'virtuous life' might refer to, and how it may shed light on this discussion. It is a question that initially seems straightforward to answer, then becomes increasingly complicated. That is because although most people have a strong sense of what it means to be a good human being and can list the kinds of traits they see as 'virtuous', as we will see, in any specific situation it may not be so easy to determine which is the best course of action, even when a person's best intentions are at work. However, such situations should not hinder us from exploring the power of setting a good life as a possible lifelong aspiration for ourselves as dance artists.

First, some contributions to this topic from the field of ethics. Virtue ethics has a long history in the West, and asks the questions 'What kinds of persons should we be?' 'How should we live?' and 'What is the good life?' It is a central aspect of the moral theory of Aristotle and other ancient philosophers, that re-emerged in the late 1950s in Anglo-American philosophy. To these thinkers, the key to ethics is understanding what makes someone a good person, rather than looking primarily at acts themselves, rules and laws, or the consequences of actions. Recognition is made that people are the initiators of action so it is important to consider their character, and what makes a person perform good actions on a consistent basis over their life time. In other words, it doesn't start with the question *What should I do?* but *Who should I be?*

Indeed, according to virtue ethics, a virtue is an excellent trait of character that is not tied to individual personality or passing whims. It is a deeply instilled disposition, that a person must continuously manifest, rather than being singular or irregular in occurrence. As Steve Wilkens observes in *Beyond Bumper Sticker Ethics*, 'Virtue is the predisposition to do good things, an internal motivation that not only does the right but also loves what is right' (2011: 115). While these traits are thought to derive from natural internal tendencies, they need to be nurtured and applied for them to become enduring. In other words, we acquire virtues through practice, by modelling good people or moral exemplars, and by refining these good habits, we will likely make the right choice when met with ethical challenges. Over time, virtues come to reside in individuals as a package that guide and direct actions in any particular situation.

However, how do we know what a good character trait consists of? According to Aristotle, any particular virtue consists of the middle ground between two extremes, popularly known as the Golden Mean, or 'a mean between two vices, that which depends on excess and that which depends on defect' (quoted in Wilkens 2011: 119). So, for instance, courage is a mean between the extremes of cowardice and foolhardiness. It is cowardly to avoid all difficult situations, and it would also be considered foolish to rush into a situation without proper preparation. And generosity means giving to others when you have enough to spare, to those who need it, rather than being either stingy or an extravagant spender. For Aristotle, a certain balance is needed to acquire genuine goodness, and practical wisdom or what you might call experience and 'street smarts' play an important role in determining where that balance resides in any given context. Ultimately, virtue becomes the appropriate response to different situations involving different people, rather than consisting of a set of universal rules or guidelines. It is something to aspire to, and is a continuing process that unfolds over a lifetime.

What is important to recognize, then, is that the 'virtue' at the heart of virtue ethics neither adheres to established or strict moral codes, as with deontological approaches, nor consequentialism, with its emphasis on outcomes. For Aristotle, virtue is a habit or quality that enables people to best achieve their unique purpose. And for Aristotle, the distinctive purpose or proper function of human life is *eudaimonia*, variously translated as human flourishing, well-being or happiness. The state of eudaimonia is not a fleeting sense of pleasure, or conceived as an end goal, but the deep joy that comes with a life well lived. It is the satisfaction of engaging in an ongoing process of fulfilling one's true nature – of fulfilling one's virtuous potentials and 'living as one was inherently intended to live' (Deci and Ryan 2006: 2). As Hank Green says, 'It is the satisfaction of knowing you've accomplished a lot, and that you've pushed yourself to be the very best person you could be' (Green 2016: n.pag.).

While virtue ethics went out of favour for a long period in Western ethics, it regained a resurgence following the 1950s when philosophers like Elisabeth Anscombe and Alasdair MacIntyre began to criticize approaches to ethics focused on rules, duties and obligations, as well as potential consequences of actions. Taking inspiration from Aristotle, modern virtue ethics shifted the focus to motives and character, moral wisdom, the role of emotions in our moral life, a deep concept of happiness and moral education. Today, one commonly finds the revival manifested in K–12 classrooms, where a great deal of effort is spent helping students to develop character traits such as trustworthiness, respect, responsibility, fairness and caring, seen as important for counteracting social ills like bullying and improving citizenship.

In the specialized field of ethics and beyond, much effort has been spent on detailing the nature of specific virtues and their meanings. For instance, being decent has been defined as having, 'a basic concern for other people, their reasons and feelings' (Risse 2000: 269). This basic concern manifests itself in 'acting proportionately in situations involving basic human needs and concerns' (Risse 2000: 269). An example would be an owner of a dance studio who pays appropriate wages, does not humiliate her employees and does not abuse the asymmetry of power that exists between herself and those who work for her or the students in her school. Meanwhile, The Virtues Project, a global grassroots initiative founded in Canada in 1991, is a great resource for those interested in learning more generally about individual virtues and how to cultivate them in all aspects of their lives. It is not affiliated with any particular ethical tradition or faith, but draws from many traditions including the oral traditions of First Nations (see virtuesproject.com).

One specific direction in which virtue ethics has developed is with regards to the ethics of care and relational ethics. As explained in the introduction, care ethics as conceptualized by Carol Gilligan and others, disputes the idea that ethics should focus only on individual autonomy and disinterested application of justice and asserts that nurturing, embodied and interpersonal relationships must also be considered. Here the emphasis is on centralizing and cultivating character traits traditionally associated with women, such as the ability to be patient, empathize and look after others in a loving manner. A range of capacities are associated with these traits, such as being attentive, able to listen and observe, be receptive to the expressed needs of others, and to respond to those in a manner committed to health and well-being. Thinking, and perhaps more importantly, *feeling*, play a major role in care ethics, as room is made for the more intuitive and emotive aspects of human interrelations. According to Cheryl Pollard, 'Embodied knowledge is another central theme in relational ethics. This type of knowledge is multidimensional [...] an integrated consciousness [...] not merely a series of rational choices, made based [on] universal rules applied systematically to each situation, it also legitimizes the need to make concrete situational judgements based on perception' (2015: 366).

Indeed, for the prominent advocate for this perspective, Nel Noddings, 'relational caring' is founded on reciprocity and mutuality, where the quality of the encounter, and its ability to relieve suffering and encourage flourishing are valued. This emphasis on interpersonal relations and human flourishing is something that numerous cultural traditions share and is increasingly finding expression in the dance field. In her book *Caring: A Relational Approach to Ethics and Moral Education* (2013), Nodding elaborates on the nature of the 'one-caring' and the 'cared-for'. She asserts that the one-caring is, '*present* in her acts of caring. Even in physical absence, acts at a distance bear the signs of presence: engrossment in the other, regard, desire for the other's well-being. Caring is largely reactive and responsive' (2013: 19, original emphasis). She elaborates that the one-caring is able to view the world through two sets of eyes, her own and that of the cared-for, a relational process the philosopher Martin Buber calls 'inclusion' (Caring 2013: 63). As for the cared-for, Nodding argues there is a receptivity required as well, in which he or she is able to receive but not out of obedience or sense of obligation. Rather, the cared-for is able to recognize that an act of caring has occurred and ideally receives it in a 'free, creative and joyous' manner that allows him/her to find contentment and grow (Caring 2013: 75).

In general, while the lists of what are considered virtues vary, many reflect similar kinds of attitudes and values. Here are some of the most commonly listed items, taken from sources ranging from Aristotle to The Virtues Project mentioned earlier. I have grouped these together where they seem most closely related, recognizing that the meanings of these terms have shifted over time and place, as acknowledged in research such as Shawn R. Tucker's book *The Virtues and Vices in the Arts: A Sourcebook* (2015):

- caring, compassionate, charitable, nurturing, helpful, loving, empathic, friendly, kind, benevolent, generous, forgiving;
- respectful of self and others, tolerant, patient, accepting of differences, cooperative, peace loving/peaceful, humble;
- courteous, tactful, gracious, considerate, friendly;
- wise, knowledgeable, understanding, prudent, foresightful, moderate;
- fair, just, reasonable, open-minded, non-discriminatory;
- responsible, conscientious, diligent, hardworking, committed, dependable, reliable, loyal, trustworthy, honest, truthful, self-controlled;
- hopeful, confident, courageous, determined, perseverant, passionate.

Looking at this list, it is hard not to take it for granted that these are the kinds of qualities one would like to see pursued by individuals in any ideal society. For this reason, it is no surprise that when I have asked students and professionals alike, what kinds of traits they believe are central to forming a 'good' human being, separate from any context of art making, most answer with some version of the earlier. Certainly, when I used to tell myself that I wanted to grow up to be a 'good' person' as well as a noteworthy scholar this general compilation of elements was what I had in mind.

Many young dancers I have met have been quite animated and vocal in their support of virtue ethics. For them virtue ethics is what underlines achieving the best life possible for oneself and others, regardless of one's career choice. As one of them shared with me when discussing this perspective:

> Instead of questioning whether or not artists should be excused from ethics, maybe observers should challenge artists to lead virtuous lives while creating wonderful work. This is a standard we set for all professionals and should be accepted for all fields. It is part of what makes the world go around. Goodness is healthy for society and by expecting it from all professionals we are reinforcing a greater good for all of our communities.[1]

Furthermore, she continued,

> I do not think it is acceptable for any individual to live unethically under any circumstances. Being an artist does not excuse a person from being humane and living to the same set of standards of other individuals. Dance is a profession just like any other and allowing artists to live unethically, society is excusing behaviour that other professionals would not be excused for.

For this student, and many others I have encountered, striving to be a good person is an important goal no matter one's career choice and should be considered in tandem with achieving artistic excellence.

The artist as a person of good character: Diverse approaches

So, despite what seems like evidence to the contrary, especially in the twentieth century, it is worth considering whether there has ever been a time in the Western art world generally and dance field specifically, that being a person of good character has been regarded as important. The answer is, perhaps surprisingly, a qualified 'yes'.

One time when artists generally have been held to a high moral standard is when they were closely associated with a metaphysical realm, and as such, believed to have the responsibility for manifesting divine qualities of goodness in all aspects of their lives. It is one of the dominant strands, for instance, during the Renaissance and into the eighteenth century. Due to the influence of Neoplatonic thought, it was argued that a man's soul is mirrored in his work. Thus, it was asserted that a depraved character cannot produce works of greatness. Such a view is well captured in quotes from Jonathan Richardson's *An Essay on the Theory of Painting* from 1715, where he writes:

> The way to be an Excellent Painter, is to be an Excellent Man. A Painter's Own Mind should have Grace, and Greatness; That should be Beautifully and Nobly form'd.

A Painter ought to have a Sweet, and Happy Turn of Mind, that Great, and Lovely Ideas may have a Reception there.

(quoted in Wittkower 2007: 94)

Rudolf and Margot Wittkower, who are responsible for tracing such trends in their fascinating book *Born Under Saturn: The Character and Conduct of Artists*, continue by observing that,

Even after the modern concept of genius had made its entry, it was first the exalted, lofty, and harmonious qualities that were regarded as characteristic of the very greatest, while the familiar association of genius with madness was not stressed until the nineteenth century.

(2007: 94)

Peter Paul Rubens, the prominent artist of the Flemish Baroque, was highly esteemed for his affability, wisdom and kindness. His biographer Gian Pietro Bellori commented, 'I found him not only an excellent artist but equally perfectly endowed with a great many virtues' (quoted in Wittkower 2007: 96).

These views seem largely borne out when looking at the early history of Western ballet. While dance certainly did not carry the status of painting, architecture, or music, until very recently its early promoters seem to have more often than not sided with those who linked the arts with nobility, intellect and refinement of character than with eccentricity, moodiness and cruelty. Dance historian Barbara Sparti, for instance, argues that when Domenico da Piacenza and Guglielmo Elbreo, two dancing masters of the fifteenth-century Renaissance wrote their dance treatises, 'their main objective must have been to convince princes and lords, and possibly courtiers and humanists, of the importance of dancing as an expression of nobility' (1996: 51). She continues, 'Domenico's frequent references to Aristotle's *Ethics*, and Guglielmo's citing of the heroes and heroines of antiquity, were an attempt to give the works moral dignity by suggesting that dance was an appropriate pursuit for a prince' (1996: 51).

Gottfried Taubert, a German dancing master of the Baroque period, is perhaps the most eloquent early advocate to draw a direct connection between dance artists and virtuous conduct. In his voluminous work *Rechtschaffener Tantzmeister* (1717, translated as 'The compleat dancing master', but which more directly translates as 'The righteous dancing master'), he saw dance as a key means for conveying 'visible ethics', by which he means conveying by example a virtuous life. He writes that when he arrived in Danzig in 1702, he decided to show the inhabitants that a dancing master 'is, by rights, a well trained teacher of morality, who must earnestly strive to conduct his life as an example of virtue to others' (2012, Vol. 1: 16). He explains:

If the true art of dancing serves as a moral example, a tutor in outward virtue and courtesy, not merely by disciplining and moralizing the human body through philosophical and mathematical ground rules so that all its parts work together and all gestures and motions are moral, virtuous, and pleasing […] then a compleat [or righteous] dancing master must necessarily be a teacher of visible ethics, and, as long as he spends some of this spare time in reading books on ethics and morality, which [activity] itself is also deemed [a form of] visible ethics and courtesy by the professors of morality, he can by no means be [considered] *inutile terrae pondus*, a useless burden to the earth. And thus the noble profession and art of dance, if its correct composition, execution, and pedagogy are applied, in which not one single indecent rule can be found […] [contributes] to the praise of God and the best interests of one's fellow man.

(2012, Vol. 2: 323–24)

The perception of the dance instructor as a moral exemplar shifted out of favour following the Baroque period. As will be discussed further in the next chapter, changes at the end of the eighteenth century brought a radically different conception of the artist, with the rise of Romanticism leading to the most dramatic change. The nineteenth-century revolt with its turn towards emotion, involved privileging the 'naïve' and intuitive' against the intellectual artist and 'self-expression' and the 'subconscious' as guiding principles. With the Romantic concept of genius as alienated from society, glorified connections were made with madness, volatility and melancholy, and varied forms of behaviour that could easily be considered immoral and unlawful. The turn of the twentieth century saw an even greater turning away from a sense of ethical responsibility. The Wittkowers observe, 'The Freudian and post-Freudian artist arrogates to himself a degree of subjective and moral freedom which would bewilder even his romantic precursors' (2007: 294).

Nonetheless, during the nineteenth century, the famous Danish ballet master and choreographer August Bournonville stands out for his seeming decency and concern for others. Bournonville was a Lutheran and devoted family man who cared deeply about how people were treated. When he travelled to Paris in the 1840s, for instance, he wrote letters to his wife in which he referred frequently to the 'moral depravity encountered backstage at the Opera, lamenting its detrimental influence on the art of ballet' (Kelly 2012: 52). During his career, he fought to pay his dancers, both male and female, a fair wage and was more generally known for his non-sexist and egalitarian values. His ameliorative moral and social ideals were closely connected with his religious beliefs, and he saw himself as a devout artist, whose destiny was to serve a higher religious goal through his chosen art form.

Moving to the twentieth and twenty-first centuries, one can see many examples of dance artists striving to 'be good', inspired by a range of motivations from the more obviously spiritual to secular humanist. Some are motivated by a strong belief in God, while others are drawn to a more Buddhist perspective or other religious tradition. Still others do not articulate a direct spiritual motivation, but their records of social activism speak of their commitment to broader humanitarian concerns. These individuals do not typically use the language of virtue but nonetheless aspire to be people behaving with integrity, generosity and care outside of, as well as within, their studios and classrooms. This comes across if one listens carefully to how they speak, reads about their accomplishments and talks to those who have worked closely with them. As I will show in the next chapter, it is also crucially evident in the ways in which they treat their dancers. For how people behave inside the walls of a studio can often be a strong indicator of their behaviour outside of it.

Judith Jamison, for instance, the formidable muse of Alvin Ailey, and artistic director of the Alvin Ailey American Dance Theater for over two decades, says during her 'This I Believe' statement for National Public Radio, 'I believe that there is sanctity in the fact that we are only on this earth for a short period of time. And I believe that with that time, we'd better be doing something good. That was the last thing my father said before he died: "Be good." That was it' (Jamison 2007: n.pag.). Elsewhere, she speaks of the importance of having a sparkle in the eyes, working in a joyful atmosphere, the thanks she feels for meeting so many amazing people, the value of treating each dancer as unique, and how living a fulfilling life outside the theatre is what provides performers with something to express and share with audiences. She also has developed Alvin Ailey's belief that 'dance is for everybody' through supporting extensive free educational and community programmes to youth of all races. These programmes target students with academic, social and domestic challenges, and welcome students who otherwise have little opportunity to develop their artistic interests. They often blend dance classes with those in creative writing, communication and personal development and provide positive adult and peer role models.

Dance artists like Alonzo King also assume a spiritual stance towards art and see dance as a 'life of service' (King 2016: n.pag.). In interviews, King observes 'Spirit inspires the mind and the mind dances the body' (King 2017: n.pag.). He speaks of art as a kind of 'knowing', an 'intellectual virtue that is possessed within all human beings – which has no limits to its diversity of expression' (King 2017: n.pag.). He observes, 'the great purpose of our lives is to realize who and what we really are, and through that discovery to serve others' (King 2017: n.pag.). He emphasizes the development of character over pure technical prowess in dance, and asserts, 'Seven qualities that are essential in the blossoming of any individual are fearlessness, will power, humility, perseverance, patience, love and enthusiasm' (King 2016: n.pag.).

King draws on a deep interest in Aboriginal and Eastern traditions, as well as Western history and culture, in his conception of the dance artist having a larger role in the universe. He notes, for instance, that 'When aboriginal cultures dance in large groups it is to participate with others as their larger Self. There has to be a plug-in to something larger than yourself, or skill is soon accompanied by conceit, and you remain in shallow water' (King 2017). King references the *Autobiography of a Yogi* by Paramahansa Yogananda as changing his life, and one can see the influence of both Western and Eastern mysticism in how he speaks of the primacy of spirituality and serving mankind as one's larger Self. This influence draws important attention to the ways in which ethical ideals central to Native and Asian cultures are fruitful to consider when thinking about the question 'what kind of person do I want to be?'

While fully exploring this subject is outside the scope of this book, non-Western theories of ethics have much to say about this question that relates to virtue ethics. Just one well-documented tradition arises from the teachings of Confucius, where ethics is discussed primarily in terms of virtues and the ensuing behaviours of the ideal person one should aspire to in order to attain harmony. Confucius identified several core virtues, including benevolence, righteousness (closely related to fairness and integrity), wisdom and trustworthiness. What is noteworthy, is that in a manner reminiscent of care ethics, for Confucius the morally exemplar human being is always defined in relationship to others. One is 'born into a unique position relative to other people, that is, one is born into a family, a community, and a nation' and in this way, 'the notion of what it is to be a person is intrinsically and constitutively social' (Santiago 2008: n.pag.). A central question thus becomes 'How shall *we* attend to others properly?' and it is with this in mind that we should direct our moral education.

While they may not explicitly reference such a theory, Asian and Asian American contemporary dance choreographers often draw on holistic concepts of humanity from their cultural backgrounds and the importance of living in harmony with others and also with nature. The Korean native Hae Kyung Lee, for instance, whose company is based in Los Angeles, stresses:

> Dance is not only dance. Dance is life. How you live is how you dance. You can see it in the work, the energy of how you live. Doesn't matter who you are...[If y]ou lie and cheat in your life, you are not an artist, doesn't matter who you are, how great everyone says you are. You must be so clear, so honest, all the time.
>
> (quoted in Hamera 2007: 190–91)

In discussing Lee's perspective, scholar Judith Hamera observes that the act of creation is cast as a consequence of responsible living and that 'this ethically-informed view of creation emphasizes responsibility to an other, here the "universe," rather than autonomous agency, which then gets transmuted into right action towards others rather than creative genius' (2007: 191).

Another example can be found in the work of the famous Japanese duo Eiko and Koma, who have performed extensively in the United States. Their work is very much about bodies taking tender care of each other and connecting with the surrounding environment. They have taught Delicious Movement Workshops, with exercises that draw extensively from nature and that focus attention on a gentle and attentive way to be in relation to others. For instance, their 'Delicious movement workshop manifesto' includes statements like the following: 'Move to experience a body as part of a landscape and landscape as a body; both breathe and move', and 'Look at dance as a flower that grows, blooms, wilts, to be noticed, be nurtured and be savored' (Candelario 2010: 92). And in relation to others: 'Feel everyone's life as an unrecoverable, transient, precious process within a larger sense of time and space', and 'Be with others (present or lost), find a way to enjoy conflicts, and negotiate', and 'Move to create a sustainable culture of peace' (Candelario 2010: 92). Having experienced one of these workshops first-hand, I can attest to how they cultivate an atmosphere of care and extreme sensitivity to one's inner sensations and those of others in the space.

Meanwhile, there are many dance artists who take a less explicitly spiritual and more secular and humanist approach to the role of the dance artist in society. Brenda Way, founder of ODC (originally the Oberlin Dance Collective), now based in San Francisco, is a person who has been explicit in her lifelong passion in connecting her ethical ideals with her life as an artist. In a 2005 interview she observes, 'Values constitute the bedrock of our lives' (Way 2005: n.pag.). Way's past includes working on housing issues as related to the displacement of low-income populations, child-care and media analysis connected to women's issues and environmental issues, among others. For her, these efforts relate closely to 'creating a small world organized around humane values [...] beauty, creativity, and reflection' (2005: n.pag.). When she has spoken about artists, she has seen them on par with others working to better the world. For instance, when discussing a piece on global warming *On a Train Heading South*, she observes,

> A key part of our purpose is to promote perception and awareness, to incite reflection and reactions. I see us as strong allies with environmental groups in the struggle for enlightened social consciousness in our shared desire for a greater humanity.
>
> (2005: n.pag.)

Perhaps the clearest examples of dance artists who currently see a direct continuum between living a life defined by values such as respect, responsibility and caring, and making art that is similarly informed are in the arena of community dance, and linked to what are variously called 'community-based art', 'public art', 'socially engaged arts practices', 'artivism' and 'arts for social change'. Although

they have deep roots in ritual, vernacular and social dance forms, these practices have gained momentum in the theatrical dance field since the 1980s, especially in the United Kingdom, Australia and Canada as well as the United States.
Community dance involves individuals, companies and organizations undertaking
projects that involve youth, seniors, mixed abilities, inter-generational participants,
incarcerated populations and members of the general public (Fitzgerald 2008).

What is so striking about many dance companies working in this realm, is
that they are founded on the assumption that there is a direct connection between
how an artist behaves in relation to society, and that quality art making can
only take place if that relationship is initially and then continually characterized
by the kinds of 'virtuous' traits listed before. In other words, it is assumed that
dance artists should demonstrate kindness, compassion, integrity, etc. in order to
even start a dialogue with other members of society, let alone gain the depth of
trust necessary for meaningful exchange to take place. Of particular importance
in this work are the kinds of qualities associated with relational ethics, which
emphasize interpersonal relationship, and traits related to receptivity, attentiveness
and responsiveness committed to beneficence. As Elizabeth Johnson, a long-time
member practitioner in this area shared with me, 'the human element is the art;
for that reason, you can't separate people from the ideas' (Johnson 2020: n.pag.).

Johnson has a longstanding connection with the company Dance Exchange,
founded in 1975 by Liz Lerman, which is considered by many in the United States
as a leader in collaborating with diverse communities, along with Jawole Willa Jo
Zollar, the founder of Urban Bush Women. Lerman's approach really took shape
starting around 1994 with the two year 'shipyard project' as described in Lerman's
book *Hiking the Horizontal*. This was the first collaboration in which the community
partners (including nuclear technicians and anti-nuclear activists, a high school band
and retired shipbuilders, among others) were treated as 'a full artistic partner from
the beginning' (2011: 50). What stands out in her description of the collaboration
is the importance of asking questions (something that Lerman stresses as a 'Way of
Life' at the beginning of her book), and inviting community members to share information, stories and ideas. She speaks of respecting the people the company met and
seeking to 'listen with openness' (2011: 52) that led to constant insights and material
for the final work. The caring character and role of the artists in these encounters is
further illuminated in John Borstel's article 'Liz Lerman dance exchange: Aesthetic
of inquiry, an ethos of dialogue', where the company members ask of themselves
questions like: 'What did we do to enable people to empathize with one another?'
and 'How did we encourage people to reveal and respond to hidden assumptions or
biases in ways that enhance rather than undermine the encounter' (n.d.: 5).

It is noteworthy that Lerman, along with many other American Jewish choreographers active since the 1950s who otherwise identify as secular, finds inspiration

in the Jewish notion of *tikkun olam* – an exhortation to repair the world and sense of responsibility to fixing the ills of society. Douglas Rosenberg, in his analysis of the strong link between Jewish dance artists and social justice, as exhibited in the efforts of such choreographers as Anna Halprin, Sally Gross and Lerman, sees their work as a manifestation of sacred traditions and a performance of righteousness (Rosenberg 2022). He observes, 'In Judaism, one measure of observance is the performance of *mitzvot*, the literal doing of ritual and deeds of loving-kindness and compassion', and he sees this as directly connected to their deep commitment to 'righting cultural issues ranging from poverty to gender discrimination, to access, ageism, and sexism' (Rosenberg 2022: 407).

Martin Buber's conception of the 'I/Thou' relationship, as outlined in his seminal philosophical essay *I and Thou* (1923), is also an inspiration for Jewish dance artists like Hannah Schwadron. Buber's central proposition is that the ideal relationship between *I* and *Thou* is 'impossible to objectify' and as such 'is the most real reality of human experience, of being wholly and uniquely "human" with humans' (Kramer 2003: 202). As opposed to an 'it' that can be organized or thingified or objectified, the humanistic relationship Buber imagines is one that celebrates the unplanned meeting as a zone of relation. Buber explains 'Betweenness' or *Zwischen*, in German, as 'the immediate presence of unreserved, spontaneous mutuality common to each person, yet beyond the sphere of either' (2003: 202). Schwadron has been devoting her choreographic improvisation practice to exploring Buber's ideas. She explains that Buber's premise 'seems to be about a kind of moving beyond the self "sphere" and into humanistic relation. I find Buber's premise a deeply humbling invitation to imagine dance practice as a sacred meeting space between self and other' (Schwadron and Marks 2022: 279).

Jawole Willa Jo Zollar, as mentioned, is another pioneer in this field, who has evolved a philosophy of art-making based on an ethos of care rooted in her early experiences of the Black community where neighbours looked out for each other. Her leadership model is

> about how do people gain a sense of their own power, and what are the tools and processes that we can impart that allow a community, a neighbourhood, an individual to feel their sense of their own power without feeling like that power has to be centered in dominating others?
>
> (Jo Zollar 2014: n.pag.)

During the Summer Leadership Institute, offered annually by her company Urban Bush Women, participants engage in such activities as the Intentional Dialogue Process adapted from Tammy Bormann and David Campt, which is designed to build trust and communication, and practice Soul Deep Listening, involving healing oneself and one's community. Reminiscent of the ideas of Aristotle regarding ethical living as a lifelong endeavour, the facilitators of the institute believe these are practices and methodologies that 'live inside of and continue to brew over a period of time – a lifetime' (Willis 2017: n.pag.).

Meanwhile, new voices have appeared calling for artists to serve as leaders and socially concerned citizens to help society determine a more desirable course. While there are a range of perspectives on this question, and an acknowledgement of its complexity, it is evident that there is a desire to move away from more traditional conceptions of artists as alienated from the rest of society and to revitalize educational reformer John Dewey's belief in art's positive, indeed critical, role in democratic societies (see, for instance, his book *Art as Experience* 1934). In his essay, 'Artistry, ethics and citizenship', Wayne Bowman observes that examining artistry and artistic practice through the lens of citizenship requires that we 'ask what kind of people artists aspire to be – the ways of being and visions of human thriving to which they are committed – and what those commitments may imply about their relationships and interactions with others' (2016: 66). He asserts that:

> Artistic practices are not merely technical or aesthetic enterprises, but deeply ethical ones – vital ethical resources where we learn some of our most vivid and durable ethical lessons by exploring questions about what kind of person it is good to be, how we should live our lives, and to what values we should collectively aspire.
>
> (2016: 66)

Engaging virtue ethics for its flexibility and non-dogmatic nature, he argues that 'Artistic citizens are (or at least aspire to be) socially engaged, socially aware, and socially responsible' (2016: 66).

The impact of such approaches on dance can be seen in increasing numbers of individuals committed to a broad range of both stage dance and community engagement activities. Contra-Tiempo, for instance, which is an Urban Latin Dance Theater based in Los Angeles, has a vision to create 'communities where all people are awakened to a sense of themselves as artists and social change agents who move through the world with compassion and confidence' (Contra-Tiempo n.d., n.pag.). The company was founded in 2005 by Ana Maria Alvarez, the child of two labour organizers, and she is passionate about bridging art and activism and modelling as a leader, character traits of joy, love, tolerance and peace. Rulan Tangen, the founder of Dancing Earth in 2004, draws on her Native American world view in seeing the alignment of all living beings. For her, an 'embodied sense of interconnectedness', is the foundation from which to, 'build confidence and compassion that counters the rampant negativity of apathy, sloth, and violence' (Tangen 2015: n.pag.). Her company frequently collaborates with Native communities around the USA and in Canada and New Zealand.

Ephrat Asherie, Aritistic Director of Ephrat Asherie Dance, takes much of her inspiration from social, club and street dance, and their inherently communal and accepting nature. She talks about how hip hop became the lens through which she came to view other parts of her life, and the importance of 'knowledge', as one of the foundational elements of hip hop culture, emphasizing peace, love, unity and having fun. Actually, as hip hop/urban dance forms like breaking, popping, locking, house, vogue and other 'street' forms are increasingly integrated into dance programmes and companies, one can see the influence of values associated with them that relate to virtue ethics and care ethics. One such value relates to the ways in which dignity and respect are often linked to ritual and spiritual processes in which the very act of dancing intensely in a communal context – as epitomized by the solo dancer getting down in the centre of the circular cypher – increases one's sense of self-worth. Yvonne Daniel argues that '[e]mbodied knowledge in African Diaspora communities has been revered and developed', and that 'dancing worshipers grow in individual esteem and dignity. They become involved in ritual community service and display social decency' (2005: 5). This same kind of sensibility is echoed by Thomas DeFrantz who observes, 'serious "body talking" dancers manifest aspects of spiritual strength displayed and understood as such by their collaborating audience' (2004: 73). Call and response, in which the dancer's sense of self is always in relation to the group, is key to this process of actualization. Rennie Harris, a professional hip hop dancer who brought the form to concert stages and actively promotes it in community partnerships with his company Puremovement, notes, 'The movement is an improvisational, spiritual thing [...] When you're at a club, you're in a circle-in the round-and energy surrounds you' (quoted in Gottschild 1999: 61).

The perceptions of community dance practitioners, along with the other examples mentioned in this section – certainly just a handful of the many actively enriching their communities – demonstrate the possible benefits of connecting ethics with artistry and linking artists with goodness of character and with notions of responsible citizenship. They offer some historical insight for this perspective as well as some of the reasons it is embraced. At the same time, it is important to take some time to recognize the potential limitations in assuming that this is a simple or unproblematic position, especially if taken to an extreme.

Recognizing complexity: Connecting goodness of character with art-making

Critics of virtue ethics are often quick to point out problems with the theory that have important implications for associating it with one's dance career. They observe, for instance, that although the traits associated with 'being good' sound wonderful, people – and communities and cultures – can interpret them very differently, just as they can what are considered 'vices', and the theory does not provide a clear method for deciding how to act in any specific context. Wilkens observes, 'The point is that differing ideas of virtues are more than just internal squabbles over which is the best of a shopping list of desirable qualities. These are serious disagreements concerning the basic questions of ethics' (2011: 131). Moreover, even if you are able to agree on definitions of good and bad traits, what happens when two or more of the virtues end up in seeming conflict with each other in a given situation, such as honesty, for instance, with loyalty? How are you to know how to do the right thing?

The dangers for artists trying to navigate this terrain are varied. First and foremost is the situation in which an artist is faced with narrow and discriminatory social ideals of right and wrong, which not only threatens their freedom of expression but their lives. Thus, for instance, in the case of Oscar Wilde, because homosexuality was regarded by Victorian society as a sin and criminal offense, he was regarded as a depraved character and accused of being a sodomite by the irate father of one of his lovers. Wilde strove to fight back by suing his accuser for defamation of character. However, because of a close connection drawn between Wilde and his writing, his words were used to incriminate him as proof of his intention to corrupt youth. In one of several court proceedings, passages were read aloud from his novel *The Picture of Dorian Gray*, arguing that Wilde had used the novel's homoerotic themes to seduce his lover. In the end, Wilde was convicted of 'gross indecency' and received two years of hard labour, which effectively ended his artistic career and his life, due to harsh conditions suffered in prison. No wonder that Wilde wished to separate art from any kind of external conditions.

Fear of being outed as a homosexual was also something that played a large role in Robbin's life and provides another take on this issue. In an unpublished journal Robbins confided, 'It was my homosexuality I was afraid would be exposed' (quoted in Jowitt 2004: 231). In the early 1950s along with McCarthyism, there was a homophobic panic known as the 'Lavender Scare', with those being targeted seen as perverts, not 'fit' to be employed by the federal government and punishable with prison. Within such a context, those sympathetic with Robbins have argued that his decision to name names, as discussed earlier, was far from an easy decision, and one where he weighed the benefits of cooperation with HUAC against the risks of loyalty to those he might name as communist sympathizers. One could argue, in other words, that Robbins was caught between numerous different virtues, including cooperation, honesty, integrity and loyalty, and that he made a pragmatic choice in this context, given that refusing to testify might have led to the end of his career and imprisonment. Some close to him did in fact assume this view and forgave him afterwards for what he did.

Undeniably, there are many examples of artists who have been directly associated with depravity of character on the sole basis of culturally skewed conceptions of sexuality, gender, race, ethnicity, nationality and religion. Under Nazism Jews and Roma, among others, were categorized as 'degenerate' and were subjected to sanctions that included being fired from teaching positions, being forbidden to exhibit or to sell their art and in some cases being forbidden to produce art. Degenerates were 'born criminals' with 'sick minds' and 'weakness of character' (Klein 2018: n.pag.). During colonialism, Aboriginals and members of First Nations were also widely regarded as uncivilized savages who were lazy, undisciplined, bloodthirsty and drunken, among other traits. In Canada, one of the consequences was restrictions on cultural practices viewed as perpetuating these vices. For instance, there was an amendment to the Indian Act in 1884 in which 'every Indian or other person who engages in or assists in celebrating the Indian festival known as the "Potlatch" or the Indian dance known as the "Tamanawas"' would be guilty of a misdemeanour (Glass 2004: 56). And in 1914, further restrictions were placed on the unregulated wearing of First Nations' regalia and dancing off one's home reserve.

Furthermore, dancers have found themselves in this very situation, when solely by their identification as a choreographer, dancer or dance instructor has meant they have been accused of indecency and wantonness of character. This is often due to the close association by different cultures and religions between dance and uncontrollable sexual urges and frivolity. Ann Wagner's *Adversaries of Dance: From the Puritans to the Present* and Elizabeth Aldrich's essay, 'Plunge not into the mire of worldly folly: Objections to social dance in nineteenth-century America', provide an excellent overview of the historical Christian polemic against dance, which illuminates the negative perceptions about the body and dance in Western, and particularly American, contexts. They outline the various arguments against the 'essential nature of dance' as disorderly, trivial, anti-intellectual and artificial, and the 'incidental characteristics of dance' as leading to sexual immorality, the squandering of time and resources, unnecessary health risks and participation in 'worldly' pleasures to the peril of the immortal soul.

Even with the acceptance of dance as an art form in America through the twentieth century, biased views remain, often complicated by conceptions of race and class. Raquel Monroe, for instance, observes that 'the cultural imaginary frames black dancing bodies, and the dances they dance as vulgar, excessive, hypersexual, and low class. While white dancing bodies and their dances enact chastity, decency, and aloofness', and upper class (Monroe 2011: 45). Monroe, along with other scholars like Brenda Dixon Gottschild, Thomas DeFrantz and Susan Manning, have traced the impact of this way of conceiving of Black and white bodies on concert dance performance and educational programmes. In their work, different values are also revealed in relation to Africanist versus Europeanist ways of interacting. An example is the principle of 'embracing the conflict' – where 'difference, discord, and irregularity is encompassed, rather than erased or necessarily resolved' (Gottschild 1998: 13). How this influences treatment of interpersonal relationships is important, because it shows that a 'caring approach' may look very differently depending on the community in which it occurs. In one setting, it may involve being soft spoken, moving gently, avoiding confrontation and seeking quick resolution, while in another, it may entail heated engagement, assertive gesturing, in your face opposition and acceptance of divergent thinking and acting (Jackson 2016).

Scholar Anthony Shay, for his part, has carefully examined the ways in which dancers in the Middle East and Central Asia have been negatively stereotyped and consequently oppressed. He demonstrates how colonialist Western attitudes, along with Islamist moral purity movements, have led dancers to be viewed as debauched, lascivious and wicked either because of associations with homosexuality, or sexuality in general (Shay 1999). In 2002, for instance, Mohammad Khordadian a celebrated Iranian American choreographer and dancer was arrested in Tehran and convicted on the charge of 'promoting depravity and corruption among the youth' along with drinking alcohol (Papin-Matin 2009: 131). His sentence of ten years in prison was later suspended but he was barred from giving dance lessons for life, even outside of Iran. Fortunately, these prohibitions were subsequently modified and he was released and eventually returned to the United States.

An overemphasis on virtuousness of character, in other words, can sometimes backfire and lead dance artists to become targets of moral reproach, discrimination, potential imprisonment or extermination, regardless of their personal views on ethics and the extent to which they live their lives with integrity. Another important point often raised is that closely aligning ethics and art can potentially limit an artists' freedom of expression. If artists feel overly driven by the need to 'be good', they may believe they should only make work that promotes a particular set of values presented in a clear and unambiguous manner. There is a dance programme in Israel, for instance, 'Orot Israel' – Academic-Religious College of Education, where young religious women create dances in line with Jewish Orthodox ideals of modesty and spirituality. Their work definitely pushes the boundaries of what has been traditionally acceptable in Orthodox circles in exciting ways, but still exists within a narrow set of beliefs that seek to avoid bodily exposure, preserve spousal fidelity and retain a sense of distinctiveness of Jewish culture (Perlstein 2022). No men, for instance, except for a woman's husband during a solo recital, are permitted to watch their performances, for fear that it will lead to immodest thoughts and actions.

Such an attitude can not only exist among the ultra-conservative, but also among the ultra-liberal. In this case, one may consider choreographers who feel the need to create overtly political dances that align with a specific leftist ideology such as Marxism, feminism, queer theory, decolonial theory or a mixture of all these. For example, Dance Brigade, based in San Francisco, is a fiercely activist dance company founded by Krissy Keefer and Nina Fichter. The woman's movement of the 1960s and 1970s, feminism and empowering women have been the driving force of Keefer's work, and the company's pieces engage text and imagery in an overt stance against war, police violence, global greed, domestic violence and racism, among other themes. At their fortieth anniversary performance in 2017, a reviewer comments on how 'Leaflet-strewn tables promoting the ACLU, the Women's March and the Living Wage Coalition greeted audience members' (Bauer 2017: n.pag.). If the work of Orot happens within the context of one clearly defined ideological and moral framework, in other words, so does Dance Brigade's.

In general, a potential drawback of focusing exclusively on 'being good' for any artist is that it might lead to a sense of sanctimoniousness, arrogance, political correctness and censorship of those with opposing perspectives – though to be sure I am not directing this at the companies just mentioned. Such a stance can be annoying, and at worst a form of propaganda that is intolerant and insensitive to human complexity, the range of possible ethical stances in any particular context and to the grey areas of life. It can lead dance artists to believe that they are the sole holders of the truth and in their heightened sense of moral superiority, abuse their authority in relation to those who look up to them and disallow any questioning of their perspectives. Such a situation has certainly manifested itself in the dance field, with its strong emphasis on gurus and disciples that I will soon be examining.

The problem is also brought home by choreographers who prefer to experience and examine the realm of moral ambiguity in their work and leave it more open to multiple interpretations – a quality that is so valuable in art. The American choreographer David Dorfman, for example, once shared with me that after many years in the dance field he has, 'come to put less import on one's life choices in relation to their artwork' (Dorfman 2012: n.pag.). The reason? He would rather, 'know and be a person who is constantly struggling with ethics, who cannot always decide where to draw the line on issues, and whose work reflects that conflict' (2012: n.pag.).

The need for a more nuanced approach is particularly evident with dance artists living in highly precarious situations who grapple with the desire to be responsible citizens as well as make complex, multivocal art. The contemporary dance choreographer Faustin Linyekula is emblematic of such a situation. Based in Kisangani, the third largest city in the war-torn Democratic Republic of the Congo, he has established the Studios Kabako to support multidisciplinary creation and performance. Linyekula has said that he feels very strongly that in relation to his life as a 'citizen' of Congo, it is his responsibility to act in a mindful manner. This is because there are people in Congo whose lives depend on him and as such, he needs to behave in a way that would not jeopardize their lives (or his own, and as a consequence, theirs) through risk of imprisonment or worse. He is also very committed to investing in the infrastructure of his country, and for that reason has financed a water treatment facility. He has stated, 'I know the state will never help us, but their capacity of nuisance is so big that they can stop any project. In such a context, I cannot say: "Fuck the state!" That will be signing up for the end of everything, including my own life.' His solution has been to activate small 'spaces of resistance', as he calls them. 'My response is not political, in that it's not programmatic', he stated in a 2005 interview with the online magazine *Ballet-Dance* (O'Toole 2016: n.pag.). Rather, his artwork exists to develop 'frames' where he feels free to ask questions of his body, explore issues and be poetic rather than didactic in his sensibility.

Striving to be a decent person while acknowledging complexity: Why it matters

Yes, consciously connecting one's world view and moral perspective to one's career as a dance artist is complicated. Virtue ethics, as outlined earlier, has its limitations, as does an ethics of care, and there is a benefit to having rules and obligations that more clearly articulate what kinds of actions are acceptable or not, within specific contexts. In other words, virtue ethics and care ethics in themselves are not sufficient to move the dance field towards a more humane way of operating. The place for more deontological theories, based on more universal principles and guidelines, including the concept of universal human rights, is also important and will be explored more in the following chapters.

At the same time, hopefully it is evident that there is immense value in striving towards being a 'good' person, especially a decent and caring person, as one pursues a career in dance. There is historical precedent, and important arguments that have been made for artists to assume this stance, from it being a valuable foundation from which to make meaningful artwork, to contributing in a meaningful way to society's betterment. Whether it be for religious, spiritual or secular humanistic reasons, many dance artists and their supporters, have and continue to, strive towards a life of ethical as well as aesthetic distinction.

Of particular significance, and why I believe it especially matters, is because dance is an art form dependent on human beings as the medium of transmission. While visual art usually relies on paint, ink, clay or other inanimate objects, and literature relies on words, dance is most often reliant and focused on live bodies in intimate relationship with each other and audiences as the means of communicating kinesthetic information, ideas and emotions. Human interaction – the I/Thou and I/We – is fundamental to the art form, and the quality of those relationships during the training as well as art making process, need to be addressed. How people treat each other is not of secondary importance, but central to the healthy functioning of the dance world.

Moreover, how dance artists interact with others, especially in the classroom or rehearsal context, can be a reflection of how they carry themselves as citizens in the broader world. Marion Kant has made the profound recognition that dance can thrive in any context, but human rights cannot. In her study of dance during the Nazi period she brings this point home. In order to achieve this, she draws on the famous observation of Eleanor Roosevelt, chair of the United Nations Human Rights Commission which drafted the *Universal Declaration of Human Rights*, that human rights begin in 'small places', close to home, including schools, and places of work. Kant writes:

> *The small places* were also the dance groups; *the schools* were also dance schools; *the workplaces* were also the theaters and studios. And it was here that human rights were violated right from the beginning of the Third Reich and without the Nazi state putting much pressure on the dancers, teachers, and their pupils. It was in *the small places*, performance sites, and rehearsal rooms that Nazi legislation took root and was put into practice. The dancers, too, belonged to the masses that made Nazism a widely acceptable and accepted movement.
>
> (2008: 9–10, original emphasis)

Through her analysis of dance during the Third Reich, Kant demonstrates, in particular, how beliefs central to the teaching and practice of German modern dance closely aligned with Nazi ideals. These ideals included self-sacrifice of the individual dancer and complete allegiance to abstract notions of 'the dance', and to genius choreographers and master teachers who held the key to the 'truth' in order to create virtuosic dancers and artistic masterpieces. The extent to which such views hold sway in the dance field generally, is something that needs further investigation. Certainly, if history is any indication, this is a tradition that is not just found in Germany, and has deep roots and a broad impact in the dance field generally. While this legacy in the concert dance realm may not have led to the horrors of the Holocaust, it has certainly entailed a great deal of physical and emotional abuse. More fully understanding this tradition is necessary if there is to be lasting change.

To conclude, this chapter has focused on the value and complexities involved in seeing a dance artist's life values and creative work linked in the pursuit of being a good human being along with pursuing artistic excellence. It argues that yes, considering the nature of virtue ethics, and especially care ethics, is extremely valuable for moving towards a more humane dance culture. It is also valuable to look to related ethical traditions of Indigenous, First Nations and Asian cultures, Jewish and Africanist ideals (among others), which emphasize the importance of character, interconnection, relationship and community. So too are these values as found in vernacular and street dance communities that are increasingly being modelled in dance companies and concert dance performances. What is needed now, however, is a closer examination of the internal beliefs and practices of the dance world that have worked against these perspectives in terms of the choreographer/dancer and teacher/dancer relationships. This is, therefore, where I will now turn our attention. Such an examination will allow us to build on virtue ethics and consider a more robust place for rights and obligations in a more humane dance world.

NOTE

1.   Anonymous sources such as this come from student papers and statements from an IRB approved study I oversaw in 2010 at Arizona State University.

3

Educating Dancers with Dignity, Respect and Care

It was and still is my belief that learning to dance should not be at the expense of being a person.

(Botham 2012: 4)

The realm of professional dance training is filled with many dedicated, passionate and well-meaning individuals who are committed to educating dancers to the very best of their ability. At the same time, it still grapples with instances of emotional and physical abuse and discrimination. These are extremely sensitive and largely taboo topics that have gained more widespread attention during the last few decades and with the recent rise of the #MeToo movement and increased attention to racial injustice in dance education. This ongoing conversation has been explosive and sporadic, with uneven results. Many dancers fear recrimination and constant re-triggering of their trauma if they go on the record, not to mention the possible end of their careers, while teachers may feel unfairly accused and misunderstood. The problem transcends individuals: in 2020, Ilse Ghekiere noted in her article '#Metoo, herstory in dance: On activism, solidarity and precision' that over the last few years a 'heated and messy social media debate took over looking for predators rather than listening to the issues of oppression at large' (2020: n.pag.). While she observes some progress in pressuring institutions to reassess their procedures, many problems remain, not least of which that there are dancers who continue to experience humiliating and otherwise unethical behaviour as 'normal' and expected, even when it harms them.

This chapter looks more closely at what these abusive and unfair situations look like, why they exist in dance training and what we can learn from the discipline of ethics. I focus on the realm of dance education, which necessarily bleeds into the realm of life as a professional dancer: pedagogy continues in learning choreography for performance, and there has been a tendency for the same beliefs and methods to be practiced in the company as well as training contexts. Readers should understand that I use the terms 'training', 'education' and 'pedagogy' more or less interchangeably throughout the book, but they do have different connotations worth noting. 'Training' tends to focus on teaching a particular set of skills, which in dance has historically meant the correct acquisition and performance of particular techniques. 'Education' is often used in the academic field of dance education to connote teaching from a holistic orientation towards the 'whole child'. Finally, the term 'pedagogy' brings attention to the 'how' and not just the 'what' of the educational process. It is for that reason that much of this chapter is really devoted to examining the kind of 'poisonous pedagogy' (Alice Miller 1990) that lies at the root of unethical behaviours that extend from formal classrooms to rehearsal studios.

My goal is to illuminate how authoritarian, disciplinary methods rooted in the eighteenth century (if not earlier) fused with early twentieth-century ideas about genius to lead to the predominant pedagogical trends of the last century. This is not to lay blame or to point fingers but to provide contextual understanding of an inherited legacy so that we might make different choices where we collectively agree they are needed. These trends reflect widely held beliefs that have become the bedrock of many institutions and also shape public perception. I then consider how a more sophisticated consideration of 'moral bads' can help to bring greater nuance to our understanding of the destructive behaviours in traditional dance education, as well as how deontological and virtue theories – in tandem with other approaches developed in progressive educational circles – can aid in building a more humane approach. Kantian ethics and work on human rights, along with care ethics, provide important insights for establishing baseline obligations as well as a more nurturing, compassionate approach for dance artists engaged in learning and teaching dance. We will see how together these approaches counterbalance a dominant consequentialist tradition that prizes end results over the training process and students' humanity. Treating dancers with greater respect, dignity and care in all aspects of dance education and then during their professional careers: this is the goal.

Understanding the traditional authoritarian model in professional dance training

When it comes to dance training, ample evidence from interviews, biographies and accounts of institutions engaged in generating professional dancers shows that results matter most. This is what is prized: producing an excellent dancer who looks and moves in a very specific way and is hired to perform the work of celebrated choreographers. Melissa Hayden, a former New York City Ballet principal dancer, once put it this way: 'The only real basis for judging a teacher is the product he or she turns out: good dancers' (1981: 33). 'Good dancers' in this context are meant to conform to very specific physical criteria, some of which are explicit and some unspoken, and perform specific technical skills associated with particular dance styles. For example, George Balanchine's influence in the United States in the twentieth century led to an ideal that still dominates the ballet world. The ideal female ballet dancer is extremely thin and lean, with long legs, narrow hips, shortish torso, long arms, small head, high arches, flat chest and a small, flat butt. The average and preferred height is around 5 feet 5 inches–5 feet 6 inches or 1.65–1.7 m. More unspoken (and just assumed) is that the ideal dancer is nondisabled, young (late teens and twenties), Caucasian or light skinned, with long and smooth hair that can easily be placed in a bun. This highly flexible body is expected to be able to perform classical ballet technique in a very fast, athletic manner and employ the unconventional arm and hand placement and other distinctive features of the Balanchine style.

The emphasis on end results often makes the issue of methods seem ancillary, although methods passed down through the centuries are usually presumed ideal. If the process worked in the past and continues to produce successful (as defined earlier) outcomes, then the approaches are deemed acceptable. Administrators, students and parents rarely question them; the focus is on *what* is passed down, rather than *how*. Traditional views towards young dancers are captured well in a statement by Bolshoi Ballet Academy teacher Ilya Kuznetsov, who formerly danced for the San Diego Ballet and Imperial Russian Ballet. He is quoted in 2010 as saying, 'I can give them a very, very, very, very hard time, and still, they will be happy with that. Their parents will say, "You can kill him, but just teach him"' (Levy 2010: A1). The messages here are that the product is what matters. That if the methods are extremely harsh, it is fine, as long as they produce a technically strong dancer and that this is something that parents and the teacher's institution support.

The reliance on, and reproduction of, training methods that have been handed down for the last few hundred years has been the norm in the mainstream professional dance field until fairly recently. In the 1950s, as Olga Maynard sums up in *The American Ballet*, her book about the School of American Ballet's approach, 'Its system is a tried and true one, existing for hundreds of years, founded on beauty and strength and a sense of order. It is an incorruptible system, to which the students strive to adapt themselves, and its rules' (1959: 294). This view is one that continues to hold a great deal of sway, as dancers often teach what they know without deep questioning. Author Deidre Kelly quotes Jeffrey Russell, an expert in treating dance injuries, as saying in 2011,

> we're still in a situation where the ones teaching the younger dancers are those who came through a system where there wasn't much being offered in the way of physical training or even healthy dance practices. In their day, you just did what you

did, and if you got hurt, tough. It really comes down to you teach what you know, and if that includes suffering for your art then that's what's also being passed down.

(2012: 181)

To be sure, one of the most important reasons for any lingering abuse and discrimination in the dance field today is because of an authoritarian 'rule by fear' approach that the dance field has replicated in some form, whether explicitly or more implicitly, since at least the eighteenth century. It was then, when ballet was first becoming professionalized, that the Paris Opera set the stage for what was to come not only in ballet but also in modern dance, theatrical jazz and the commercial dance sector. A manuscript from the turn of the eighteenth century describes the conditions of the dancers from that early period:

> Their fate depends on the one man who reigns as an absolute monarch over the Opera [the director], one who decides on whims their wages, whether low or high, and who stands above control or supervision. They are devoted to him like slaves in their constant fear of losing their position.

(quoted in Kelly 2012: 17)

Here power was concentrated in the hands of a single (traditionally male) leader or small elite at the expense of individual freedom; strict obedience to authority was enforced mostly through fear and a slave-like mentality.

This hierarchical, patriarchal model, its continued institutional support and the accompanying pedagogical methods that evolved as a result have been well documented and analysed by Robin Lakes (2005, 2008), Deidre Kelly (2012), Sho Botham (2012) and Doug Risner (2008), amongst others, who have explained the various factors making up the discourse. In general, the teacher is an absolute authority and can treat dancers in any way they wish; the teacher knows what is right and the students must obediently, and silently, follow their directions. As well, the teacher expects students to accurately perform specific steps and combinations quickly when they are presented, and the focus is on pointing out what is wrong and correcting mistakes. Finally, teachers in this tradition believe in a disciplinary approach to maintaining control, especially by punishing those whom they perceive to be making errors or misbehaving. These views continue to haunt the dance field. In 2002, when an outside agency brought a blazing critique against the 'Dickensian' conditions at the Paris Opera Ballet School. Claude Bessy, the school's headmistress and a former star of the main company, proudly stated, 'I was brought up with the stick' and lamented, 'Today, when you make a stupid mistake there is no punishment' (quoted in Webster 2002: n.pag.). Bessy's remarks capture a deeply entrenched notion that in order to become a professional dancer, students must go through the wringer physically and emotionally, and that training that does not do this is somehow amateur and subpar.

In her article 'The hidden authoritarian roots in western concert dance' (2008), Lakes describes typical authoritarian teaching behaviour as including rote imitation with unchanging verbal prompts, silencing students' questions, exhibiting impatience when there is no immediate mastery of the material and 'both physical actions and verbal attributions that seek to render the student powerless' (2008: 112). As Lakes observes, whether it be their literal use of a large stick, as common in the nineteenth century, or less explicit means of exercising control through eye-rolling, tone of voice and other non-verbal communication, authoritarian teachers' behaviour often escalates into acts of humiliation, bullying and outright abuse. Later, in the chapter I will more closely examine the full range of these problematic behaviours through an ethical lens – for now, suffice it to say that Lakes shows that 'Teaching behaviors and methods teach a set of rules, beliefs, and ideologies as powerfully as does the curriculum, the syllabus, or the lesson plan' (2008: 112).

Lakes proceeds to demonstrate how this authoritarian disciplinarian model connects to a variety of traditions that greatly influenced the theatrical dance field as it evolved in the West over the last few hundred years. One of the most important of these concerns the history of the general educational system. Here, Lakes traces how seventeenth-century teachers viewed students as passive receptors of knowledge for the teacher to mould. As she puts it, 'Metaphors for students such as blank slates, empty vessels, and balls of wax emanate from this era' (2008: 119). Lakes also points to the impact of vocational training as an early model for preparing dancers for professions in the theatre. Vocational training includes a clear master/apprentice hierarchy, replication of behaviour modelled by the master and product-oriented teaching and learning modes. Throughout the twentieth century, more progressive, holistic pedagogical approaches focusing on the education of the whole child gradually replaced such approaches in public K–12 education systems. But the realm of professional dance training largely remained steeped in this older model.

Lakes also considers the nineteenth-century attitudes towards children and child-rearing that stressed harsh discipline and the father's total control. Within this context, mistakes or any signs of misbehaviour were rewarded with the cane, and a 'spare the rod, spoil the child' attitude prevailed. Since many professional dancers are young women trained from very young ages, traditionally by male teachers, Lakes argues that the dance field adopted these paternalistic views and perceptions of the need for harsh punishment. Indeed, there are reports that Romantic ballerina Marie Taglioni was pushed so hard by her own choreographer father that she did not have enough energy to put on her nightgown; others would help drape it over her as she dropped into bed. The exhausting schedules of other dancers also appear in newspapers and diaries of the nineteenth century and are well documented by Deirdre Kelly in her detailed analysis of the lives of *corps de ballet* dancers at the Paris Opera during the period. Known as *les petits rats*, these were very young dancers, usually from poor households, who studied at the school and laboured long hours for little pay. They took class six days a week, followed by a full day of rehearsal, plus performances at night. The hard work and long hours, often on an empty stomach, made the dancers appear exhausted and nearly dead.

The familial and often patriarchal nature of dance training continues to help perpetuate abuse in the dance field. Young students devote many hours to studying dance, whether at elite schools that may include boarding or at a local studio, which becomes a second home. In these contexts, students feel compelled to believe what is said to them, similar to what happens to young people seriously involved in sports and gymnastics (Brackenridge 2001). As one dancer observes, 'your studio becomes your home, and your teachers become like your parents, and they're telling you these things [while yelling and cursing]. You're a susceptible adolescent, and it's hard for that not to impact your psyche' (quoted in Kelley 2019: 17). In many instances students' actual parents – known popularly as 'dance moms' – are highly involved, putting their children in questionable situations and becoming complicit in perpetuating the authoritarian model. During one of my interviews, a dancer shared that her mother encouraged her to have plastic surgery on her face at the age of 14 to improve her chances of getting into an elite ballet company. While there is likely much love and genuine desire for success that directs this kind of behaviour, it also comes at the cost of breaking young dancers' spirits and undermining their belief in themselves. It did in this case, although eventually this dancer found her way back to a very successful professional career after a liberal arts college education allowed her a period of intensive self-reflection and means to find her own voice.

Lakes also links dance's authoritarian tradition to early trends in physical education training, and from there, to military pedagogy. In the military, the soldier is conceived as a well-oiled machine that can follow orders without question, similar to a dancer who has been objectified and dehumanized. Sho Botham has additionally likened dancers in this tradition to the 'docile bodies' of the army, which French philosopher Michel Foucault described as resulting from new coercive strategies of control arising during the eighteenth century. These bodies are aggressively disciplined; their existing subjectivity is destroyed through constant humiliation. The result is a being who will follow orders efficiently and without question, who can be moulded to the desires of those in power. Lakes observes that 'Military "drills" set the pedagogical model that became transposed onto American physical education and later influenced the teaching practices of concert dance' (2008: 122). A quote about the film director Busby Berkeley, who started his career in the army and created elaborate dance sequences known for their choreographic precision, provides a great example of this tradition in the commercial dance sector:

> Famous for his 'combustible personality', Berkeley was most often unconcerned with the feelings – or the safety – of his dancers. Since his rants often took place during the many hours of preparation required to set up his sequences, working on a Busby Berkeley set was often described in the same manner as warfare: boredom punctuated by terror.
>
> (Stephens 2011: n.pag.)

In other words, it was not only concert dance where this kind of behaviour became the norm; but it was also evident in early Hollywood.

Indeed, it is important to recognize how this way of approaching dancers resonates in the competition dance circuit today, where many dancers get their start. Competition dance is one of the most common forms of training today for young dancers in the United States. In 2019, over 50,000 dancers competed at Showstoppers, a dance competition that was founded in the 1980s. The goal is to win; the training in private studios with this focus is often geared towards producing what scholar Susan Foster (2010) has dubbed an 'industrial body' that is frequently objectified and sexualized through social and popular media. This body is long and lean (read: 'thin'), displays extreme flexibility of the legs and affirms youth and heterosexuality. The pressure to master acrobatic tricks often comes at a price of safety. Brandi Dawn Kelley reports in her dissertation, 'Contesting bodies: Former competitive dancers' perceptions of their own bodies', that one of the participants in her study said she was forced to 'push the body in unhealthy ways to reach positions' (2019: 16). And another spoke of feeling pressured to make her body do whatever her teacher asked of her, with little guidance on how to avoid injury. This person shared, for instance, that:

> I knew I had a flexible back, and I crunched into my spine to force things because she was like 'I want you to get your scorpion', and I'd wack [my leg and back] until I got it. And I'd hear everything crack and it would hurt, but it wouldn't matter to her because I got the trick.
>
> (Kelley 2019: 16)

This same dancer recalled that 'Our teachers would yell at us and curse at us, and eventually you start to believe them. It's hard to pull yourself out of that environment' (Kelley 2019: 17).

Taken as a whole, these various influences converged to create the kind of results-oriented, authoritarian and disciplinary approach to professional dance education that continues to pass down in Western concert dance through many teachers and the institutions that support them. However, this approach is not the only reason for the lack of respect often accorded dancers. A significant amount of the emotional and physical abuse that continues to plague the profession is also due to the rise of the concept of the choreographer as a genius and the moral freedom awarded that new status. This took place at the turn of the twentieth century, and its impact exacerbated an already autocratic paradigm. It is to this development that I will now turn, before considering how the field of ethics can shed more light on the problems with this legacy.

Fusing new concepts of genius with authoritarian pedagogical perspectives

In the dance field, the perception of the choreographer/dancer as a 'genius' took hold relatively late, at the dawn of the twentieth century. This new status arose in response to developments in the other arts in the nineteenth century and the impact of the Ballets Russes and the expansion of modern dance, with its emphasis on individual artistic vision, spiritual uplift and devotion to abstract ideals. Together with a legacy of authoritarian teaching methods, this new conception of the choreographer contributed to a pedagogy in both classrooms and rehearsals that disempowered dancers. Here then is another contributor to a legacy primed for treating dancers without inherent dignity or respect.

During the rise of Romanticism in the nineteenth century, a particular conception of artistic genius arose in which the artist was seen 'as a kind of being elevated above the rest of mankind, alienated from the world and answerable in thought and deed only to his own genius' (Wittkower 2007: 95). The new Romantic vocabulary shaping visual art, literature and music consisted of intuition, spontaneity, feeling, autonomy of artistic creation and totality of vision. One of the most visible manifestations – the Bohemian artist – led an unconventional, vagabond, unruly lifestyle characterized by eccentricity, promiscuity, moodiness, drunkenness, poverty and overall lack of responsibility to anything other than himself and his creative impulse. Rejecting the masses as a stifling group, along with their perceived petty bourgeois taste and restrictive morality, led some artists to see themselves by the dawn of the twentieth century not only as answerable solely to their own vision but also beyond the claims of morality. Whether tongue in cheek or not, Wilde is famous for claiming that 'the sphere of Art and the sphere of Ethics are absolutely distinct and separate' (Wilde 1905: 191).

Dance historian Lynn Garafola has argued that in Western concert dance, the conception of the unfettered, single-minded genius is most clearly traceable to Serge Diaghilev's Ballets Russes, which toured from 1909 to 1929 in Europe, South America and the United States. For her, the rise of the choreographer/dancer as a person of privilege became possible because of this company's new framing of the choreographic process as 'a creative art, one steeped in a personal vision that broke with fossilized convention' (2010: 78). Before the twentieth century, choreographers were usually tied to major bureaucratic institutions, where they worked in collaboration with composers and librettists who enjoyed greater status. Marius Petipa, for instance, was a servant of the crown in his position as first ballet master of the Saint Petersburg Imperial Theatres. In the nineteenth century, meanwhile, the profession of a dancer was associated with virtuosity in terms of technical ability rather than original creation, which Hanna Järvinen has also observed, changed with the rise of Vaslav Nijinsky, who came to be seen as someone whose dancing was individualistic, unique, new and transcendental – all qualities of the discourse of genius (2004: 67).

The Ballets Russes, in contrast to previous ballet companies, was a privately run organization under the auspices of a single director – Diaghilev. The company's various choreographers, such as Nijinsky, were thus given previously unimaginable freedom. Garafola observes that

> collaboration had vanished, leaving in its stead a relationship of dominance and subordination. Free of the bureaucratic constraints of a traditional theater, Nijinsky, literally, could do anything. Thanks to Diaghilev's unconditional support of his choreographic ambitions, Nijinsky demanded – and received – unlimited rehearsals, the absolute obedience of the dancers and the surrender of their creativity.
>
> (2010: 83)

Here we see the important role of organizational structure in supporting a power imbalance that favoured the choreographer, giving them complete authority – a structure that remains largely in place until today.

The change also accompanied the broader economic transformations taking place with increased industrialization. Insensitive bosses interested in producing profitable end products increasingly perceived people as tools or instruments. D. H. Lawrence provides a wonderful example of this trend when he writes of a manager in his novel *Women in Love* (first published in 1920):

> His vision had suddenly crystalized. Suddenly he had conceived the pure instrumentality of mankind. There had been so much humanitarianism, so much talk of sufferings and feelings. It was ridiculous. The sufferings and feelings of individuals did not matter in the least. They were mere conditions, like the weather. What mattered was

the pure instrumentality of the individual. As a man as of a knife: does it cut well? Nothing else mattered.

(1955: 257)

The way workers appeared like cogs in a wheel paralleled the hierarchical and authoritarian world of dance. Utilitarian conceptions of the human being as an instrument for the choreographer's use later resonated in the words of Balanchine, as I will discuss later. It was a further step in dehumanizing dancers, leaving them vulnerable to mistreatment.

Kelly (2012) too points to this period as the dawn of the cultural phenomenon of the choreographer as an artistic genius and the dancer as a less-than-fully human instrument of his vision. While the status of the professional ballet dancer before this time could be extremely difficult, as noted earlier, there are examples of dancers who took advantage of the system to carve independent lives for themselves. Those who reached star status in particular were able to live with some degree of comfort and freedom. Kelly documents several courtesan-ballerinas during the eighteenth and nineteenth centuries who led such lives. Following Anna Pavlova, however, ballerinas would come to lose control over their own careers in

> subordinating themselves to the new star of twentieth-century ballet – the choreographer. Typically male and sometimes doubling as an impresario, the choreographer had begun nudging the ballerina from center stage during the Diaghilev era. [...] A Svengali-like figure, the choreographer demanded that the ballerina become his inferior, a docile handmaid serving his artistic needs more than her own.
>
> (Kelly 2012: 129)

Even more so than before, in other words, dancers fell to the mercy of the dance teacher-cum-choreographer: artistic freedom came first, and everything else became subordinate to his (or her) genius. This view haunts the dance world to this day, as when Ghekiere observes, 'Artistic preferences, artistic oeuvre, artistic methods, artistic freedom [...] all these artistic "whatevers" function as perfect excuses for basically any type of behaviour, harassment and abuse included' (2020: n.pag.).

Indeed, the dawn of dance modernism at the turn of the twentieth century saw an important shift in ideology that centred the individual artist's vision. The call of the new generation, from Isadora Duncan to Martha Graham, was for each person to discover their own 'secret language' of the soul and manifest it through a unique movement language. 'There is only one of you in all time', Graham famously espoused, and 'this expression is unique. And if you block it, it will never exist through any other medium and it will be lost' (quoted in De Mille 1992: 264). Within this paradigm, the act of creation assumed a quasi-religious experience of divine fulfilment. The body was a sacred garment, and dancers were God's athletes. In rejecting the dictates and conventions of tradition, many modern dancers (in the mould of the Romantic artist) turned to intuition, notions of authenticity of emotional expression and placed themselves at the mercy of their art, which spoke to and through them. Dance was not just a profession but a guiding principle, a higher form of living, to which one totally devoted one's life. Within this discourse, the individual choreographer was a servant of a greater force, an example their dancers were expected to follow without question. This ideology shaped not only the traditional modern dance world but also others working towards innovation and continues until today. In 2018, when the Flemish experimental multidisciplinary choreographer Jan Fabre was accused of a range of sexual harassment and psychological cruelty, he invoked the 'sacred bond between the choreographer and the dancers' as under threat (Flanders Today 2018: n.pag.).

Thus, one sees during the first part of the twentieth century a variety of changes that newly emphasized the choreographer's role and would strengthen authoritarian rule across the genres of ballet and modern dance and then theatrical jazz and commercial dance. With the transformation of the choreographer into a star and quasi-mystical figure, companies and their associated schools' success or failure depended increasingly on, as Garafola says, 'what the choreographer had to say and how he (or she) chose to say it' (2010: 83). As she observes,

> With so much riding on outcomes, the emphasis lay on product rather than process: the end justified the means, even if this transformed the studio into a site of humiliation, coercion, and violence. Like Nijinsky, but to far greater degree, Martha Graham, Antony Tudor, and Jerome Robbins treated the dancer as a mute, unquestioning instrument of the choreographer's imagination.
>
> (2010: 83–84)

In other words, the situation was ripe for abuse.

Tracing examples of authoritarian pedagogy in the twentieth-century United States

To understand the impact of this new conception of genius on the treatment of dancers within classrooms and then subsequent company contexts, it is valuable to take a moment to look more closely at a few examples from across different dance styles. It is evident that many European and Russian-trained ballet teachers who immigrated to America had tremendous influence. These teachers, highly revered, were afforded supreme power at the institutions where they operated and touched the lives of a broad range of dancers who ended up as choreographers working in all aspects of the dance field, including ballet, modern, theatrical jazz and the commercial realms. Their autocratic methods converged with the new ideas about genius just described to create a pattern that continues to play out. This pattern involves a hierarchical pedagogical style that arouses both awe and fear in students, and because it is supported systemically, sets the conditions for dancer-abuse to flourish unchecked and unregulated. This behaviour has manifested itself along a continuum from the official teaching spaces of dance schools to company classes and the rehearsal process. It has meant that even with progressive changes in formal dance education, especially later in the twentieth century, these traditional behaviours have often remained in private studios, companies or other professional settings.

Luigi Albertieri was just one such personage who can serve as a starting point. An Italian ballet master who had trained under Cecchetti, he was the premier danseur of the Empire Ballet in London and also worked at Covent Garden. After moving to the United States in the early part of the twentieth century, he initially was ballet master of Chicago Lyric Opera (1910–13) and then active in New York as ballet master of the New York Metropolitan Opera House (1913–27) and the Century Theatre. He also opened his own school in New York City in 1915, where many aspiring dancers flocked to study. The American-born Margaret Severn, who became a celebrated vaudeville and concert dancer, attended classes there. She described him as having 'a terrific egotism and narrow intolerance for any method other than his own' (1992: 259). In her reflections on his behaviour, she continued:

> His enemies, of whom there were many, could not help but respect him for his knowledge of and devotion to the art of dance as he conceived it, even though his most adoring pupils all became at one time or another the target of his almost insane – but fortunately shortlived [sic] – rages. He knew no restraint when it came to insulting a rival or, in fact, anyone who displeased him. [...] However, in spite of his idiosyncrasies, he was a great teacher and the unquestioned master of his art.
>
> (Severn 1992: 259–60)

Severn's comments point to the volatility and rage that could be unleashed on students, behaviour made tolerable by the teacher's greatness and devotion to dance.

The example of Jack Cole illuminates how this same pedagogical style, and accompanying justifications, found its way into theatrical jazz dance. Cole had begun by studying ballet with Albertieri in New York and was a lifelong adherent of the Cecchetti ballet technique. The influence of Albertieri's temperament on Cole could not be more evident. In a candid article published in *Dance Magazine* in 1983, author Glenn Loney does an amazing job of capturing Cole's larger-than-life character and tumultuous treatment of dancers starting in the 1930s. He observes:

> Cole's dancers and co-workers were hardly blind to his faults, though love and admiration must have dimmed their sight now and then when the great artist was behaving like a madman. Yet, mingling with the awe, respect, infatuation, and fondness expressed by Cole's associates is always a mix of darker emotions, inspired by memories of angry outbursts, cutting remarks, grueling [sic] practice sessions, and some totally irrational behavior.
>
> (Loney 1983: 76)

Loney's interviews with many of Cole's dancers consistently reflect their belief in his superior talent and their simultaneous recognition that his intense, manic approach 'wrecked many of us' (1983: 77). The dancers speak of his dragging female dancers across the room by their hair (1983: 78), trying to 'throw a girl out of a second-story window' (1983: 78) and how 'when he got really angry, he could become absolutely deranged' (1983: 78). Gwen Verdon captures the acceptance of this dynamic within the industry when she observes:

> When someone is as creative as Jack Cole was, I figure they're entitled to be a little eccentric – or whatever you want to call it. If he hadn't been so talented, I don't think anybody would have accepted how angry he could become.
>
> (1983: 78)

Meanwhile, in the ballet realm, Balanchine intensified artistic directors' tyranny for generations to come. Balanchine, the last major choreographer for the Ballets Russes, came to the United States in the early 1930s, where he became the driving force behind the School of American Ballet (SAB) and the New York City Ballet (NYCB). He was a godlike figure who demanded of his ballerinas total devotion bordering on self-sacrifice. Balanchine is famous for saying 'dancers are instruments, like a piano the choreographer plays' (quoted in Sarkis 2012: n.pag.). As such, he moulded dancers according to his own aesthetic desires. Ballerina Natalia Makarova commented, 'He is the conductor, the choreographer, the creator, the demiruge' (quoted in Caute 2008: 496). Most regarded him, like Patricia McBride said, as 'the father whose wishes were never questioned and who always knew what was best' (quoted in Taper 1996: 344). After his death Rosemary Dunleavy-Maslow claimed, 'He's Become the Messiah' (quoted in Pogrebin 2004: n.pag.).

Kelly demonstrates that Balanchine's unquestioned demands led to incredible suffering for many students at the SAB and in the company. His desire to see the bones of the sternum and rib cage sparked the epidemic of eating disorders rampant especially in the ballet world since the 1970s, and he

> subtly and systematically degraded [his dancers], denying them sex (unless it was with him) and sustenance, both in the form of food and domestic fulfilment. If his ballerinas married or had babies, he grew angry and was known to shun them.
>
> (Kelly 2012: 129–30)

The tragic effects of this patriarchal system are echoed by dancers to this day. In describing the boys club mentality of SAB and the company, Alexandra Waterbury, who came forward in 2018 with allegations against some of the male dancers who had swapped images of their partners performing sex acts or stripped naked, stated, 'It's like Balanchine is like a god. It's like a cult' (Villarreal 2018: n.pag.).

Moreover, the hiring and support of Jerome Robbins in 1949 as Associate Artistic Director at NYCB secured validation of the more diabolical aspects of dancer treatment in the name of genius. In her memoir, the teenage prodigy Barbara Bocher sums up the feeling by passionately speaking out at the age of 77 against the treatment she received at his hands: 'The army camp behavior that had just taken place in the […] rehearsal was a clear breach of children's human rights and certainly had no place in a civilized society, then or now' (Boker and Darius 2012: 26). However, as Bocher sarcastically put it, 'No one was to question a man who, despite his steamrolling methods, invariably turned even theatrical brass to gold' (2012: 19). The continued male choreographic dictatorships at NYCB and elsewhere have meant a lack of accountability until very recently. Peter Martins, who succeeded Balanchine, faced allegations of violent outbursts and assault as well as sexual misconduct during the #MeToo movement. He retired in 2018 but has faced few other consequences. In other words, while things seem to finally be changing, it is important to recognize the deeply engrained institutional support of artistic directors that sets the structural and systemic conditions that enable sexual and other forms of abuse. In 1997, when sexual allegations were first formally brought to light against Paul Mejia at the Fort Worth Dallas Ballet, the board's executive committee responded 'with what amounted to a shrug, as if to say this sort of thing is to be expected of *any* artistic director' (Goad 1998: n.pag., original emphasis).

Turning to the modern dance realm, a similar dynamic can be seen going back (at least) to Denishawn, the school and company founded by Ruth St Denis and Ted Shawn in 1915, which was the training ground for many of the leaders in this style. The lofty, egocentric persona cultivated by St Denis echoes those of 'Old-World' European teachers like Albertieri. Added into the mix was the modernist, quasi-mystical devotion to 'the dance' that demanded complete submission from students. Jane Sherman, who danced for the company as a young girl, notes St Denis' famous discourse on the 'spiritual' nature of dance, while highlighting St Denis' ongoing 'insensitivity and self-centeredness' (Sherman and Schlundt 1986: 318) and 'cruel treatment of people' (1986: 316). When she was in her eighties, St Denis herself confided to the photographer Marcus Blechman that, 'I've climbed, to use a *cliché,* the ladder of success higher than any American dancer since Isadora. And now I look back in horror and realize that the rungs of that ladder were people' (quoted in Sherman and Schlundt 1986: 318).

That approach continued with Martha Graham, who was inspired by seeing Ruth St Denis perform and began classes at Denishawn in Los Angeles in 1916. Graham demanded complete compliance to her will from the students and dancers in her company. She is known to have raked her nails down a dancer's chest to get him to perform a 'contraction' more deeply and across his inner thighs to turn out more (Lakes 2008: 121). Again, these actions were part of a broader discourse of self-sacrifice to 'the dance', conceived as a spiritual quest involving 'authentic' emotional expression, and were met with a combination of adoration and fear by those who studied and worked with her. A dancer who was a 14-year-old in a class in 1952 wistfully recalls being slapped in the face as a way to better connect with the movement. She raves, 'that gave me Martha unmediated [...] [I] received the gift of Martha's sacred self' (quoted in Lakes 2008: 116). Those less invested in the process, however, were able to see how Graham's emotional outbursts and physically abusive actions negatively impacted her dancers. In 1935 an outside evaluator for a funding organization advised against financial support for the Martha Graham Dance Company on the grounds that:

[H]er methods were in direct opposition to his strongly held convictions concerning democracy, women's rights, and human dignity. He was startled by Martha's relationship with the members of her group, concluding that she not only ignored many people's individual rights but actually trampled on them. [...] He felt strongly that whether people worked in a factory or a mine or in the arts, [...] they should be treated with dignity and consideration. His conclusion was that he could have awarded the money to Martha on artistic merits, but hers was not a democratic organization. He went so far as to say that some members were treated as if they were slaves.

(Bird and Greenberg 1997: 105–06)

As Lakes has highlighted, there is much irony in the way the authoritarian model reveals itself in many of the famous modern as well as postmodern and ballet companies from the 1930s onward. Incongruously, many of the choreographers whose actual dances often critiqued hierarchies, disrespect, lack of compassion, cruelty, etc. acted (and still act) in these very ways towards their dancers in class and rehearsal settings – thereby demonstrating the extent to which the norms remain deeply entrenched despite shifts in aesthetics and political identification. Anna Sokolow, for instance, created dances about the devastating effects of the Holocaust yet would readily hurl a chair at her performers because she believed it was the best way for them to feel 'real' fear. In class and rehearsals, Antony Tudor – known for his sensitive portrayals of human interaction on stage – 'slashed people to pieces [...] People were always hysterical crying. Sometimes they could leap from there and make progress. Other times it just destroyed them' (Lakes 2008: 112).

These attitudes and actions are not only excused but also constantly defended within and outside the profession on the basis of artistic genius, artistic freedom and the ability to produce excellence. Just consider a 2002 feature on Mark Morris from *New York* magazine. Writer Jennifer Senior remarks of his company:

> They're used to this: the brusqueness, the impatience, the periodic flare-ups that could spook a Buddha. To work with Morris, one must never confuse frustration with anger. His circuits work much faster than most [...] [As Morris observes] 'I'm very bossy, and I'm very, very demanding, and I'm specific and not very patient. And though I don't mean to be particularly vicious, I know I can be.'
>
> (2002: n.pag.)

In this quote, Morris admits to being unnecessarily cruel at times, but he dilutes the significance of his behaviour by painting it as a feature of his perfectionism; the author excuses his viciousness even further by asserting Morris isn't really cruel so much as brilliant – after all, he has such fast 'circuits'.

To conclude, this section provides insights into the ways in which authoritarian teaching methods, in combination with ideas of choreographic genius, have laid the groundwork for the ongoing mistreatment of dancers. It has become a normalized narrative within the profession and in the broader culture, with organizational structures that support and perpetuate it and parents and a public that largely accepts it. When an organization is in thrall to a 'genius', or, in a lesser version of this dynamic, when an organization declares all artistic matters as off-limits for non-artistic staff or board members, situations for abuse arise because there is no real oversight or opportunity for critique. In other words, this is not just a case of a few bad actors but of a system and culture that allow teachers and choreographers to assume extensive control and dominance over the dancers (and staff) in their charge. The dynamic is captured well in the popular series *Glee* when the main character Rachel Barry goes to New York to study at the New York Academy of the Dramatic Arts (NYADA), a fictional college that is supposed to be a top school in the nation for performing arts. There she encounters teacher Cassandra July, who is presented as the epitome of successful dance training. In the first episode of season four, July is shown to humiliate her students by insulting them and telling them how badly they are doing. She summarizes her disdainful view of Barry with 'You suck'. When Barry queries 'Why are you picking on me?' she responds, 'I'm not! I'm motivating you.' This episode premiered in September 2012. The question remains – how can this narrative be effectively challenged? As Julia Buckroyd proclaimed in her 2004 presentation, 'Ethics in dance: A debate yet to be held', 'We need a paradigm shift whereby the dancer will no longer be seen as an "instrument" for the choreography or a success story for the teacher but rather as an equal collaborator in the creation of an art form' (2004: n.pag.). The second part of this chapter considers how the field of ethics can help us in addressing this problem.

Understanding moral bads in dance pedagogy

One valuable way the field of ethics can assist in making sense of the traditional mistreatment of dancers is by bringing a more nuanced understanding of the problematic behaviours displayed in traditional dance pedagogy. The concept of 'moral bads' can be helpful in pinpointing a range of behaviours that ethicists today generally identify as wrong. In the dance field, these include various forms of humiliation, degradation, coercion, deception, harassment, betrayal, domination, exploitation, cruelty, malevolence, manipulation, discrimination, negligence, aggression, sadism and violence. While a full analysis of all these is not feasible here, the following section outlines how they operate and provides examples of how they often co-exist. I will next examine why we perceive these as wrong by looking at the specific ways they disregard human dignity, fail to demonstrate care and compassion and fall short of contributing to human thriving.

The examples of moral bads can be seen to exist along a continuum and may be exhibited in an active or more passive manner. For instance, negligence can be as subtle as consistently ignoring certain students or dancers or as overt as neglecting student safety or emotional well-being by having dancers repeatedly perform movements to the point of risking injury or experiencing unnecessary levels of pain. Degradation can be found in a choreographer calmly telling a dancer he is a half-wit or angrily dragging a dancer by the hair across a studio in front of fellow performers. Deception can arise when an artistic director offers a role to a dancer who they know will not be able to successfully perform (for instance in order to have them fail and thereby keep them in the *corps de ballet*), or when a teacher or choreographer purposefully withholds information that would allow their students to perform a sequence in a particular manner (for instance, failing to describe the intention behind the movement when it is clearly very important to the teacher).

I draw the examples in this section from a range of scholars who have questioned certain long-standing approaches and from my own experiences and those reported by students, professional dancers and choreographers working primarily in the United States and Europe in the areas of ballet, modern, theatrical jazz and commercial dance.[1] Many of these incidents occurred within the last three decades, or in other words, within living memory. The latter point gives the lie to the frequent claim that these approaches are 'old school' and no longer resonant. They remain alive and well, deeply affecting the well-being of those who have experienced them. Since the intent here is not to point fingers at particular individuals, I preserve the anonymity of those voicing their concerns. I want to provide insight, individually and collectively, into behaviours that have frequently been normalized and expected in the dance field and expose them as unnecessarily cruel and disrespectful.

One of the most common forms of mistreatment of dancers occurs when teachers or choreographers make derogatory remarks, mock and/or shame a person in front of their peers. These often relate to making fun of a physical feature that falls outside the norm of the ideal dancer body, especially remarks about the stomach, bust, hip or butt size. Examples are many. They include a dance teacher in a private studio commenting on a teenage dancer's stomach, asking 'When is the baby due?' and then parading around the class with a pillow under his shirt, saying, 'Look at me, I am pregnant – don't I look like Jessica now?' Or, 'He insulted me on a regular basis ("Tuna-belly", "Cheese on the back of your legs").' Or, 'You don't belong in the classical ballet world because your feet are too flat. Your butt is too big.' Or, 'The situation in which [he] publicly drew attention to a dancer's weight was witnessed by some of us and involved a long and painful humiliation game in which [he] insinuated that she must be pregnant. This bullying went on until the performer started crying.'

Actually, demanding a single ideal body type often still drives dancers to extreme actions to achieve that look (e.g., anorexia and bulimia, plastic surgery). These demands can take the form of regularly weighing students and/or telling them what to eat without reference to nutrition or health or otherwise telling them they are not pretty enough. For instance:

A teacher told us one night that if we were serious about dancing we each needed to lose five pounds. [...] for Saturday class and rehearsals lasting up to six hours, we were told that one banana and several bottles of water would be a healthy way to eat for the day.

And, 'He would also say horrible things about our bodies, say phrases like "Nothing is sexier than a hollow stomach", and "Eating lunch makes your body and muscles cold, so it's better not to eat at all".' These are examples of negligence and even reckless harm, intimidation and coercion, if following the regime yields more attention, getting hired or better roles. On her YouTube channel, ballet dancer Kathryn Morgan highlights the long-term mental toll of such body shaming, as in her post from 29 February 2020, during which she mentions an artistic director suggesting to one of her dancer friends that she try cocaine to lose weight; Morgan says in response: 'This is not OK anymore.'

Other examples of shaming involve insinuating that dancers are stupid and lazy, even when they are striving their utmost to grasp the material. These include the following:

> My friend always seemed to be a target of my teacher because of her awkward muscle tension […] This time she did it particularly more extreme than normal and at the same time happened to curl her fingers up, as if she was making a claw. My teacher started yelling at her and proceeded to stop the music. She then exclaimed, 'Stop doing that! You look like a complete monster! Are you trying to look retarded?'

And, 'You are beautiful, but you don't have a brain, like a chicken without a head.' And, 'Once, after I incorrectly executed a barre combination, he asked if my mother knew I was autistic yet. On a separate occasion, he said I danced as if I had down syndrome.' These are all examples of humiliation, degradation, intimidation and domination. The dancer can feel diminished relative to their peers even as they feel unjustly accused and frustrated given their sincere effort to perform the movement correctly. They can feel ashamed and afraid because they have been verbally attacked. They may also live in constant fear of being called out again in front of their peers. Ironically, dancers can even be berated for stupidity in an environment that traditionally disregards higher education. For example, one of my students shared that she was scheduled to take the PSATs (pre-university entrance exam), but the test interfered with Saturday class and the beginning of rehearsal. Her teacher told her that she was not excused and was required to be at the studio – that if she was serious about dance, then she wouldn't consider going to university.

Another problem is playing favourites while ignoring other students and/or not providing individual feedback or support. Students who are favoured, moreover, may be so because they are boys or men, Caucasian or light skinned, non-disabled, single or childless, youthful and/or family or friends of the teachers. For example:

> What truly frustrated me was that my instructors would correct the best students in the class, as if they even needed any correction, and then they would just watch me and not say anything […] Being ignored for years was not what I deserved.

Or, 'Maybe you shouldn't be in this ballet class because you won't have a career' (to a Black dancer). Or,

> A programme director who paid careful attention to a young male dancer's recovery from injury, asking him to take time off until it was healed, and then refusing to discuss a female dancer's similar injury, saying 'it could wait until evaluations'. Evaluations were five months away.

And, 'I remember one dancer telling me about a conversation with a choreographer about her pregnancy. The choreographer had said he couldn't work with her anymore, because "mothers were not interesting artistically".' These are all examples of discrimination, whether based on ability, gender, race or parental status; in other words, dancers being treated unjustly and not afforded fair and equitable attention and support.

Angry outbursts and shifting between emotional extremes are another tradition that involves manipulation, intimidation, coercion and control. For instance:

> I was in one company where a choreographer screamed at us during a rehearsal that what we were doing was crap and he fired us. Then after the break he couldn't understand why so many dancers were missing – he said he was just joking.

And, 'One day, he puts a performer on a pedestal; the next day, he systematically breaks him/her down, often scapegoating one person and stirring tensions in the group.' Or,

> He left me walking on eggshells by constantly gaslighting me (telling me one thing in private, then saying another in front of the company to make me look forgetful or stupid) [...] He would sometimes call me after working hours to further control my emotions.

In these examples, the erratic behaviour places dancers at the mercy of the person in authority and instils fear because they are never sure of where they stand. In extreme cases, the anger can escalate into outright assault, as in the following example: 'He's yanking me around to the left and to the right, he's digging his left thumb and his middle finger – I felt like he was piercing my muscle.'

Another unfair situation, although less common today, involves allowing a person to dance at only one studio or desiring the student or dancer to sacrifice themselves completely to a single teacher or choreographer. To do otherwise is considered disloyal. This is an example of coercion: if a dancer does not comply, they are punished. As one of my students shared,

> At one particular dance studio, I clumsily mixed up my checks and handed in a payment that was made out to a different studio I was attending. My teacher sternly handed it back to me in disbelief with a firm 'This does not belong to us!' […] To make me aware of her anger, when we began rehearsing for our upcoming performance, she moved me from front and center straight to the back.

Here the student is being unfairly penalized for exercising freedom of choice of where they want to study.

In terms of unethical behaviour of a more physical nature, one of the most common is pushing dancers to perform work in an unsafe manner. This can include forcing them to repeatedly run through routines to the point of exhaustion and injury, not providing regular water or bathroom breaks, allowing students to perform injured, not treating injuries seriously enough and having dancers perform in dangerous conditions without protecting them (from extreme heat or cold, unwanted touch, etc.). These are all examples of negligence, recklessness and needless cruelty. For instance: 'The [guest artist] insists that we leap across the space with our faces completely raised to the ceiling. She keeps pushing harder and harder until one dancer leaps into the mirror, completely shattering it.' And,

> As [he] landed a particularly challenging jump combination across the floor in modern class, his ankle made a loud cracking sound. His body immediately collapsed as a result, but the teacher kept the class jumping by [him] at high velocity. She yelled at him to get it together and to keep going, which [he] did, overlooking what he later learned was a second-degree sprain.

Notably, some famous choreographers, like Paul Taylor, readily admitted to physically assaulting dancers: 'I've actually hit dancers. I've bitten little fingers that stuck out too much' (quoted in Lakes 2008: 113) – and justifying his actions in a manner similar to Bessy, continuing, 'People don't usually learn unless there's a little pain involved' (Lakes 2008: 113).

Sexualizing dancers by touching private body parts or referring to private body parts and to dancers' sex lives also occurs. These situations involve humiliation, degradation, exploitation and violence to bodily integrity and to dancers' sense of agency. For example: 'A female guest choreographer approaches me in rehearsal, asks me if I know where my passion is, lifts up my T-shirt (I was braless), and begins hitting my naked chest, exclaiming, "This is where your passion is!"' Or, 'The male ballet teacher who needlessly encompassed my thigh with both his thumbs and pointer fingers very near the base of my pubic area and dragged both hands down my entire leg to remind me to lengthen.' Or,

> I once worked with a guest choreographer while I was in school. He would harass many of my female classmates in front of everyone. He would go up to someone, get very close to her, and whisper things in her ear as he stroked her arms or back.

These cases demonstrate the unnecessary violation of students' privacy and sense of control over their own bodies and sexuality.

The most extreme cases involve overtly harassing dancers – by requesting they engage in sexually explicit communications or acts with teachers/choreographers – and coercion because those acts are tied to much-coveted roles. Dancers become dependent on the authority figure for approval only for them to use that influence to establish sexual intimacy. For instance: 'He walked in as they changed, touched their backsides and commented on genitalia – rewarding dancers who kept quiet with ballet roles [...] [he] befriended ten students on Facebook before coaxing them to send intimate photos.' And, he 'would only assign a solo or lead role to them if they agreed to sleep with him [...] No sex, no solo'. And finally,

> this director was consistently having inappropriate sexually motivated encounters with several of the women in the company. But none of the women felt comfortable talking about what had happened to them so most of them kept the stories to themselves or just amongst the girls and that was that. To add insult to injury, his wife was a dancer in the company at the time. So it was sensitive. The people that knew what was going on had no idea how much she knew or if she knew anything at all and no one I guess wanted to be the person to stir the pot. So, silence.

That 'silence' echoes loudly, clamouring for positive change. All of these 'moral bads' that still linger in dance pedagogy are holding the dance field back from being as humane as possible. They demonstrate the range of ways that dancers, first as students and then as professionals, can be mistreated. Taken together, moreover, they shed light on the fundamental wrong: dancers are treated as less than full persons. As Doug Risner explains,

> Whether the particulars specifically concern verbal harassment, sexual abuse, eating disorders, or inhumane teaching approaches, the larger concerns – without diminishing any of these palpable dilemmas – focus on the manner in which these issues profoundly compromise the human dignity of dancers.
>
> (2002: 72)

It is this question of human dignity to which I will now turn, to understand more fully how the field of ethics can help us understand the need for more rights (and attendant obligations) in the dance field.

Some views on dignity and respect from the field of ethics

Problems with attitudes and behaviours that consider the student or dancer to be a less-than-fully developed human being (such as a tool, animal or childlike creature) have been wonderfully critiqued in the fields of dance education, dance science and somatics, as indicated in Chapter 1, with suggestions on how to address them. (For instance, see the highly pragmatic and useful *Safe Dance Practice* by Edel Quin and Sonia Rafferty, published in 2015.) In this book, however, I am interested in looking at ethics as an influential tradition that denies the tolerability of conceiving of humans in such ways and provides some guidance on challenging these conventional narratives. Some of the strongest arguments are those that derive from a deontological tradition and claim that regardless of specific circumstances, human beings must *never* be used merely as instruments, that they have basic rights that guarantee a baseline treatment of respect and that they are treated with dignity. According to this logic, there is also a parallel obligation on behalf of those in authority at schools and companies to develop policies and procedures to protect these rights. Here I draw upon and briefly present four convincing theorists and documents that assert and explain this position: Immanuel Kant, the authors of the *International Declaration of Human Rights*, Avishai Margalit and Margaret Walker.

Kant is probably the most famous philosopher to argue for all human beings to be treated equally and as creatures with free will. He argues from the position that all ethical knowledge derives from human rationality. Since all humans have a reason, we can all make moral decisions. Based on this idea, Kant came up with what he called the 'Categorical Imperative', meaning that it is always universally true. One version of the Categorical Imperative reads, 'Act always so as to treat humanity, whether in your own person or in that of another, always as an end, and never simply as a means only' (Rachels 2007: 131). According to Kant, all (and only) humans have dignity, a status above all relative value (which is a quality of everything else). To recognize people's dignity is to respect them as moral agents: they may never be used only as a means, or in other words, treated merely as instruments, utilities or commodities by another human being.

We can see Kant's ideas in the stance of the drafters of the *Universal Declaration of Human Rights*, which was ratified in 1948, following the atrocities of the Second World War. The authors of this document spent a great deal of attention on the very opening statement of the Preamble. Here it proclaims that 'recognition of the inherent dignity and of the equal and inalienable rights of all members of the human family is the foundation of freedom, justice and peace in the world' (www.un.org). As a result, the Declaration establishes that by simply being human, individuals have a universal claim to dignity and certain equal and inalienable rights. These rights counter many forms of human cruelty, whether more mental or physical in nature. Again, like Kant, the claim is universally applicable regardless of context.

Meanwhile, philosopher Avishai Margalit, author of *The Decent Society* (1996), argues that the *decent society* is one whose institutions do not humiliate people and which fights conditions that are reasons for members to consider themselves humiliated. As he puts it, 'A society is decent if its institutions do not act in ways that give the people under their authority sound reasons to consider themselves humiliated' (Margalit 1996: 11). For Margalit, humiliation is any behaviour or condition that results from human acts or omissions and gives a reason for someone to feel their self-respect is injured (even if the behaviour is not intended to humiliate); where 'self-respect' is our attitude towards ourselves as being worthy of respect just because we are human. Going even further, Margalit outlines three primary forms of humiliation: (1) treating human beings as nonhuman, as if they are animals, machines or subhuman; (2) forcing upon human beings a loss of basic control over their lives; and (3) rejecting people's humanity – 'rejecting a human being from the "Family of Man"' (Margalit 1996: 144).

Lastly, the ethicist Margaret Walker argues in 'The politics of transparency and the moral work of truth' that having dignity is really about being recognized as a full moral subject. This requires that one is a 'self-accounting actor in relations of mutual accountability' (2007a: 232), which is only possible if one is free to express one's distinct subjectivity and experience and to provide this option to others, especially in situations involving injustice and cruelty. Dignity also involves having physical integrity and self-possession, such that others cannot simply disregard bodily boundaries or a person's sense of somatic wholeness. To lack dignity, consequently, is to 'stand in something other than reciprocal and symmetrical relations of accountability' (2007a: 232).

All of these positions claim people inherently deserve to be treated with dignity. This dignity involves treating people as full moral subjects rather than subhuman or less-than in some way. Being a full moral subject means existing in a reciprocal and symmetrical relation to others. For the purposes of this book, this means recognizing dancers as full persons. They deserve to be treated with dignity and allowed the freedom to voice their unique experiences within a context where they will be heard and respected. They have an inherent right to ask questions and discuss concerns with teachers, choreographers and artistic directors. To reiterate, this neither depends on the character or actions of those in power nor depends on any specific context – it is the universal right of all human beings to be recognized as having inherent worth.

Rights, moreover, imply duties. Every right has a correlative obligation: all of us, along with our educational and cultural institutions, are responsible for upholding those rights. In this context, the right to be treated with dignity and without humiliation or abuse means that we all have to find ways to ensure that this is the case. To this end, thankfully, there have been important steps during the last couple of decades to draw up more rigorous contracts and establish ethical codes of conduct to bring greater regulation to the dance field. This is evident both in the more structured realm of large dance companies as well as within the freelance world. Much work remains, but these provide a good foundation of certain rights, standardized rules and guidelines for the field.

The American Guild of Musical Artists, for instance, has been especially active in fighting for the rights of dancers in a range of large ballet and modern companies in the United States. In particular, the 'Harmonious Workplace' section in these contracts addresses many concerns and has become increasingly robust. The one for the San Francisco Ballet for the period of 1 July 2016–30 June 2021, is particularly detailed. It states that the 'EMPLOYER and ARTISTS agree to endeavor to promote mutual respect, a positive atmosphere, and harmonious working relationships' and further stipulates that the employer

> prohibits all forms of harassment in the workplace. This includes but is not limited to sexual harassment and harassment based on race, color, religion, ancestry, sex (including breastfeeding and medical conditions related to breastfeeding), pregnancy (including childbirth and related medical conditions), age, national origin, genetic characteristics and information, disability, marital status, military or veteran status, sexual orientation, gender identity, gender expression, or any other factor prohibited by federal, state or local law.
>
> (Basic Agreement 2016–21: 73)

What is then particularly helpful is that the section outlines that harassment may take many forms. These include: verbal conduct such as name calling, innuendoes, derogatory comments, slurs or inappropriate sexual remarks, solicitations or invitations; sexually explicit or racially derogatory gestures and gestures, posters, cartoons or drawings that ridicule a particular group; requests, threats or demands (whether implicit or explicit) to submit to sexual advances in order to obtain or maintain employment, promotions or benefits or in order to avoid negative consequences; unwanted physical contact such as blocking normal movement, interference with work or inappropriate touching; behaviour that creates an intimidating or hostile work environment or substantially interferes with an employee's work performance; and retaliation or the threat of retaliation for having reported the harassment. Finally, the section explains that an employee who is found to have engaged in harassment will be subject to disciplinary action up to and including discharge and lays out the process by which to report harassment (Basic Agreement 2016–21: 73).

Nora Heiber, who is the West Coast AGMA representative and a former professional dancer with LINES Ballet, has been promoting collaborative leadership and strategies for addressing concerns and new challenges facing the dance and opera world with the advent of COVID-19. Inspired by work on Nonviolent Communication (NVC) by Marshall Rosenberg – through her work with CNVC Certified Trainer Aya Caspi, and restorative justice, Heiber supports the creation of mutually supportive processes that facilitate ongoing collaboration between management and dancers to resolve issues and promote healing and transformation to inspire the best in everyone. Rather than using the language of blame, shame, fear or domination, her driving question for the dance field to move forward is, 'What are life-serving strategies to care for everyone involved?' (Heiber 2020). Following Rosenberg, she observes that all human beings have certain basic needs, such as autonomy, physical nurturance, play, acceptance and appreciation, and the key is to have people connect on that deeper level emotionally and then collaborate on the strategies that might resolve the concern for all affected parties. For Heiber this transforms the field of 'right/wrong' and opens new possibilities to care for everyone's needs in a way that boosts morale and allows for well-being above and beyond issues covered in the formal AGMA contracts. There is much in her approach that relates to care ethics – as will become clear in the discussion later – because of the emphasis on deep listening, compassion and interest in human thriving.

For freelance dancers, the situation is much less secure, but there have been some attempts at establishing best practices. In 2002, a group of New York City-based dance artists wrote 'The Dancers Forum Compact' to 'promote communication and respect among dancers and choreographers, and to enhance the creative act' (2002: 1). It further states that 'dancers and choreographers together must insure [sic] that they work in a manner that addresses the well-being and dignity of all involved in the act of creating dances' (2002: 1). This document emphasizes clear communication around topics like pay, scheduling, safety and conflict resolution. It also has sections addressing discrimination and harassment. Similar to the language in union contracts, it lays out forms of verbal, physical, visual and sexual harassment. Some choreographers still follow the Compact's guidelines, although, according to a 2018 *Dance Magazine* article, its use has declined (Allison 2018: n.pag.). Even more recently there have been discussions about whether freelance dancers need a union and how to improve conditions through greater regulation across the dance field. These have been led by such organizations as the Dance Artists' National Collective (DANC), which was founded in 2019 to create safer, more equitable, more sustainable working conditions for dancers (danceartistsnationalcollective.org). It follows up on a call made by Sara Wookey in 2011 for basic standards of labour. Wookey made waves as a freelance dancer who dared call out performance artist Marina Abramović and the Museum of Contemporary Art, Los Angeles for unfair treatment during the process for auditioning for a gala event. In her letter, she rightly observed that this is a 'situation of injustice in which both artist and institution have proven irresponsible in their unwillingness to recognize that art is not immune to ethical standards. Let's have a new discourse that begins on this thought' (Wookey 2011: n.pag.).

As regulations and ethical codes become more prevalent, it is, however, important to understand their limitations. In her 2012 study, Sho Botham observes many cases of new guidelines existing on paper but not necessarily put into practice. She writes, 'although there might be these "good intentions" to move forward towards person-centred practices […] this has not happened as claimed […] although these claims exist on paper in the syllabi, for example, they have not been embodied into practice' (2012: 168). Furthermore, she observes:

> Paying lip service to improving standards in this way is not helpful to anyone, least of all for the teachers who are led to believe that these courses are promoting one way of doing things when in reality (as we will show) they are just doing what has been done in the past.
>
> (2012: 65)

Meanwhile, Susan Stinson recognizes the contextual, subjective, changing and complex nature of ethical dilemmas that present themselves in educational settings and the need to remain flexible and engage students in applying any set of formalized codes. In her presentation, 'Professional ethics and personal values: Intersections and decisions in dance education', she provides a compelling case for subjecting ethical codes to critical thinking. She observes, for instance, that in her research, 'I realized that I want my students to recognize that sometimes the rules may be wrong, and sometimes the only moral response is to disobey authorities, despite the consequences' (2004: 29). The recognition that critical thinking plays an important role in applying any set of rules reveals the limitations of deontological theories of ethics and demonstrates the value of virtue ethics, with its emphasis on practical wisdom and care.

Teaching dance with care and compassion

Rules and regulations are particularly helpful in outlining what should *not* be done. However, dance training should entail more than non-maleficence (a commitment to avoiding harm to the student) and autonomy (respect for the student's right to be self-governing). While these are clearly crucial, we should also consider beneficence – a commitment to positively promoting the student/dancer's health and well-being. In 2018, Christopher Hampson, the Artistic Director of the Scottish National Ballet, wrote a statement regarding 'Behaviour in the ballet world' where he called out the 'despicable' behaviours of humiliation and harassment he had witnessed in his past and how some leaders 'did little to support artists in achieving their potential' (2018: n.pag.). Instead, he says leaders should be asking questions like, 'Do you inspire working practices that bring out the best in others?' (2018: n.pag.). In the field of ethics, we can again turn to virtue ethics – especially care ethics – for guidance. We will see how this ethical perspective complements existing developments in dance education that stress a holistic approach to student engagement and encourages 'the flourishing of each individual, valuing each dancer for what he/she is as well as what he/she can do' (Botham 2012: 95).

Indeed, before focusing on care ethics, it is important to once again acknowledge the long and substantial contributions of the academic field of dance education to 'bring joy and satisfaction to their [children's] lives, challenge their minds, stimulate their imaginations, and exalt their spirits' (NDEO 1998: n.pag.). Since at least the work of Margaret H'Doubler, many who are active in the dance field – especially in public K–12 education and liberal arts dance programmes in the United States – have focussed on the 'whole child' or student. They have also applied scientific understanding of the body and brain to achieving physical virtuosity and creating a healthy and emotionally fulfilling approach to dance training. The integration of somatics from such mind/body practices as Alexander Technique, Feldenkrais, Laban Movement Analysis and yoga has especially emphasized the importance of first-person experience in this process, along with anatomy and kinesiology (Rouhiainen 2008). Contact Improvisation from the 1970s onwards has brought attention to the need for openness, sensitivity and receptivity in intimate dance encounters (Albright 2013). These practices offer a powerful antidote to old-school methods of humiliation and use of the 'stick' by providing insight into how to perform a movement from a scientifically informed and individually appropriate base that is non-threatening and life-affirming to self and other. Meanwhile, feminist, constructivist and critical pedagogies have all offered further tools for centring student experience and recognizing the role and value of collaboration and exchange in learning and meaning-making.

Virtue ethics, and specifically care ethics, continue these developments and have been increasingly incorporated by dance educators since the 1980s and 1990s. As applied in the realm of teaching dance, they emphasize modelling, explaining and cultivating behaviours conducive to human thriving. At a general level, this means educating dancers in a holistic manner (taking into account body-mind-spirit connections), working with the strengths of each student and encouraging every student to emerge as a fully expressive human being. Susan Koff (2004) observes that this shifts the focus of 'success' from the end product to the quality of leadership in the classroom and the educational process itself, where 'technique' no longer drives learning but develops in the course of it. In other words, 'good teachers' are evaluated on both how well their dancers embody a particular aesthetic ideal and to what degree they foster an environment in which students can feel deep fulfilment and joy. Mary Cochran, who danced for the Paul Taylor Dance Company from 1984 to 1996, expressed it well when she shared with me,

> In terms of leadership in the field, I learned more from the bad examples than the good ones. I learned deep in my bones what not to do and how not to foster excellence and creativity – and, once I escaped from these people, I ran in the opposite direction as fast as I could.
>
> (2010: n.pag.)

She explained, 'I did not find it [the traditional authoritarian approach] productive. Free, open, happy – such an atmosphere is much more productive' (2010: n.pag.).

In his important essay 'Who cares? Teaching and learning care in dance' (2004), Edward C. Warburton dives deeply into how care manifests itself in the dance context. Drawing on the work of Nel Noddings and the field of psychology, he outlines the kinds of cognitive processes that 'inform emotional receptivity and response' (2004: 90). He argues that different stages ebb and flow between our thinking and feeling minds: (1) sensitivity to a caring encounter in which we shift from a self-centred to an us-centred perspective; (2) receptivity, when we become open to an encounter with another person; (3) inclination, a readiness to engage and willingness to feel and understand; and (4) motivation, in which we extend our emotional energies to another and engage in a compassionate encounter. In addition, care also means having emotional flexibility and kinaesthetic empathy, having the capacity for active listening and knowing when those who are the 'cared-for' need to care for themselves. Warburton stresses that 'Caring is a moral orientation that obliges us to move beyond simple ideas about "being there for people" or "becoming a good listener"' (2004: 91). It is an ongoing relational stance that takes effort and is a shared, two-way responsibility between the teacher and student. As he observes,

> In the final analysis, perhaps the biggest test of a caring teaching practice is the will to maintain a rigorous commitment to prolonged dialogues, be they verbal or non-verbal, tactile or visual: to a conversation that conveys care so convincingly that the desire for what is best is unmistakable.
>
> (Warburton 2004: 95)

For Warburton, as with others who promote care ethics in dance education, 'the number-one ethical principal must be responsiveness not only to the moment of encounter but also to our students' long-term intellectual, emotional, and physical growth' (2004: 93). This 'responsiveness' manifests itself in numerous ways as the educator models deep listening to the spoken and unspoken needs of the students, individually and as a group, and attends to concerns and blockages as they arise. In 'Location of possibilities: Exploring dance technique pedagogy through transformation and care' (2019), Jamieson Dryburgh elaborates how care takes place when teachers demonstrate vulnerability and avoid an all-knowing stance, let students lead reflective moments that enable them to make connections and model 'how to deal with conflict, disagreement and ambivalence rather than attempting to eliminate it' (Dryburgh 2019: 95). Dryburgh emphasizes that 'the studio is inhabited by learners of diverse and changing readiness for assuming shared responsibility and therefore I, as teacher, must adapt, be responsive, and respect this diversity' (2019: 92).[2]

Meanwhile, in 'A collaboration in care: Re-visioning teacher-student dialogue in dance education' (2018), authors Rebecca Gose and Grace Siemietkowski assert that a collaborative practice of care in dance is centred on the open dialogue between teacher and student and that each has the choice to be active in any conversation. Their point is that not speaking out could be potential grounds for miscommunication and spreading untrue beliefs or hurting feelings. Surrounding this open dialogue is teacher reflection and teacher application as well as student reflection and student application. This observation reinforces the idea of individuality that is necessary for students to both be seen and take responsibility in this relationship for a continued successful practice of care. Reflect, participate in dialogue, then apply: a cyclical practice. The article ends on this note:

> Lastly, caring communication evolves from an individual's own volition. It must come from a personal desire to understand the needs and concerns of others in the teaching and learning cycle [...] it is only through a committed engagement by willing participants – leaders willing to facilitate a discussion process, for example – can a sea of change in dance education potentially spring forth. Through active listening and caring encounters, empathetic and caring relationships can begin to transform the educational setting and the implicit pedagogy therein.
>
> (Gose and Siemietkowski 2018: 32)

Like many readers, hopefully, I have been fortunate to experience and witness dance teachers skilled at establishing climates of care, empathy and trust across a range of dance styles, although they may not explicitly reference care ethics as an inspiration. I have observed teachers like Cynthia Roses-Thema, who has written powerfully about the dancer as a 'rhetor' (2008), engage students in ballet classes in thoughtful real-time dialogues where they put into words their experience of embodiment directly after completing an enchaînement (ballet routine). Teachers of voguing and waacking, like Marcus White, or breaking, like Serouj 'Midas' Aprahamian and Edson 'House' Magana, cheer on students as they enter the cipher and find their inner power. Their teaching shows important connections with hip hop as pedagogy that Daniel Banks powerfully articulated when he observed the importance of building 'trust, mutual respect, and collaboration, so that everyone has 'buy-in' and is empowered to take responsibility for the collective experience' (2015: 252). Meanwhile, ballroom teacher Larry Caves and mambo specialist David Olarte teach partnership dancing as intimate, non-verbal dialogues similar to Contact Improvisation, where roles of leader and follower constantly shift regardless of gender. And recently, one of our graduate students who specializes in Bharata Natyam, Sumana Mandala, has drawn on somatics, feminist and critical pedagogy to empower the young women in her private studio through more student-centred approaches to instruction (Mandala 2020). Without sacrificing the rigors of 'technique', she asks them to find new ways to experience Bharata Natyam that are meaningful to their twenty-first-century lives by being receptive to a more relational approach to teaching.

Melissa Rolnick, meanwhile, is an example of a dance teacher who has striven to 'say goodbye to poisonous pedagogy' (in the words of one of her conference presentations in turn inspired by the work of psychologist Alice Miller who describes 'poisonous pedagogy' as including behaviour that is intended to manipulate children's characters through force or deception) in the modern dance realm. A former professional dancer for Margaret Jenkins, she has evolved an approach to teaching dance, at Arizona State University and then at Gustavus Adolphus College, that supports those who hope to pursue professional careers and those who experience dance more broadly as an enriching and meaningful pursuit. She names her practice MEISA (movement, exploration, imagination, sensation, awareness), through which she seeks to 'inspire students to engage with movement as embodied research and an opportunity to validate their experience of being human' (Rolnick 2020: n.pag.). She has shared with me that MEISA arose out of a desire to create a practice that would 'recognize and honor the whole person and their expressive possibilities […] I invite them to discover and in so doing am recognizing the fullness of their humanity' (Rolnick 2020: n.pag.).

Rolnick explains, 'After a lifetime in dance, creative, somatic and contemplative practice, I felt the need to unify elements of those practices together under a thematic umbrella to create one practice.' The current MEISA objectives are as follows:

1. To cultivate movement exploration and expression through the imagination and attentive presence.
2. To create an atmosphere that empowers practitioners to discover movement choices that feel 'right' for them.
3. To cultivate enlivened physicality and sensate experience through intentional practice and developing the 'inner witness' (a processing/noticing of sensation, emotion, movement from the inside; one is attentive to their internal experience as a source of knowing).
4. To encourage playful practice, curiosity and creativity without judgement.
5. To offer an experience that cultivates enhanced movement possibilities, balance, flexibility, strength and range of motion.
6. To cultivate community connection and engagement (and develop the 'external witness' – where one is attentive to the outside world and others).

(2020: n.pag.)

Rolnick's teaching reflects many of the values discussed earlier in relation to treating dancers with respect and dignity as well as approaching the classroom from a position of care ethics. For instance, she encourages individual agency in her classes by advocating for students to listen to what their bodies need and to be responsive to that. She sees them as the final arbiters of both the movement they will explore and how they will explore it. Although she leads them through an experience that she commits herself to being present and attentive to, she does not

> presume to know beyond myself/my experience and in fact look[s] to the students as partners in discovery. They are my collaborators. I facilitate an experience but am continually informed by their responses in embodiment, actions, drawings, verbal and written reflections. My intention is to be fluid in this dialogue.
>
> (2020: n.pag.)

Rolnick believes that cultivating community between herself and students and among the students creates an optimal environment for learning that includes exploration, creativity and honest sharing. She allows herself 'to be real and vulnerable with the students to create an environment in which the students feel they too can be vulnerable and share. I talk about vulnerability and the necessity for respectful engagement' (2020: n.pag.). As she further explains, 'language and delivery of language matters' in order to ensure a safe environment for all. For example, when students are acting as external witnesses, they are reminded that as viewers they are being given an 'offering' (2020: n.pag.). To that extent, the students practice how they give feedback, following a process that involves describing what they see, what they feel within themselves as they witness, asking questions and checking in with the mover if they feel complete in their feedback experience.

I have myself observed and experienced that one of the most valuable contributions for demonstrating respect and care across all of these different classes and regardless of dance style is when dancers are reminded of their own agency. This happens when teachers provide them with opportunities to act on their own volition and make choices on how they perform movement, either in terms of how they interpret a given phrase or through designated periods of improvisation or 'freestyling', depending on the style in question. Clearly, there is a long history here of improvisational strategies that can be considered and engaged. In the modern dance realm alone, these are evident in the Nikolais/Louis legacy, contact improvisation and practice of Authentic Movement, to just name a few.

For Rolnick, for example, this means the extensive incorporation of options in her contemporary modern classes. While she believes that she still has the responsibility as a technique teacher to teach students to 'see a phrase, learn it and reproduce it as this is still a requirement for much of the dance world' (2020: n.pag.), her main interest has become the use of guided invitations for movement investigation as a way to challenge the students to be more 'invested in the process of creating and embodying movement material by leading them through explorations that encourage them to define and clarify a movement image or concept' (2020: n.pag.). As she says, in these cases, 'The students are given permission to drop into themselves and given the freedom to discover what moves them. Often there is a considerable emotional response in and to their experience as the movement takes on personal meaning' (2020: n.pag.). In this practice, there is no clear-cut right and wrong. There is an opportunity, and challenge, for someone to 'move by focusing on the internal, being able to be present enough for others to be able to witness and to own one's experience as a witness' (n.pag.). She shares, 'To be "seen" is to be honoured and is an empowering experience' (2020: n.pag.).

Conclusion

In her 2018 *Washington Post* article, 'Why this is the moment for dancers to behave badly', Sarah Kaufmann observes:

> Valuing dancers is the key issue. Is a dancer who is yelled at in rehearsal [...] being valued? The intrinsic value of a human being seems to fade in and out of the picture

when you look closely at the dance world. It can be the most difficult concept for dancers to get across to their leadership.

(2018: n.pag.)

For his part, Christopher Hampson stresses, 'Dancers today are not "behaving badly", they are asking more of us as leaders. That's a good thing and we should deliver' (2018: n.pag.). He argues that 'there is no need, ever, to cause hurt intentionally to another person to deliver your own high standards' (2018: n.pag.). It is not a question of achieving artistic excellence but is the 'fool's way', often at the hands of the 'insecure or emotionally immature and self-absorbed' (2018: n.pag.). He recognizes that 'this type of behaviour guarantees resentment, perpetuates mistrust, generates fear and compliance; it is uncreative and it is damaging' (2018: n.pag.).

In this chapter, I have traced some of the reasons for abuse of dancers across the dance realm and the ways in which the field of ethics can provide arguments for more respectful and caring treatment. These perspectives are drawn both from deontological traditions, focused on recognizing the inherent rights of dancers as human beings, as well as virtue ethics, which seeks human flourishing through cultivating and practicing nourishing character traits, especially of care and compassion. Taken together, they provide important contributions to a rich tradition in dance education that has striven to bring a more humanistic approach to dance training. They offer an introduction to the value of ethics for the dance field, something that can be pursued in more detail through texts like *Ethical Dilemmas in Dance Education: Case Studies on Humanizing Dance Pedagogy* (2020). This book, edited by Doug Risner and Karen Schupp, provides an in-depth examination of the complexities involved in actualizing these approaches and the extent to which they require ongoing commitment. The many case studies illuminate that this is by no means an easy or well-defined process and is perhaps most about the willingness to be receptive and responsive to others, as defined at the root of care ethics.

Together with the first two chapters, the discussion here provides foundational arguments for dance artists to consider the importance of ethics for artistic concerns as they pursue a career in the dance field. While the previous chapter outlined the implications of seeking to be a decent human being (alongside being a dance artist) as related to broader societal participation, this chapter has examined the art form's foundations in human-to-human interaction in dance education. The intimate nature of this interaction demonstrates just how important it is to rethink any traditions in dance that separate artistry from ethical considerations or assume a stance that exclusively measures value in terms of final products. In the next chapter, I will continue to probe these issues by looking more closely at the creative process and the kinds of ethical issues that arise specifically in making dances. While some of these issues continue the discussion of pedagogical matters, they also shift to other considerations that are unique to choreographic investigation and performance, thereby offering important insights into the need for ethical awareness in that dimension of a dance artist's life.

NOTES

1. Anonymous sources include student papers from an IRB approved study I oversaw in 2010 at Arizona State University, personal interviews, articles and blogs.
2. Also, see Tanya Calamoneri, Colleen Dunagan and Nyama McCarthy-Brown (2020), 'Ethical dance pedagogy', *Journal of Dance Education*, 20:2, pp. 55–64.

4

Ethics and Dance Making

Attention to safe practice and awareness of risk factors supports choreographic creativity, effective rehearsal and optimum performance. Dance leaders can get the best from their sessions and their dancers by planning appropriately and regularly evaluating their methods and strategies.

(Quin et al. 2015: n.pag.)

This chapter focuses on dance making that typically occurs in educational, community and professional theatre situations and the kinds of key ethical concerns that may arise during its preliminary, rehearsal and even performing stages. While some of these relate closely to the topics discussed regarding dancer treatment, as outlined in the previous chapter, there are significant differences that arise in the specific context of making a dance piece with particular aesthetic goals and intentions regarding communication of specific meanings and emotions. Discussed here are both more traditional guidelines that might be offered for responsible artistic practice as well as suggestions for how to approach work that is intentionally more provocative and purposely controversial. In this chapter, I draw upon established ethics protocols from the realms of education and community engagement to stress the importance of establishing guidelines and best practices. I also consider social contract theory as a helpful source for developing mutually agreed upon ethical principles for a particular piece, event or company, especially with regards to work that is purposefully pushing boundaries in form and content.

Creative practice in educational settings

I begin with dance making in the educational setting, since that is where some of the clearest guidelines can be found regarding ethical protocols. Specifically, higher education, especially in research-oriented universities, has many resources that can be helpful for choreographers who want to learn more about ethics. While these resources have historically been oriented towards scientists, they are relevant for dance makers, especially those who see their work as a form of research. In effect, as more and more choreographers within university programmes frame their creative practice as some variation of 'embodied research', 'practice-as-research', 'arts-based-research', 'action research', 'recherche-création' and 'performance-as-research', participating in these trainings and processes is becoming more and more common (Schiller 2015).

At the heart of ethical guidelines in higher education and other research institutions is concern over any kind of in-depth inquiry involving 'human subjects'. In this context, human subjects are 'living individuals about whom an investigator conducting research obtains information through interaction with the individual or uses, studies, analyses or generates identifiable private information' (US Department of Health and Human Services n.d.). This interest in protecting human subjects is a response to well-documented cases of inhumane treatment of individuals that occurred during the twentieth century under the guise of scientific research. These were instances where human beings were treated merely as means to particular ends, disregarding Kant's mandate, as described earlier in this book, to always treat people with dignity as moral subjects. Such studies included experiments conducted by German physicians on concentration camp prisoners during the Holocaust without their consent, who subsequently died or were crippled as a result (the Jewish dancer Miriam Dajches was among such victims), and the Tuskegee Syphilis Study (1932–72), in which hundreds of low-income African American males in the United States with syphilis were deliberately not informed about their disease and denied treatment once penicillin became available.

As a consequence of these and other cruel and inhumane studies, several documents were produced to oversee ethical, risk-minimizing conduct in research, where 'research' came to be defined as 'systematic investigation, including research development, testing and evaluation, designed to develop or contribute to generalizable knowledge' (US Department of Health and Human Services n.d.: n.pag.). Here, the three key attributes of research are that the investigation is *systematic,* intended to contribute to *generalizable* knowledge, and is *published* or otherwise widely disseminated, usually through some kind of peer-reviewed process. These are common characteristics of scientific research, where investigators are expected to outline clear hypotheses, gather data, apply a reproduceable method, make observations, formulate conclusions and share their findings for others to assess and build upon.

Researchers working in the performing arts, especially in the university setting, are increasingly likely to carry out research that falls somewhere within these general parameters. This is not only true of recognizable scholarly studies in the arts but also those that are more studio based, as the realm of what is considered research expands to include practice-based activities. Thus, for example, a study in which a dance professor interviews students participating in their choreography to better understand some element of the choreographic process would be considered research with human subjects if the professor then disseminated their findings through a conference presentation or publication. Similarly, a graduate student's observational study for a final written thesis – say, research on how a select group of children in a dance programme engage in a class of contact improvization over a period of several months – would count as research along these lines.

Indeed, the rise of 'Practice as Research' (PaR) has increasingly challenged more traditional concepts of research and knowledge production within an academic, primarily scientific, paradigm to acknowledge the rigor and insights gained from experiencing and doing that the arts make possible. In *Practice as Research in the Arts: Principles, Protocols, Pedagogies, Resistances*, Robin Nelson points out that with the increase of artists in institutions of higher education, especially at the Ph.D. level, it has become possible for the arts *in and of themselves* 'to be recognized as knowledge-producing and submitted as research for PhDs and professional research audits' (2013: 4). While PaR remains a highly contested area, the turn towards acknowledging *praxis* (theory embedded in practice), or what might be called 'material thinking' or 'intelligent practice', as a form of knowledge production has expanded conceptions of 'legitimate' academic research. The kinds of pedagogy involved in PaR, and the evidence and documentation of the process and final product serving as the means of assessment, are now being debated and formulated. For Nelson, a PaR submission might comprise various aspects: for instance, a product (e.g., performance or video), different forms of documentation of the process and 'complimentary writing', which includes 'locating practice in a lineage of influences and a conceptual framework for the research' (2013: 26).

Dance practitioner-scholar Sarah Rubidge outlines three different strands of PaR as specifically related to dance. The first is 'practice-based research', which 'uses practice as a means of interrogating a pre-determined theoretical or technical issue' (Rubidge 2004: n.pag.). This might include an investigation through dance-making of a choreographer or theorist's claim concerning the nature of choreographic practice. She observes that in projects such as these, the research question tends to be clearly stated at the start of the project, and 'practice is used as one mode of interrogating that question, and may play either a supporting or a dominant role in the research methodology' (2004: n.pag.). Second is 'practice-led research' or 'discovery-based research', in which the 'research is initiated by an artistic hunch, intuition, or question, or an artistic or technical concern generated by the researcher's own choreographic practice which it has become important to pursue in order to continue that practice' (2004: n.pag.). An example might be, 'What would happen if […]?' (2004: n.pag.). Finally, she discusses 'research into artistic practice, through artistic practice' (2004: n.pag.). She associates this with the efforts of outstanding practicing artists in the professional world who 'have pushed the boundaries of the discipline forward, but have never become involved in articulating their reflections on their practice in conventional theoretical terms' (2004: n.pag.).

What is important here, however, is not so much a detailed understanding of different conceptualizations of PaR but recognizing that choreographic practice shares similarities with traditional modes of research in its contributions to the advancement of knowledge and/or generation of significant insights into the field of dance and other fields of inquiry. As choreographer Gretchen Schiller observes in her article 'Grasping gestures: Practice-based research', dance produces

> reflexive activities and processes which generate modes of thinking, sensing and concept building. The reflexive methods address and materialize the ways in which we make and think our visceral, imaginary and conceptual understandings of movement efforts in space, through time and with weight.
>
> (2015: n.pag.; also see Pakes n.d.)

And this means that, like traditional research in the sciences and humanities, we *should* consider ethical concerns related to the research process in the performing arts. In fact, given that dance making most often engages living performers (and sometimes audience members), one could argue it is particularly valuable to consider the resources guiding academic researchers and any additional issues that may be unique to the dance context.

Luckily there is an excellent foundation to work from. Within the educational context specifically, multiple resources are available. These derive from several codes and reports that were developed during the latter half of the twentieth century, such as the Nuremberg Code, The Declaration of Helsinki and the Belmont Report, which outline key requirements for ensuring ethical conduct in research. At a foundational level, this involves participants' voluntary consent and perceived benefits that outweigh harm. More specifically, the *Belmont Report: Ethical Principles and Guidelines for the Protection of Human Research* (1978) outlines three fundamental ethical principles. These are respect for persons, beneficence and justice. The first recognizes that individuals should be treated as autonomous agents, and as such should have the opportunity to freely choose what shall or shall not happen to them based on clear and complete information. It also recognizes that for a variety of reasons, some people are not capable of full self-determination (such as children or the mentally challenged) and require special protection. The second stresses that research should maximize possible benefits and minimize possible harm of those involved – that there is an obligation to not only protect people from harm but to secure their well-being – and, for that reason, researchers should assess the nature and scope of risks and benefits in a systematic manner and communicate these to participants. Finally, the principle of justice calls for fairly distributing the research's benefits and risks. For instance, there should be fair procedures in the selection of research subjects such that no one group is chosen over others due to researchers' prejudice or participants' vulnerability or privileged status.

The National Research Act of 1974, which was responsible in the United States for the Belmont Report, also led to the creation of Internal Review Boards (IRBs) to review biomedical as well as social and behavioural research involving human subjects. Since then, IRBs have been established at universities and other institutions where research is regularly conducted. These boards are formally designated to review and monitor all research involving human subjects, including as it relates to the arts. An IRB has the authority to approve or disapprove research or require modifications to research plans prior to re-application for IRB approval. The purpose of the IRB review is to assure, both in advance and by regular, continuing appraisal, appropriate steps to protect the rights and welfare of those participating as subjects in the research. To accomplish this, IRBs use a group process to review research protocols and related materials (e.g., informed consent documents and questionnaires) with clear requirements for researchers at different stages.

Perhaps one of the most valuable parts of the IRB process for creative artists is its required training. In the case of my home institution, Arizona State University, this training is provided through the Collaborative Institutional Training Initiative (CITI Program), a nationally available online programme (see https://about.citiprogram.org/en/homepage/). Those in the arts conducting research that is more qualitative in nature (rather than a study, say, related to dance science) are required to take the social-behavioural-educational research course. It offers valuable insights into historical and current information on regulatory and ethical issues important to the conduct of working with human subjects. The modules present case studies to convey key concepts, such as voluntary participation, informed consent, risk of harm, confidentiality, anonymity and right of service within the project.

While all of these factors may not ultimately be desirable, possible or even appropriate for a particular creative endeavour involving dance, they bring awareness to the kinds of issues that are important to treating people with respect, care and fairness during the choreographic process. Voluntary participation and informed consent draw attention to providing, for instance, dancers and collaborators in a creative project with as much information as possible up front to make informed choices about participating. Respecting persons means avoiding coercion and being as transparent as possible about one's intentions. Meanwhile, concern over confidentiality and anonymity allows choreographers to consider the extent to which they should acknowledge dancers and collaborators by name in the creative process – something I address later when discussing ethical concerns regarding intellectual property and cultural appropriation. 'Risk of harm' allows dance makers to think through whether they are planning a piece that will expose the participants, either dancers or audience members, to any discomfort – whether psychological or physical – and how to minimize dangers and warn those involved (again, so that they might make an informed decision on whether or not to partici-pate). And finally, 'right to service' can allow choreographers to pause and consider whether their selection processes, for instance, are equitable or unintentionally but unfairly favour people from certain, say, racial, ethnic or socio-economic backgrounds (see Chapter 6 for an example of unfair processes in creating and performing Deborah Hay's *Blues* for the Museum of Modern Art in 2012, which led to dancers feeling frustrated and unsafe).

For those dance makers who do proceed with a formal IRB application, direct engagement with such concerns is necessary and can also be an excellent exer-cise in ethical decision-making. The application requires explicitly addressing the following areas: the purpose of research; identification of subjects: demograph-ics and whether subjects are physically, psychologically or socially vulnerable and need added protections; recruitment/selection procedures and materials that assure fairness; study location, to ensure the space is safe; an explicit description of activities – procedures, kinds of data gathered, how the data will be securely main-tained, etc. – to indicate that these issues have been responsibly thought through; the research's benefits (or lack thereof), to demonstrate a concern for beneficial outcomes and human wellbeing; risks and discomforts of any kind – physical, psychological, professional, financial, legal, spiritual or cultural – so that they can be communicated to participants; description of how deleterious effects will be minimized; and evidence of the methods of protection of personal privacy within the project to protect individuals from unwanted public exposure.

It should be noted that while this process may seem daunting, extensive assis-tance is provided along the way, and once the proposal is submitted, approval can be relatively quick, especially if the work falls within a minimal risk category. There are three levels of review outlined in federal regulations: Exempt, Expedited and Full Board.[1] Exempt research will not require any further review after the initial approval and only needs to be reviewed by the chair of the IRB. Categories that qualify as exempt are generally low risk, such as studies that are conducted in established or commonly accepted educational settings, involving normal educa-tional practices and/or accessing publicly available information, where confiden-tiality of any personally identifiable information will be maintained. A research project is appropriate for Expedited review if it involves only minimal risk but is not classified as Exempt. Minimal risk is defined as risk that is not greater than what one encounters in ordinary daily life or during the performance of routine physical or psychological examinations or tests.

Many choreographic processes, especially in educational settings, fall under one of these two categories and benefit from the IRB application's questions and feedback for avoiding ethical dilemmas in the long run. For instance, imagine a dance professor or a graduate student wants to create a piece on undergraduate students that involves having them observe everyday people's behaviour in public parks. This necessitates a close look at how that process will unfold. What parks will the dancers be asked to visit, at what times of day and are they secure places? How will the students be asked to record their observations – with note taking, photographs or video? (Video requires a higher level of review.) Will the students be speaking with any of the people they observe and if so, what kinds of questions will they ask? Will the identities of the individuals be kept confidential? Through the back-and-forth dialogue that occurs during the proposal process, these kinds of questions would be addressed, allowing a dance maker to proactively resolve potential ethical problems.

If a creative project involves more than minimal risk to participants, it may be extremely beneficial for such a project to require a Full Board review, in which a group of experts weigh in on the activity. Research involving any of the following typically require Full Board review, since they involve vulnerable populations and potentially cause harm or involve unjust, coercive practices: minor subjects (children 17 years of age or younger); special populations (i.e., prisoners, pregnant women, individuals with disabilities); the use of video or audiotape to record subjects; asking questions that may be highly embarrassing or compromising (e.g., in relation to sexual behaviour, sexual orientation, alcohol consumption, illegal drug use, medical conditions, violations of the law, personal finances, problems in the workplace, etc.); inflicting physical pain upon subjects; creating high levels of stress, fear, discomfort or tension; threatening subjects in any way; providing some subjects with benefits denied to others (this includes payments or rewards for participation, e.g., offering extra credit to participants, etc.); causing physical or mental exhaustion or engaging subjects in intense exercise; placing individuals in confining physical settings or attaching other devices; and exposing subjects to extreme conditions (e.g., bright lights, loud noise, intense pressure, strong odours, complete darkness, extreme heat or cold, etc.).

For dance makers accustomed to complete artistic freedom and interested in pushing boundaries, this list may seem limiting and curtailing of creativity – a straight-jacket of sorts. Not to mention that dance in and of itself is undoubtedly stressful on the body, and sometimes those movements that are most exciting are also the most physically challenging and possibly painful. I take up these legitimate concerns later in this chapter. Within the educational context, however, these kinds of safeguards may be extremely valuable insofar as most of the performers and participants within pieces created within higher education are students, and as such, form their own vulnerable population to whom those in authority have a set of moral responsibilities. Undergraduate dance majors are often young people away from home for the first time, eager to please their faculty mentors and perform in original works created on them by faculty, graduate students and guest artists. Within this context, there is a responsibility to be sensitive to the kinds of power dynamics at play and the extent to which the primary focus should remain on the educational value of the experiences provided. In other words, it is constructive for choreographers in higher education to have clear educational goals driving their creative processes – i.e., the knowledge, skills, competencies and qualities that their work provides the participants – and ensure students understand why that is important for their evolution as dance artists.

For example, consider a situation in which a choreographer on a dance faculty wants to create a piece around sexual assault using undergraduate dancers in their dance programme. If this choreographer proceeded without IRB training or submitting a proposal for review, several ethical problems might arise. Students might audition or sign up for the piece without fully understanding the extent to which they would be asked to learn about, or disclose, intimate experiences of sexual assault and then feel they have no way out of the process for fear of alienating a professor and/or losing needed credits towards graduation. Or the choreographer might transform students' own highly personal stories in ways they do not fully explain or manipulate movement material without consent and leave dancers feeling violated. Or the final piece may involve partial or full nudity and exposure of intimate body parts, which may cause some students extreme embarrassment or place them in uncomfortable situations in relation to family members, peers and/or other faculty members in the audience. All of these kinds of issues could be avoided or minimized through an IRB review. It is an opportunity to explain the project's educational goals and think through and address ethical challenges and implications in advance.

The IRB process is also very helpful for a choreographer interested in creating work involving children, minors or adults unable to give consent. In this case, the requirement is for each person from a special population to give 'assent', where assent is defined as an 'agreement by an individual not competent to give legally valid informed consent (e.g., a child or cognitively impaired person) to participate in research'.[2] The assent process, while not legally binding, involves taking the time to explain to a child (for instance) what is going on in the proposed study, why the study is being done, what they will be doing, and that if they object, they can opt out without punishment. Just as with informed consent, and following the perspective of care ethics, the emphasis here is on sharing information and values and jointly making decisions. The assent process should use language that is appropriate for the subjects' age level and mental capacity, which will vary depending on the individuals involved. For children and minors, a parent or guardian would also be required to provide consent.

Another area often involving special consideration is research involving Native Americans or tribal land, which is critically important for choreographers interested in drawing on Native traditions. There are at least 565 federally recognized Indian tribes in the United States. Due to historical abuse and mistreatment of Indigenous populations in the USA and abroad, there should be a particularly high level of scrutiny for such projects in the arts as well as sciences. Researchers must recognize and comply with the intent and spirit of laws and policies relating to American Indians and enacted by tribal governments themselves.[3] Before undertaking any activity or project that has the potential to affect a tribal government, its community or tribal members, faculty, staff and students at an institution must first determine whether tribal government input, participation or approval is required. The emphasis is on facilitating a culturally respectful process in which concepts of sovereignty, government-to-government relations and trust are understood. Respectful collaboration and consultation with appropriate formal and informal points of contact are critical. And researchers – including artists – are required to educate themselves about tribal cultures or systems where necessary to sensitively and equitably deploy the creative process. The same goes for choreographers working in Canada, for example, who engage in research involving First Nations, Inuit and Métis, and in other countries where there are Aboriginal peoples.

The dance anthropologist Joann Kealiinohomoku recognized many of the potential issues involved in interacting with dancing within Native American communities in her essay 'Ethical considerations for choreographers, ethnologists and white knights'. Here she describes how her goal during Hopi-Tewa ceremonies was always to 'try and behave appropriately and to be sensitive to the situation' (1981: 14) and to delineate the various problematic ways that often 'well-meaning but ill-informed and naïve persons insert themselves into alien situations' (1981: 15). As part of her analysis, she characterizes several different types of outsiders. Some of these include the 'great appreciators' who inappropriately idolize and 'feed on ethnic mystique' (1981: 16). She also calls out 'the category of outsiders who perceive themselves as the powerful archangels who will save dance cultures, even though ripped from context, and whether that is culturally appropriate' (1981: 17). These include choreographers who are not trained in the social sciences and are likely unaware of the ethical issues involved. She writes:

> It seems to me that any group of dancers that wants to save someone else's dance culture is monumentally and paternalistically insulting. After all, in this day of mass media and vast communication networks, Indians, Blacks, Mexican Americans, and so forth, all know there are ways of preserving their dances if they want to [...] we should seek collaboration rather than informants.
>
> (1981: 19–20)

Indeed, it is incredibly valuable for dance makers to recognize the need for respectful, mutually beneficial processes and define ethical protocols for any creative
research involving community members. In the college context, along with other
research institutions, there is an increasing attention on community-engaged
research (CEnR). CEnR can come in many forms and involves working collaboratively with groups affiliated by 'geographic proximity, special interests, or similar situations with respect to issues affecting their well-being' (NIH Principles of
Community Engagement 2015: n.pag.). In the dance field, socially engaged arts
practices, community theatre and dance, public art and arts for social change are
just some of the terms for activities that relate closely to this kind of research. In
these contexts, dance artists may collaborate with youth, seniors, city workers,
the terminally ill, incarcerated populations, etc. in the creation of original work.
Community engagement in the realm of CEnR is about relationships between
and among communities, researchers and research institutions, and, for that
reason, presents some unique challenges that need to be considered from an ethical perspective.

The Yale University CTSA's Community Alliance for Research and Engagement (CARE) Ethical Principles of Engagement Committee (2009) developed an
expanded set of principles relevant to this discussion. The committee's position is
that ethical review should apply 'not only to individual research subjects but also
to interactions between the research partners' (2009: 2). The committee explains:
'Each partner has certain responsibilities. Among the most important of these is
that each should recognize the other's needs and empower the other to assert its
unique rights within the relationship' (2009: 9). Part of ethical conduct within the
context of community-based research is developing a dissemination plan for the
findings of the proposed research that will meet the needs of both communities
and researchers. In addition to its emphasis on ethical and empowering practice
among partnership organizations, the CARE Committee extends the principles
and protections of the Belmont Report to communities:

> University Researchers should involve Community partners as early as possible in
> discussions about the potential uses of all data to be collected, including a dissemi-
> nation plan for the sharing of the research findings with the wider [non-academic]
> Community, and should develop a process for handling findings that may reflect
> negatively and thus cause harm to one or both partners.
>
> (2009: 3)

I will discuss the kinds of ethical principles guiding community engaged dance-
making later. For now, an example of related creative activity within a university
is a dance faculty member working on a community-based project with refugee

women who have experienced trauma. The goal of the project might be to see how working collaboratively to create a dance piece provides them a means of healing and well-being. Going through the IRB process for such a project would entail identifying the key agencies involved and consulting as necessary with the leaders of the communities engaged. It would mean identifying off-campus rehearsal spaces and the degree to which the choreographic methods, movement vocabulary, costuming and music/aural aspects respect the cultures of the women participating in the project. For instance, in the case of devout women following Muslim customs, the choreographer would need to ensure that rehearsals were in a women-only space, where the women felt they have permission to move and express themselves freely. Initial discussions with key stakeholders would determine how and whether a final performance of the work would take place and the extent to which observations and data are collected (say, from watching videos of rehearsals, or interviews with the women) and made publicly available. Throughout, the women's wishes should be honoured. Project leaders would need to sensitively address concerns as they arise and promote what is best for the women in the project, even when it may mean curtailing aesthetic concerns and/or production values.

These examples all illustrate the kinds of ethical concerns that one may face when doing research as a dance artist in higher education (see Risner and Schupp 2020 for detailed case studies). Some readers might question the point of choreographers following IRB processes in the case of more typical choreographic efforts that engage students to create a dance work that is primarily focused on formal concerns – such as the use of space, timing, weight, momentum, focus, etc. – and only peripherally on content, or on a subject matter unlikely to be traumatizing or controversial. In those cases, it is true that such creative activities are not usually viewed as traditional research, and as such, not seen as needing to undergo formal review. They are typically regarded as a part of regular educational instruction in dance, and because they are often limited to a single or short run of a specific artwork on a university stage, they are not perceived as furthering general knowledge of a particular issue. Finally, since the findings from the process are not intended for publication in research literature, they do not fall under the typical definition of research provided.

However, as pointed out in Chapter 2, even in such cases, there is a possibility that dance makers may mistreat dancers during the choreographic process as part of a more general historical authoritarian, hierarchical tradition of dance pedagogy, an engrained discourse of the dancer's self-sacrifice on the part to the choreographer's vision, or simply out of lack of awareness of ethical concerns. If a formal IRB process is not carried out, it still remains for dance artists making work in the educational context to stay vigilant to the kinds of mistreatment I discuss in this book. While the core ethical principles from the Belmont Report may not need to be as thoroughly addressed, the notions of respect of persons, beneficence and justice, remain important and should be considered. Even if a dance is solely concerned with exploring different rhythms made by tap shoes, for instance, the choreographer should treat their students with respect and care, making sure to avoid favouritism, communicating clearly and approaching everyone in the cast fairly. They should be concerned with the kinds of space where rehearsals take place and attempt to have a surface that will not injure the dancers. They should consider the roles of dancers in the creative process and the extent to which they will credit students for their contributions. When these kinds of issues arise during the creative practice itself, they require 'exercise of discretion, sound judgment and flexibility commensurate with the level of risk and potential benefit' arising from the activity (Government of Canada 2018: n.pag.). All of these issues are especially important because of the educational context in which the creative process is taking place. Dance students attend institutions to develop their craft, and artists working with them have a unique responsibility to honour the broader pedagogical goals by modelling best practices when it comes to ethical behaviour.

Creative practice in professional settings

For dance artists working in the professional dance realm, ethical guidelines are often less well defined and understandably vary greatly depending on the context. Choreographers who work with companies, private studios and/or for television or film, and/or are hired by government or community organizations, will likely face different levels of expectations with regards to ethics. Many of these overlap with the kinds of concerns already discussed in relation to dance in education, such as around respect, concerns over health and safety and fairness/justice. However, other topics frequently arise that deserve special attention. These include intellectual property, or choreographers' responsibility for how they use material generated by their dancers or others involved in the process of making work, and sensitivity to how certain themes are presented on stage. In approaching these topics, the realm of ethics provides guidance. For choreographers particularly interested in complete artistic freedom, social contract theory may provide the best approach.

To begin, however, it is important to reiterate that in professional dance contexts outside regular educational boundaries, choreographers should be sensitive to how the authoritarian pedagogical tradition has often bled into the functioning of dance companies. In professional ballet and modern dance companies, for instance, there may be a direct continuation from the company's school or pre-professional programme to the company, where personnel overlaps and the hierarchical relationship between student and teacher is mirrored in the relationship between dancer, choreographer and artistic director. As I discussed in earlier chapters, such a situation can easily lead to situations in which a dancer's role in the choreographic process is compromised and their humanity diminished. This is particularly likely wherever a single choreographer or artistic director's vision directs the overall company or project. For that reason, it is valuable for companies (and independent dance makers) to develop guiding ethical principles and/ or codes for choreographers concerning dancer treatment and assure that both parties are protected. As the Dancers Forum Compact (2002) observes,

> The degree of comfort, receptivity, and cooperation, or lack thereof, demonstrated toward one another by dancer and choreographer, affects the experience and development of work. Each party is responsible for cultivating and maintaining a relationship supportive of the artistic process and product, and all other activities.
>
> (2002: 2)

Of particular import is the matter of credit and acknowledgement. Unlike in traditional research within universities, where the norm is to protect the confidentiality of those involved in the research process, in the professional context, choreography is usually recognized as an aesthetic product of a particular artistic vision and performed by dancers who are publicly named. In this context, it is seen as a sign of respect for the choreographer to accurately identify and state each individual's involvement in creating and presenting the artistic product, along with any additional collaborators. Terms such as 'choreographed by', 'directed by', 'conceived by', 'created by', 'in collaboration with', 'with input by', 'performed by', 'danced by', 'originally performed by' and 'originally danced by' are appropriate.[4] The Dancers Forum Compact recommends that, 'The choreographer should use her or his best efforts to ensure that credit and acknowledgment appears in programmes, press releases, photos, videotapes, and related marketing materials' (2002: 4). And, 'In cases where a work is remounted after some or all of the original dancers have left the work, the original performers and their role in the process should continue to be acknowledged in the above stated materials' (2002: 4).

Recognizing dancers' role in the creative process is particularly important in illuminating the often deeply collaborative nature of dance making, treating dancers with dignity and challenging the notion of the lone artistic genius. While there are certainly cases of choreographers setting pre-existing material that they have developed on their own, more common today is for choreographers to work closely in real time with dancers trying out different movement ideas or conceptual prompts. For instance, a choreographer may have a general idea for a lift but will try out different possibilities with the dancers before settling on one they prefer. Or a dance maker may provide dancers with a structured improvization to enact as a means of generating material that is recorded using video and then used to draw set material. In such cases, failing to recognize the role of the dancers, either explicitly through public acknowledgment or through more informal means, is to miss out on treating dancers with dignity and honouring their contribution. It also makes their labour invisible and potentially means less pay and lead to burnout. I have heard dancers voice frustration over unfair compensation and insensitive handling in return for choreographers' mining their kinesthetic and expressive capacities.

To be sure, some companies highlight the collaborative nature of their process in ways that demonstrate how a more overtly collectivist approach can work effectively. Pilobolus, a company founded on collaboration in 1971, has valued mutual responsibility between individuals and the group since its inception. 'Other dance companies are about the individual [artistic director] and the power of the individual', former co-artistic director Michael Tracy argues. 'What is interesting about our group is that however powerful we may individually be, we always focus on the perspective of the group' (quoted in Chremos and Catrambone 2012: n.pag.). The company uses a collaborative, creative and education process when designing each new work, inviting a diverse group of artists, choreographers and dancers to create as a team who are then acknowledged in programme information. One of the founding members, Robby Barnett, explained to me in an interview that this means engaging dancers who are willing to 'investigate themselves' (2010: n.pag.) and treating dancers as full players in the choreographic process. Barnett described the company's fundamental expectation of play, improvization, problem solving and disagreement – the choreographic process follows a kind of 'Darwinian logic' in which 'the strongest ideas win out' (2010: n.pag.). Ultimately Barnett's highest values were respect for others, higher-order thinker, appreciating difference, being honest/authentic and perhaps most basically, getting things done. Barnett explained that if a problem arises, they all talk about it, and try to accommodate the dancers and make them happy. He observed that the 'dancers are exceedingly explicit about what they want' (2010: n.pag.). The artistic directors found that in striving to meet their needs one loses some control – but 'get in return complete commitment and dancers who really care about the company' (2010: n.pag.).

Within the realm of more traditional research, the idea of acknowledging sources is more than an issue of dignity or treating dancers well, however. It is also part of responsibly building an argument for the solidity of your conclusions and how you provide proof and evidence for the credibility of your original findings. Accurately and honestly citing the work of others is seen as a moral imperative of good research and 'academic integrity', where academic integrity may be defined as a commitment to honesty, trust, fairness, respect and responsibility. Within this context, plagiarism is regarded as fraud. The expression of original ideas is considered intellectual property and can be protected by copyright laws, just like original inventions. Presenting someone else's work as your own, copying part of another person's work without giving credit, giving incorrect information about a source, changing some aspects but copying the broader structure without giving credit, etc., are all considered plagiarism and are violations of copyright and denounced in academia.

It should be noted before going more deeply into intellectual property issues in dance that strict guidelines surround the use of music in choreographic endeavours; the music industry is extremely organized in this regard. These regulations ensure that the musician or composer receives credit and compensation for their original work. Generally, a recording of a piece of music has two sets of copyrights. The sheet music itself, the melody and lyrics, belong to the artist, often represented by a publisher. The recording of that song/piece belongs to the music label. A choreographer needs to request and receive permission from both in order to use a specific recording. For music used for live performance, the choreographer usually needs to check with large performing rights organizations like the Broadcast Music Inc. (BMI) or American Society of Composers Authors and Publishers (ASCAP). Each of these has a database of millions of songs, including who owns which rights to each one. There are sites on the internet that offer royalty-free music in order to make music available to anyone and encourage free exchange of ideas. Sites like YouTube have also developed a workaround for obtaining permission that is regarded as fair to music artists. If you intend to post your dancing as a video online, software will check for copyright infringement; if the owner consents, YouTube will put an advertisement before your video, and the profits from that ad (or a portion thereof) will go to the copyrighted content's owner.

However, a major challenge persists: how to address the question of influence and drawing on others' movement material in the choreographic process. This especially holds within the professional dance realm, particularly when moving beyond original movement generated by the dancers and into movement and dance phrases from other sources beyond the dancer or the choreographer. In other words, what about when a choreographer draws directly on gestures, motifs, sequences, costuming, music choices, etc. of another choreographer or another culture's dance forms? What is the ethical responsibility in this case to explicitly assign credit?[5]

Unlike music, choreographic processes or final choreographic products, i.e., dance pieces, have rarely been formally copyrighted or carefully regulated. Part of this is because according to the law, for dance to be copyrighted, it must be fixed in a tangible form, such as recorded in a notation system or a film recording. This has been difficult for many dance artists in the past; they did not have easy access to either of these means of documenting their work or the money to pay for filing copyright fees. In fact, the first copyright ever granted to a recorded dance composition was not until 1952 for the Labanotation score of Hanya Holm's choreography for the musical *Kiss Me Kate*. Moreover, the amount of money generated from original choreography, especially in the realm of traditional concert dance, is small compared to the kind of revenues generated by sound recordings. Most dance companies are non-profits that exist through grants and private funding rather than profits from purchased recordings of dance pieces, as with music CDs and downloads.

Another reason, however, may well be that many dance traditions thrive on a dialogic engagement by practitioners – a kind of call and response between mentor and apprentice, or between peers, that ranges from unconscious and simply accepted as inevitable, to recognized and appreciated as part of the life force of the dance form. For instance, a dancer who performed for most of their career with George Balanchine is expected to choreograph in his style. Peter Martins once said, 'I don't even want to think about where he [Balanchine] stops and I come in because it's something I don't analyze [...] Everything I do and think is informed by Balanchine' (quoted in Pogrebin 2004: n.pag.). In social and popular dance forms like breaking, a bboy or bgirl is expected to reference another person's steps in a battle or cypher as a means to provide his/her own original commentary on them. Serouj Aprahamian observes in 'Going off! The untold story of breaking's birth':

> The legacy of 'competitive interaction' (Malone 1996: 5) seen throughout working-class African American dance history reemerged once again within this youth-oriented practice, as teenagers tested one another through various unconventional gestures and movements. For instance, one might put a more creative twist on a popular step, act out a humiliating insult, or drop to the floor and come back up with their hand directly in an opponent's face. These mostly upright sequences could be interpreted as displaying everything from wit and playfulness to aggression and intensity. It all depended on the situation, but the main aim throughout was to exchange with a competitor in your own unique way.
>
> (2021: 60)

In neither instance is explicit acknowledgment of mentors' or peers' influence seen as necessary or even desirable.

Indeed, the movement of postmodernism in the arts, especially since the 1980s, overtly recognizes and celebrates the intertextual nature of dance and theatre, playing with notions of collage and bricolage, where the conscious playing of diverse citations is part of the style, and is perceived as a positive characteristic. As choreographer Stephen Petronio states in the 1988 film *Retracing Steps*, 'I feel like I can put anything next to anything else that's proceeded me in history. You

may just see a flash of movement, but I'm seeing a kind of ticking through history'
(Blackwood).

There are definitely ways that viewing dance as always necessarily intertextual
can be justified as good from a moral perspective. The proverb that imitation is
the highest form of flattery points to the idea that one copies someone else because
one admires that person or values what that person has done. For instance, the
dance artist Richard Move assumed the guise of Martha Graham in his work
Martha @ – and performed sections or full pieces from her repertoire out of his
admiration for her. These were deeply appreciated as amusing yet sensitive paro-
dies of Graham's work. And/or it may be the only way to continue the legacy of
an individual or a group that would otherwise be forgotten, lost, overlooked or
discredited. For instance, in his 2007 memoir *Frankie Manning: Ambassador of
Lindy Hop*, Manning notes how 'stealing' steps at the Savoy Ballroom was para-
mount to ensuring the continual development and preservation of the Lindy Hop.
He reflects:

> Nobody ever thought of copyrighting their moves [...] If you stop and think about
> it, how far would the dance have gone if people didn't steal from each other? Back
> in the early '30s, there weren't any dance schools that would even teach the Lindy
> because they didn't accept it as a dance. It wasn't until the latter part of the decade
> that Arthur Murray and other dance teachers decided that this thing was so big,
> they might as well put it in their schools. So the only way we could learn was by
> exchanging steps. If another person learned your step, they might improve on it,
> which happened all the time. Then when someone else did it, it could spread, and
> the dance could advance.
>
> (Manning and Millman 2007: 101)

In these cases, the very act of imitation itself demonstrates one's admiration, and
one's value of others and wish to perpetuate creative work, which might all be
seen as definite virtues.

Another justification comes from the idea that 'nothing is original' and that
artists have always been engaged in borrowing methods and ideas while honing
and perfecting their own style. Or, as stated before, that being engaged in a 'call
and response' model between dancers or dancer(s) and musician, or dancer(s)
and audience, for instance in particular Africanist dance traditions, is an admired
aesthetic practice. Within these contexts, citation may not only be considered a
way of achieving artistic excellence but also an important vehicle for social transformation and spiritual transcendence. As Thomas DeFrantz has observed in his
article 'African American dance: Philosophy, aesthetics, and "beauty"', 'Black
performance prizes referential logics and spontaneity as foundational creative

approaches' – what he calls its 'citational – its "signifyin" – ethos' (2005: 97). When the dancer is able to fully become the dance and does so in the presence of an appreciative audience, the 'flash of the spirit' is evident, i.e., 'the contingent presences of immaterial, animating, vital forces'. In this way, dialogic body-talk connects with notions of the sacred in a way that moves Black dance into the moral realm and helps to heal communities that have experienced trauma. Here the consequences of the actions are seen as morally good and provide justification for the actions involved, including the use of citation and allusion.

On the other hand, there are important ways in which failure to acknowledge the sources of choreographic material, or failure to do the necessary research into the authentic experiences of those one is representing, can lead to real moral bads. In these cases, 'borrowing' original material from another person or culture really is an example of unfairly stealing; a lack of due diligence means misrepresenting an individual or group in a manner that, whether intentional or not, harms them. These situations are particularly wrong when there is a significant financial and/or power imbalance between the parties involved, and the person or culture whose work is used/imitated does not receive significant benefits and/or ends up being overlooked or perceived in simplistic or stereotyped ways that are hurtful. Since a person cannot file a lawsuit for copyright infringement unless they have registered copyright for their dances, this means that in such cases there is little recourse for justice. From the perspective of the Belmot Report, the choreographer would have failed to respect persons – in this case the original artists – and unfairly assess and distribute risks and benefits.

For example, Beyoncé's extensive appropriation of moves and staging from the Belgian choreographer Anne Teresa de Keersmaeker in her 2011 video *Countdown*, is arguably an example of stealing. This is because, if you are familiar with de Keersmaeker's work, especially *Achterland* (1994) and *Rosas danst Rosas* (1997), you will see nearly identical moments in *Countdown*'s movement phrases, costuming, setting and filming. This is not simply an instance of a few imitated gestures or movements here and there. Entire choreography, staging and production elements are copied. While the *Countdown* video co-director Adria Petty stated that, 'It was always meant to be a straight homage', and that she was 'disappointed that she [de Keersmaeker] wasn't credited on the video' (quoted in Kaufmann 2018: n.pag.), Beyoncé herself said her work wasn't the only 'inspiration' and that it was just one of 'many references' for the video (n.pag.). In this specific instance, such a defence seems disingenuous, given the extent of the imitation. In addition, the economic disparity and difference in status between the two artists was fairly large. While de Keersmaeker at the time was a relatively fringe choreographer known in limited contemporary concert dance circles, Beyoncé was a super star with global renown and an estimated worth of $350 million. It was demonstrably unfair for Beyoncé to leverage de Keersmaeker's unique choreographic style for her own gain and recognition. Andy Horwitz, writing on the controversy at the time observed, 'This is an egregious example of the devaluing and exploitation of contemporary performance by mainstream, commercial culture' (2011: n.pag.).

Meanwhile, Anthea Kraut has observed that with her actions, Beyoncé assumed a position of power traditionally reserved for white artists in terms of authorship. For Kraut, 'The history of dance in the United States is also the history of white "borrowing" from racially subjugated communities, almost always without credit or compensation' (2016: 4). In the case of Beyoncé, her failure to seek permission and to give credit, as well as her

> levelling of any distinction between her pop culture and high art sources, function as a usurpation of what has typically been white privilege. Claiming the experimental artist's prerogative, Beyoncé does more than reproduce choreography in *Countdown*: she also rescripts racialized norms of authorization, authorship, and ownership.
>
> (2016: 321)

However, as Miriam Giguere states, 'This argument does not dispute the importance of sampling or cross-cultural and cross-general exchange, but rather it highlights the issue of attribution and the importance of an awareness of the ethical issues involved in movement transmission' (2019: 31).

The unacknowledged usage of characteristic gestures, movements and choreographic material of minorities and disenfranchised peoples, including lesser-known artists from the contemporary dance realm, is an example of a lack of justice that has long been taken for granted in the dance field. But it is receiving increasing scrutiny. In her now celebrated book *Digging the Africanist Presence in American Concert Dance*, Brenda Dixon-Gottschild traces various Africanist aesthetic principles woven into the work of choreographers like Balanchine, to show how such elements form a critical, yet previously overlooked, part of his aesthetic. These qualities include the syncopation, aesthetic of the cool, acrobatics and unexpected movement juxtapositions that he developed from his interaction with Black artists on Broadway and in Hollywood. Other studies consider the work of early modern dancers like Ruth St. Denis and Ted Shawn, revealing how their work recycled materials sourced from other cultures as an important means of defining their avant-garde style. In her article 'Dancing out the difference: Cultural imperialism and Ruth St Denis's "Radha" of 1906', for instance, Jane Desmond examines the ways in which *Radha* drew on images of India available to her in books, without having studied actual Indian dance. She demonstrates how, in her piece, St. Denis presents a 'hyperbolization of categories of otherness, mapping markers of race, Orientalism, and sexuality onto the white middle class female body' (1991: 30–31).

Meanwhile, in her book *The People Have Never Stopped Dancing: Native American Modern Dance Histories* (2007), Jacqueline Shea Murphy considers how modern dance pioneers such as Shawn infused modern dance with simplistic and unnuanced Indigenous themes and aesthetics. Although Shawn visited American Indian peoples in the Southwest United States and observed their dance traditions, Murphy asserts that, ultimately, he made simplistic use of Indian materials for his own purposes and did not engage meaningfully with Indian worldviews. For instance, in her analysis of Shawn's two-minute version of the *Hopi Indian Eagle Dance* (1926), she points out that he 'makes no attempt to recognize the function and power of the Eagle, or of the Hopi ceremony he is embodying' (2007: 122). The piece 'evades the cultural, religious, and healing aspects of the Eagle Dance' (2007: 122). While he admired the skill and spirituality that infused actual Native dances, Shawn's reductive choreographed imitations here and elsewhere served more to fulfil his own ideas of a virile, athletic and ritualistic masculinity than to share the stage with Native peoples or cede them 'any control in the [early] development of an American ballet' (2007: 122).

Shawn's efforts, like those of certain other choreographers drawing on non-Western dance forms can provide a valuable means of bringing attention to styles and traditions that have otherwise been under appreciated on the concert stage. In Shawn's case, for instance, his long-held interest in American Indian Dance eventually enabled the development of American Indian stage dance by American Indian dancers at Jacob's Pillow, his Berkshire Farm that has since become a renowned international centre for diverse and inclusive dance performance. At the same time, his own choreographic process demonstrates the complex ethical issues involved in making work that uses source material or themes inspired by cultures other than one's own.

Have you, as a choreographer, considered why and how you want to draw on and represent an 'other's' cultural heritage? How much research have you done or plan to do on the dance form and its place and meaning for the culture or community involved? To what extent are you appropriating the dance form for your own ends or for monetary gain? Do you recognize the potentially radical value of engagement with the dance form for transforming your own ideas about dance? Are you taking into account how insiders to that culture will experience your work once it is completed and performed? To what extent are you collaborating or consulting with experts in the dance form while creating your work?

All of these questions are important to consider in terms of ethics, and circle back to the kinds of issues I raised earlier when discussing IRB review. They bring attention to core ethical concerns from the Belmont Report: respect, beneficence and justice. Here, respect is both of persons and their cultural traditions. Beneficence is about weighing the benefits of drawing on these foreign cultural expressions in one's own choreographic process against the risks of doing so, especially for the groups one is 'borrowing' from. And justice is about paying attention to the power imbalances involved in the choreographic process and striving to address them fairly and equitably. Attending to these concerns will allow a choreographer to provide greater transparency into the creative process and assign credit where and when it is due. As Miriam Giguere observes at the conclusion of her article,

> The topic of choreographic plagiarism is complex [...] There are issues of ownership that do not have clear answers and there are instances where U.S. copyright law leaves gaps for potentially unethical omissions of credit. By raising some of the key issues that choreographers [...] will encounter, the hope is for us to have the resources to make informed decisions on copyright issues and to recognize the importance of crediting those who inspire us and fuel our creative practices.
>
> (2019: 32)

The case of The Nutcracker

A terrific example of shifts taking place in how professional dance companies and choreographers engage with non-Western cultures can be seen in recent developments related to *The Nutcracker*. This now popular ballet was originally choreographed by Marius Petipa and Lev Ivanov in Russia, with music composed by Tchaikovsky, and premiered in 1892 at the Maryinsky Theater in St. Petersburg. Over the last two decades, various troubling Eurocentric, Orientalizing aspects of the original staging have been questioned and, as a result, are being transformed. This brings to light the ways in which choreographers can become more sensitive to the communities in which they work, and adapt and change when it seems the responsible approach to take. As Jennifer Fisher observes in her article, '"Arabian coffee" in the Land of the Sweets', 'Just as *The Nutcracker*'s second-act dances vary in choreography, they vary in terms of their potential for producing and reproducing potentially injurious stereotypes' (2003: 150).

The story of *The Nutcracker* is based on the story 'The Nutcracker and the King of Mice' by E.T.A. Hoffman. It follows a young teenaged girl Clara, through various adventures on Christmas Eve. After receiving a Nutcracker doll at her German family's festive Christmas party, she falls asleep and has vivid dreams related to the Nutcracker, various toys and mice, which she imagines coming to life. One of the high points of the ballet is her magical trip to 'The Land of Sweets' in the second act, where she is entertained by a series of dances, including The Arabian

Dance and The Chinese Dance. These dances are particularly problematic and fall under the umbrella of 'Orientalism', a term made popular by the writings of Edward Said in his famous 1978 book of the same name and the subsequent field of postcolonial/decolonial studies.

In brief, Orientalism is the highly biased and often unjust process by which the colonial powers of the West, and especially Europe in the nineteenth century, constructed images and ideas of the East. Said asserts that rather than representing the so-called 'Orient' (in itself a nebulous, problematic concept) in a manner that was authentic to the peoples of those regions, and their own world views, traditions, beliefs, etc., Westerners created images based on their own desires, fantasies and fears. Artists and scholars, whose depictions of the peoples and practices of places like the Middle East, India, Southeast Asia, Japan and China often created simplistic, stereotyped representations that involved some kind of denigration. They may have created their art or writing with the best of intentions and out of genuine curiosity about those with different traditions and values. But the results could be, and certainly today reveal themselves to be, inaccurate and disrespectful. People from these cultures were frequently represented as lesser or subhuman, as overly sexual, effeminate, weak minded, unchristian, childish, sly or dangerous.

While many variations of these particular dances have appeared since the first production, an Orientalist perspective can often be seen in popular stagings of both The Arabian Dance and The Chinese Dance. In terms of The Arabian Dance, the duet between a male and female dancer often emphasizes stereotypical conceptions of the Middle East as mysterious, feminine, sensual and lavish. The focus is on the female dancer, who is usually dressed in chiffon harem pants with sexy slits, and a bejewelled bra top that reveals her midriff. Sometimes veils are involved to indicate the thrill of the unknown. The languorous, slinky movement of both dancers features difficult acrobatic steps, deep back bends, hip movement and overextended ballet vocabulary like high leg extensions, suggesting sexual availability, danger and excess. The woman's seductive movements portray a common stereotype of Near Eastern women as exotic and sensual, existing solely for men's pleasure. Meanwhile, the usually bare-chested man who lifts and manipulates the woman evokes the dangerous yet alluring male Arab stereotype. As Fisher states, the duet is often 'replete with echoes of pernicious stereotypes – sexually available women; lazy, avaricious men' (2003: 148). Fisher demonstrates that these stereotypes have circulated throughout the twentieth century in Europe and in America in ballet, and on Broadway and in Hollywood films:

> The image of the 'low Arab other' was forged by depictions of moral laxity and excessive indulgence in sensual pursuits: Arab women were portrayed as

sexual slaves, dancing for depraved masters or reclining passively on the floor; Arab men moved with stealth and cunning, or were seen sitting or squatting on the floor.

(2003: 151–52)

Meanwhile, The Chinese Dance can be equally troubling in its reliance on and reproduction of stereotypes. The male dancers traditionally wear a Fu Manchu-style moustache, and all the dancers may apply elongated eyeliner to imitate 'Asian' eyes. The choreography, meanwhile, features tiny scurrying steps, frequent bowing, bouncy jumps and upwardly pointed index fingers, which combine to suggest obsequiousness, simple-mindedness and childishness. Ronald Alexander, programme director of the professional training programmes at Steps on Broadway and the director of Harlem School of the Arts Prep Program, observed in 2013 that the way in which Asians have been portrayed in the Chinese variation – 'heads bobbing up and down, index fingers protruding, and happy smirks of joy plastered on the dancers' faces – is insulting and embarrassing'.[6] Georgina Pazcoguin, a City Ballet soloist who is part Filipino, has also stated, 'I struggled internally with being cast in Tea as a person with Asian heritage' (quoted in Pogrebin 2018: n.pag.). While she was excited to have the exposure of a featured role in a popular ballet, she 'never felt quite comfortable with the depiction of the culture' (2018: n.pag.).

Choreographers and artistic directors sensitive to racial stereotyping have stepped up to make changes in the production elements and choreography. Pazcoguin has been a major catalyst for these changes. She teamed up with Phil Chan, an arts administrator and former dancer, to form Final Bow for Yellowface, committed to 'eliminating outdated and offensive stereotypes of Asians (Yellow-face) on our stages'.[7] The two were inspired by the changes they helped instigate at the New York City Ballet in 2017. City Ballet's changes to their Nutcracker included omitting the moustache and the wide hat; toning down the eye makeup on the man; replacing the geisha wigs with a headpiece on the two women; and modifying the shuffling and bowing choreography, with more generic hand gestures in place of the pointy fingers. Other companies that had previously changed the choreography and costuming to be more authentic and culturally sensitive include San Francisco Ballet, which features a Chinese warrior fighting a Chinese dragon, and the Richmond Ballet, which asked the Chinese American dance artist Michael Lowe to reconceive the dance, also with a focus on a Chinese dragon. As they proceed with their efforts, Pazcoguin and Chan encourage dance makers to engage in 'creative questioning' to help dance productions become more respectful to Chinese culture while remaining faithful to the artistic visions of the past (Chan and Pazcouguin 2019: n.pag.).

Involving people of Asian and Middle Eastern heritages in these processes is of particular value. This not only offers the possibility of more authentic representations but provides a voice to those who have been previously disenfranchized, maligned or overlooked in the creative process. Pazcoguin and Chan, for instance, offer their consulting services for companies looking to avoid insensitive portrayals of people from different races. A current project of Final Bow for Yellowface is to gather a group of choreographers and other creative artists of Asian descent as potential collaborators on ballets. Assembling such groups can provide an important resource for those striving to make changes to their repertoire, who may not have the know-how or connections to do so on their own.

Collaborative choreographic practice as embodied ethics

There are, in fact, many dance artists and scholars who view collaborative creative processes as a central means to embody, model and attain various ethical ideals in society. These artists and scholars exist in both the educational and professional realm, and, as I discussed in chapter two, closely connect their personal values with those of their work in the studio. The focus in many of these cases is on dance making's relational and improvizational nature, both in rehearsal and performance contexts. These draw on a variety of recent and historically relevant philosophers' ideas as a reflective practice for capturing their experiential perceptions and for developing and supporting their arguments. There is an emphasis on the close connection between mind and body, and seeing decision-making as an embodied praxis, where ethical ideas may be attained through doing, experiencing and reflecting. I discuss a couple of these approaches here as examples of this perspective.

In her book *Considering Ethics in Dance, Theatre and Performance* (2018), Fiona Bannon considers the practice of joint authorship in the performing arts as interweaving aesthetic perceptual processes with an ethical practice of living a reflective life in relation to others. In other words, she views collaborative art making as the key to living a fulfilling life. Bannon has experience working as a Dance Animateur (a community artist) in the United Kingdom and Australia and is Chair of *DanceHE*, the representative body of dance in higher education in the UK. As Einav Katan-Schmid writes in her review of the book,

> The explicit goal here is to articulate the ethos within the practice of making collaborative performance works and, in return, to ask the readers to consider shared performance as providing a valuable training ground for cultivating ethical ideas as embodied habitus.
>
> (2020: 102–03)

Bannon avoids a didactic approach to either ethics or aesthetics, instead empha-sizing the *process* and *experience* of shared art making as a means to engage with applied ethics, conceived as a situational, ever evolving practice oriented towards a better existence. Her work proposes a 'reflective culture-making' that regards collective engagement in aesthetic projects as providing valuable opportunities for sensitive negotiations of selves to imagine and generate better futures of our 'being-in-common' in contemporary society. This is because (and here she draws heavily on John Dewey's ideas of art as experience, and aesthet-ics as perceptual process) collaborative creative processes in dance, theatre and performance, engage in embodied acquisitions of knowledge, involve coordi-nating visions and creative goals and encourage constant reflective practice by individuals and between co-creators. These same qualities align with views of ethics from the perspective of embodied action: as relational and fluid in nature, part of our changing circumstance, 'an identifying and identifiable feature of our work and of who we, ultimately, may aim to be' (Bannon 2018: 27). Bannon turns to Baruch Spinoza, among other philosophers, to provide philosophical justification for her position. As case studies, she considers the work of Meg Stuart, Rosemary Lee, the duo Deufert & Philschke and Fevered Sleep, among others, who create work in Europe.

At the heart of Bannon's view is the notion of 'relationality' and a conception of art and ethics as existing within a dynamic, lived exchange between the self and others. In this way, it resonates with care ethics, as I discuss in earlier chapters, and a focus on listening and responding promoted by philosophers like Martin Buber in *I and Thou*. This is, in fact, the main point of another recent book that also regards creative practice in dance as a model for ethical living. The edited collec-tion *Performing Care: New Perspectives on Socially Engaged Performance* (2020) provides an argument for, and examples of, how an ethics of care is shown and valued within original dance and theatre projects involving diverse communities. It considers 'creative practices that are generated through an interrelated engage-ment with artistic creation and social responsibility and obligation' (2020: 7) and the ways in which collaborative performances, especially based on improvizational structures and real-time composing, foster attentiveness, encourage embodied connectivity and cultivate practices of deep listening and a readiness to respond to, and accommodate with sensitivity, the needs of the 'other'.

James Thompson's chapter 'Performing the "aesthetics of care"' in that book provides a foundational perspective on how dance making can become a means of recognizing the value and necessity of interdependent relationships as a crit-ical component of creative endeavours. He asserts that an 'aesthetics of care' is about a set of values realized in a relational process that emphasize engage-ments between individuals or groups over time. It might consist of small creative encounters or large-scale exhibitions, but it is always one that 'notices inter-human relations in both the creation and the display of art projects' (2020: 44). He outlines valuing openness and honesty of intention, mutual regard, the reciprocity of gradual creation and 'building mutual activities of sharing, support, co-working and relational solidarity within a framework of artistry or creative endeavour' (2020: 46). He argues that 'the aesthetics of care seeks to focus upon how the sensory and affective are realised in human relations fostered in art projects' (2020: 43). To that end he emphasizes aspects like the quality of touch between participants and the attentiveness with which people engage one another. Importantly, he avoids a solid distinction between process and product, instead observing that

> this is an aesthetics that could both present those mutually beneficial structures and foster them. It would not pretend to a distinction between a process and an outcome because both might stimulate affective solidarity between people – perhaps participant to participant or performer to audience.
>
> (2020: 44)

A wonderful example of such a caring process and ensuing collaborative performance can be found in *Men & Girls Dance*. This production, by Fevered Sleep, a company based in England devoted to making collaborative cross-disciplinary art projects for adults and children, features men and girls dancing together. The initial performances began in 2016 and are semi-improvized and co-created through residencies in different locations initially across the UK, and now internationally, partnering a group of male professional contemporary dancers with different groups of local girls from the community 'who dance for fun'. As Amanda Fisher demonstrates in her article 'Performing tenderness: fluidity and reciprocity in the performance of caring in Fevered Sleep's *Men & Girls Dance*', the creative process required the dancers to 'not only engage with their bodies but also their selfhood and feelings, and it was the dancer's perceptions, joyfulness and sense of vulnerability that became central to the development of each performance. Care emerges in *Men & Girls Dance*, then, not as a representation of a caring encounter but as a form of embodied knowledge whereby the dancers come to know each other through an emerging and embodied understanding of caregiving and care receiving' (2020: 55). This is made evident by Fisher's analysis of the process involved in designing and building the piece, as well as the performances she encountered as an audience member and witness to motifs of interdependence and cooperation through game play and lifting sequences, and the tender, attentive and joyful ways in which the girls and men interact.

Responsible risk-taking during the creative process

In 'Mapping responsible conduct in the uncharted field of research-creation: A scoping review' (2019), the authors consider the issues of responsible conduct of research that can arise in the practice of arts-based research, which in Canada is called 'research-creation' (RC). They refer to this as an 'emergent, interdisciplinary, and heterogeneous field at the interface of academic research and creative activities' (Voarino et al. 2019: 311). One of their key observations is that art's transgressive nature does not always align with traditional research ethics criteria, such as the principle of beneficence. In particular, they reference Barbara Bolt, who argues in her article 'Beneficence and contemporary art: When aesthetic judgment meets ethical judgment' that art is unique in that its purpose may be to create discomfort and harm. She writes:

> What is the value of art to a society if it doesn't confront the key issues that threaten fundamental human rights? What if art becomes so comfortable that it no longer provokes artistic shock? Thus the question of minimizing risk and discomfort that is inherent in the notion of beneficence becomes a key point of tension when artists become engaged in artistic research.
>
> (Bolt 2015: 57)

According to Bolt, for some artists, 'art's beneficence lies in its capacity to create trouble and discomfort, rather than minimise discomfort' (2015: 64). In addition, the authors observe the tension between the need for participants to provide informed and free consent and the often inductive and unpredictable nature of RC. Artistic creation often evolves in unforeseeable ways that cannot be fully explained at the beginning; attempting to do so would damage the integrity of the process. For those dance makers who are especially engaged with these characteristics of art-making – its transgressive nature and inherent uncertainty and even multi-layered ambiguity – is it possible to address these in a responsible manner?

For artists drawn to risk-taking while engaging with living organisms – animals or humans – within the educational realm, there is an incentive to find ways to do so responsibly, in the ways I outlined earlier in this chapter. The authors of this report recommend adapting existing guidelines for RC's unique approaches. For instance, rather than engaging with regular IRB boards, they suggest ensuring review committees with art expertise are in place within universities and that there is dialogue with those involved in traditional responsible conduct of research to understand how artist-researchers' needs can be met. They also recommend monitoring the research-creator's position of power and encourage all involved to log emotional effects, with an overall recommendation of 'protecting participants versus creation excesses' (Voarino et al. 2019: 333). This implies that activity should be curtailed or ended if participants or attendees' discomfort (or even harm) becomes too great.

Within varied professional contexts dance artists who want to push the boundaries of what might be considered aesthetically, socially and/or politically acceptable can do so to a more or less responsible degree. *Men and Girls Dance* addressed many traditionally taboo topics regarding appropriate gender roles and interactions between children and adults – and yet that did not mean the process of making the piece was, or needed to be, unethical. In fact, the sensitive handling of those issues was arguably what has made the work possible and ultimately successful, both aesthetically and in terms of its ethical impact on the participants and audiences. The integrity of the process imbued the production with the virtues of care, honesty and tenderness, allowing empathy among the performers, which then could be shared with spectators.

There remain, however, those artists who are interested in challenging what is morally permissible – from intentionally using nudity as a provocation to engaging in pornography, mutilation, bondage, defecation, masturbation, violence, torture, manipulation of animals, deception and lying, verbally or physically attacking audience members, or some other generally taboo behaviour in the process of making and performing their art. How might such projects be approached ethically? This is a question such dance artists may not have confronted, preferring instead to single-mindedly follow their artistic vision and world-view and believing, as indicated by the historical tradition in dance, that their genius either allows them to function outside of regular societal boundaries concerning right and wrong, or that their own ethical compass is the only necessary guide in making their work. Today, with increased awareness of the relationship between art and ethics, and concern for dancer safety, wellness and sustainability, there is greater commitment to addressing the issues raised by such work. The organization ironically titled, 'Trust Me, I'm An Artist', for instance, is an example of a recent attempt to provide artists, cultural institutions and audiences with the skills to understand the complex ethical issues that arise in creating and exhibiting controversial artworks made specifically in collaboration with biotechnology and biomedicine.[8]

For the purposes of this book, what I propose for such dance-makers – assuming they are engaging with others and not just their own bodies, over which they might be seen to have sovereignty – is to consider some kind of variation of social contract theory, as described in the introduction to this book. According to this ethical perspective, people's moral obligations arise out of, and are dependent upon, an agreement among those involved. It is not reliant or answerable to universal codes or laws, or based on individual beliefs.

It also does not rely on believing in the need to ascribe to particular virtues, or an ethics of care. Rather, it is a set of guidelines regarding behaviour that a group of people collectively agrees upon. One of the key points of contractualism is that the guidelines are freely chosen by rational individuals with agency who are capable of making such a decision. If this process informs the creation of a dance company or a specific dance project, and it is made clear that participating in the artistic process will bring grave, serious and potentially life-threatening risks, whether physical or emotional, one could argue that such an endeavour was handled responsibly, in so far as the participants provided informed consent.

A formal contract drawn up in advance by a production team or company and/or a working agreement created collectively by those involved in the creation of a particular work should cover a lot of ground. It could describe the mission or goals (to create work that deviates from societal norms, stating why this is valued), the kinds of unconventional choreographic processes that might be involved (such as involving participants in con games, 'dark play' or using prosthetics or potentially invasive new technologies), the types of challenging conduct to be expected (like defecation, masturbation, biting, self-cutting, dangerous suspension devices), and the extreme conditions in which dancers might find themselves rehearsing and performing – such as performing in extreme heat, cold, water and rough terrain. Participants should be aware of what might happen if they do experience severe psychological or physical hardship – whether they are responsible for their own care or if the choreographer, company or producer might assume some liability. If the dancers can be expected to *not* be treated with respect during the process, and purposefully lied to, screamed at, coerced, etc. as part of the creative process, that should also be made clear.

Not surprisingly, it is not easy to find examples of written contracts, agreements or concrete policies that explicitly lay out how such 'risky moves' will be handled during creative dance processes. Rather, they exist as a combination of implicit understandings, informal conversations, pedagogical processes and formalized procedures. Along these lines, Elizabeth Streb's company Streb Extreme Action seems to be an example of responsible risk-taking. Streb is known for creating work that is committed to pushing boundaries of what the human body can do, and she is forthright in discussing her interest in exploring the 'edge' of the possible. It is part of the company culture to have open and constant dialogues around the kinds of risks being taken. Dancers have agency as 'action engineers' in realizing Streb's vision as the 'action architect' in a manner that minimizes harm while achieving the desired artistic effect. Interestingly, a commitment to physical safety and responsible performance of movement is built into the very pedagogy and training the dancers receive in 'PopAction' classes. Training in skills and Streb's movement vocabulary is progressive, and dancers learn, from the teachers and senior dancers, the best way to protect their bodies as they proceed from one movement to the next. Dancers are also asked 'Are you ready?' before combinations, and can either say 'ready' or 'stop' in response (not 'no' because it sounds too much like 'go'). This is an example of how the notion of 'informed consent' can occur on a constant basis to mitigate serious injury during the creative process and also in the performance context.

In addition, engineers check new apparatuses for stability and structural integrity, and the technical director is present during the creative process to assure safety protocols are followed. Also, as employees, dancers are not hired on a project basis but become members of the Streb organization. As such, they are protected by normal state and federal laws; if they are injured, they file an incident report and are covered by worker's compensation, as in any regular job. Moreover, if a dancer is injured, the organization will attempt to find another role or opportunity for them while they heal. For example, Leonardo Giron Torres, one of the performers from 2007 to 2017, hurt his toe on one of the machines. During his recovery, Torres recalled having the chance to capture moments of a performance on video, and how much he learned from being a spectator (Torres 2020). When another dancer, Felix Hess, was injured, he filled out an initially conceptual part of a piece into a full theatrical scene and began creating intricate and personalized chalk drawings that he continued even after returning to fully performing (Hess 2020).

Meanwhile, in the United Kingdom, dance companies are seen as any other companies; leaders are expected to, 'protect your employees, and others, from harm' according to the Management of Health and Safety at Work Regulations 1999. Under these regulations, at the very least, employers should identify anything that could cause injury or illness and minimize and control the risks.[9] These regulations strongly encourage involving employees in risk assessment and mitigation to best accomplish these goals. According to the guidelines, 'Collaboration with your employees helps you to manage health and safety in a practical way' (n.d.: n.pag.). It achieves this by helping to spot workplace risks, making sure health and safety controls are practical, increasing the level of commitment to working in a safe and healthy way, and providing feedback on the effectiveness of health and safety arrangements and control measures. While not all dance companies complete risk assessments to the same degree, this mandate goes a long way in protecting dancers and audience members during the creative process in Britain.

Conclusion

One of the greatest challenges with regards to ethics and dance making relates to the pervasive and continuing discourse that positions the choreographer as the visionary orchestrator of (dancers') risk and as a positive force with the power to bring about transcendence and social transformation. Antonin Artaud called for a theatre in which 'a little real life blood is immediately necessary' (Artaud and Morgan 1958: 77) in order to incite audiences to change, and Marinetti, founder of the Futurist movement, encouraged performers to 'sing the love of danger' (Harari 2009: 176) to bring about 'real' transformation for both performers and spectators.

The normalization of this view within contemporary concert dance making, moreover, means that dancers often expect such risks to occur and accept them either because they revere a specific choreographer's ideology or aesthetic and the 'high' that such risks elicit within themselves and/or because they have a pragmatic understanding that this is simply what is expected of dancers today. Fabien Prioville, a former member of the Tanztheater Wuppertal Pina Bausch, provides an example of the latter when he argues that the dancers in Bausch's company take no risks beyond what live performance ordinarily entails. He explains that what might appear to audience members to be authentically risk-inducing activity is the result of carefully controlled and constructed choreography that is very precise and has been meticulously rehearsed. He states, 'Even when we literally play with fire on stage, there's no risk because it's so clear what each step is' (quoted in Dawkins 2010: 28). For the performers, 'it's just work' (2010: 28), and nothing above and beyond the norm: 'we take risks because we are dancers and it's our body and you never know what will happen. You take a risk as soon as you step on stage because you are exposed and vulnerable' (2010: 28).

In response, this chapter outlines how the field of ethics can bring attention to issues too long overlooked or downplayed in relation to making dance. At the very least, there are ways to mitigate both the unnecessary confusion around expectations of performers and the unfair favouritism that can occur during the choreographic endeavour, each of which may damage morale and affect the work. The chapter also provides guidelines for responsibly thinking through how movement material is used by dancers and how material from other sources may be integrated into a dance work. Keeping in mind and collaboratively developing strategies to address the three core principles of the Belmont Report – respect of persons, beneficence and justice – can go a long way in transforming the creative process into a more humane endeavour that allows performers and choreographers to bring their best selves to the practice, to make and perform work with sensitivity and awareness for those most affected.

NOTES

1. See for instance: 'Determining if a project is exempt, expedited, or requiring full board review', http://www.uwgb.edu/UWGBCMS/media/irb/files/pdf/Exempt_Expedited_FullBoard.pdf. Accessed 26 June 2021.

2. See 'Special considerations', Research Integrity and Assurance, Arizona State University, https://researchintegrity.asu.edu/human-subjects/special-considerations. Accessed 26 June 2021.

3. See for instance: 'Guidelines for working with Indian tribes or on projects having the potential to impact a tribal government, its community or its members', https://researchintegrity.asu.edu/sites/default/files/2018-04/Guidance-Native-American-Tribal-Consultation.pdf. Accessed 26 June 2021.

4. Many other kinds of roles for the choreographer are possible, such as choreographer as pilot and dancer as contributor; choreographer as facilitator with dancer as creator; and choreographer as collaborator with dancer as co-owner. See: David Zeitner, Nicholas Rowe and Brad Jackson (2015), 'Embodied and embroidery leadership: Experiential learning in dance and leadership education', *Organizational Aesthetics*, 5.1, p. 171, https://core.ac.uk/download/pdf/47189897.pdf. Accessed 15 July 2022.

5. In 2016, a joint CORD (Congress on Research in Dance) and SDHS (Society of Dance History Scholars) conference was held at Pomona College in Claremont, California, that explored some of these issues, titled 'Beyond authenticity and appropriation: Bodies, authorship, and choreographies of transmission'. See Conference Proceedings, http://s3.amazonaws.com/dance-studies-association/downloads/All_2016_Proceedings_Combined.pdf. Accessed 15 July 2022.

6. See Dance Magazine (2013), 'Burning question: Is *Nutcracker* racist?', *Dance Magazine*, 1 December, https://www.dancemagazine.com/burning_question_is_nutcracker_racist-2306921922.html. Accessed 26 June 2021.

7. See 'Our vision: Why are changes needed?', https://www.yellowface.org/our-vision. Accessed 26 June 2021.

8. See http://trustmeimanartist.eu/about/. Accessed 5 July 2021.

9. https://www.hse.gov.uk/simple-health-safety/risk/index.htm. Accessed 19 July 2022.

5

Ethics and Critiquing Dance

The ultimate aim of criticism in an open society is the criticism of life in the furtherance of humane values.

(Smith 2006: 38)

While Chapter 3 concerns the creation of dance, this chapter addresses its reception. More specifically, I consider important ethical issues involved when critically assessing dance works and dancing, either verbally or in writing. These include responsibility, truth, honesty, fairness, respect and care. I also examine questions regarding how a critic assigns meaning to a dance and responds to its perceived expressive or communicative qualities in terms of morals or ethics. The first part of the chapter provides some historical context and focuses on these issues in relation to *how* critique often takes place. I especially focus on traditional written dance criticism of live performances, with some reference to verbal critiques of dancing in televised game shows, feedback sessions following informal choreographic showings and critiques on individual blogs. The second part of the chapter more closely considers the place of ethical considerations in the actual critique and the nature of 'ethical criticism' in dance. In other words, when and why might critics include an ethical component in their interpretation and evaluation of dance? How important is it that a dance work is perceived to expresses a moral, ethical or political point of view? Taken together, these two parts allow us to both celebrate, as well as recognize some serious limitations with, conventional modes of dance critique, and offer approaches that are sensitive to context, strive for a balance between different ethical ideals and aim to treat those involved in the critical process with greater dignity, care and compassion.

Introducing the limits of traditional dance criticism

Before digging more deeply into the ethical values at the root of critiquing dance, it is helpful to sketch out some of the major limitations of conventional dance criticism both in print and more generally. One of the most commonly described roles of a professional dance critic in recent history is that of providing a deeply informed response to a dance performance. In her well-known article 'On your fingertips: Writing dance criticism' (1994), Sally Banes outlines four 'operations' for good dance criticism. These include providing a neutral *description* of the dance, *interpreting* the dance in terms of discerning associated meanings, offering *contextual information* on its creation, and *evaluating* the dance, in terms of assessing its merit. As Banes observes, these are not '*the* explicit rules of our profession; many critics perform some or all of these operations intuitively' (1994: 25, emphasis in original). It is by interweaving and achieving a rich balance of all of these four operations, however, that the critic is able to reach their objective, which in Banes' opinion, 'is to complete the work in the reader's understanding, to unfold the work in an extended time and space after the performance, and to enrich the experience of the work' (1994: 25).

At face value, this conceptualization of dance criticism seems reasonable enough and a great model. It paints a picture of an expert who is well educated in dance vocabulary and can record their experiences of movement, choreography, sets, costumes, lighting and sound in words that resonate with a reader. Such a person knows the history of dance, is familiar with different dance styles and traditions and can contextualize the dance for readers. They are also aware of the conventions and frameworks for evaluating dances and dancers in various styles and can therefore fairly assess the piece. In this way the informed critic can speak intelligently about the feelings and references the dancing evokes. They can also compare and contrast the dancers' performances and choreography to established criteria for that genre to reach a reasoned and sound judgement – as Banes puts it, to judge 'whether the piece is good according to certain standards' (1994: 39). Through their efforts, the critic deepens the reader's understanding and appreciation of the dance work, beyond the time of the actual performance, and the assumption is that we are all better off for it. As celebrated dance critic Deborah Jowitt has observed,

> Any writing that illuminates whatever is written about is capable of opening the mind of a reader. And anything that enlarges someone's perspective, or gives him/her something new to think about or bounce her/his ideas off should be helpful in creating a better society, on however tiny a level.
>
> (2011: n.pag.)

Unfortunately, however, history has revealed some problems with how dance critics and criticism have actually functioned. To begin with, many newspaper critics hired to review live dance performances, in the past and even up to today, have not come from backgrounds in dance, but in other fields, such as music, theatre, philosophy or English literature. For instance, Theophile Gautier, Stephane

Mallarme and Paul Valery, who were early writers on dance in the nineteenth and the early twentieth century, were from literary backgrounds. Henry Taylor Parker, who wrote on drama, music and dance for the *Boston Evening Transcript* for twenty-nine years between 1904 and 1934 had attended Harvard but was said to have left over the limited number of courses in drama and literature available to him. Carl Van Vechten, another celebrated dance writer of the early twentieth century, was a photographer and initially known as a music critic. While an education in dance is not in itself a guarantee of a sound review, the lack of such specialized knowledge can mean inadequate attention to detailed movement description or to subtleties of performance and choreographic design, since the critic may not have the necessary expertise to be able to accurately represent what has taken place. Instead, dancers might be said to 'twirl' or 'bound about' in a vague and general manner, and the critic may focus on the physical appearance of the dancers, along with the interpretive and evaluative components, leaving out the kinds of careful movement and choreographic analysis on which to build an informed argument. This is a problem because, as Jack Anderson has observed,

> Critics I particularly enjoy reading are those who can make a dance seem to come alive on the page so that I can experience it vicariously. Should I later see that dance on stage, my reaction may differ from the critic's, yet good writing can make a plausible case for differing viewpoints.

(2014: 160)

Another major issue has been the overall paucity of dance criticism in the dance field as a whole. Very few publications have full-time dance critics or specialized contributors on dance. As blogger Tonya Plank observed in 2007, 'The problem with dance criticism I feel, and the reason why fans get so upset, is that (unlike, say, film criticism or theater criticism), there aren't enough critical voices out there offering different perspectives, leaving one person's opinion to have HUGE repercussions, especially when that one person writes for the New York Times' (n.pag.). More recently, in her article 'The death of the American dance critic' (2015), Madison Mainwaring lamented vanishing space allotments and opportunities for professional dance critics. She observed that in October 2014, word counts for *New York Times'* reviews were reduced by 20 per cent (averaging about 400 words), and that *Dance Magazine* put its reviews on the web before doing away with them entirely in 2013. Many of the members of the Dance Critics Association (DCA), which was formed in the mid 1970s and used to hold conferences and publish a newsletter, now basically have a Facebook page to connect them. The current followers are mostly freelancers who work for multiple publications to whom they often need to pitch stories. The disappearance of full-time dance critics is a real problem. As Laura Cappelle observes in her 2019 *Dance Magazine* article 'Five major dance critics stepped down last season: What does that mean for the future of the field?':

> As the material conditions of the job become tougher, individual knowledge and independence will be harder to build up and retain. Increased diversity is hardly a guarantee either: It's easier than ever to share a review online but much harder to get paid for it. Few young writers have the means to see hundreds of performances.
>
> (2019: n.pag.)

In addition, the lack of widespread and sustained professional training for writers of dance criticism, and largely ad hoc means by which they become or are hired as dance critics, has meant that critics may approach performances with limited stylistic knowledge that is skewed in particular directions. In other words, rather than being able to draw on a comprehensive understanding of dance history, a critic might only have intimate familiarity with one or two dance forms from which to derive their interpretations and assessments. Historically, the genre most familiar to Western concert dance critics was classical ballet, followed by modern dance and then postmodern dance and to some extent theatrical jazz. However, this has meant that when such a critic encountered a dance performed in a style outside of their movement or cultural expertise, for instance, in Flamenco, hip hop or Bharatanatyam, this could lead to misconceptions and not understanding the appropriate meanings to attribute to the movement, let alone applying a valid method of evaluation. Such a critique of traditional dance criticism has existed since at least the 1990s and found in various dance writing along with attempts by critics to address it (see Gere 1995). More recently, in 'Dance, culture and the printed word: A call for the cosmopolitan dance critic', Samantha Mehra discusses cross-cultural reviewing from the point of view of a journalist writing in a multi-cultural Canadian context. She argues that Euro-American ballet and modern dance continue to be foregrounded as 'high art worthy of specificity and expertise' (2010: 434), and charges critics with paying insufficient attention to the detail of less familiar forms. Mehra reflects: 'I became overwhelmed with the idea of critical power and responsibility, and how the use of language in major publications (newspapers, magazines) can either perpetuate or undermine latently stereotypical language and the thought patterns associated with it' (2010: 434).

For many choreographers and dancers, in particular, an overemphasis on evaluation has been deeply upsetting and at times, enraging. Here, a major problem is found with a 'thumbs up' vs. 'thumbs down' approach to dance criticism, which major news outlets often demand, encouraging a 'rank and recommend' approach. This places the majority of energy on assessment – rather than say, on describing or interpreting the work – and/or does so in a manner that certainly fails to consider the artist's intentions or their humanity (something that falls out the traditional mandate for critics but that I will address in more detail later in this chapter as a valid concern). Here I recall performance historian Michael Kirby's characterization of standard theatrical criticism as 'primitive and naïve, arrogant, and immoral' (1974: 59), because of its overly subjective and ill-informed, biased nature. In many ways, this kind of judgmental criticism connects with the hierarchical, authoritarian approach to pedagogy explored in earlier chapters in this book, where those in authority routinely humiliate dancers. Choreographer Liz Lerman reflects the sentiment by speaking of being 'bruised' and 'black and blue' from her experience of professional dance criticism (2011b: n.pag.). Contemporary ballet choreographer Gabrielle Lamb refers to less favourable reviews as 'a bit of an out-of-body experience' and observes that 'Most often negative reviews are dismissive and don't contain much in the way of information' (quoted in Wozny 2018: n.pag.).

Modern art criticism's focus on assessment is part of a legacy dating to the seventeenth century. There are two definitions in play through the seventeenth to nineteenth centuries that lead to the kinds of tension we still see in discussions of criticism today: art criticism as either involving evaluations that stress a work's positive aspects or criticism as inherently negative, aiming to entertain through a scornful sense of humour. For instance, in 1677, the English poet John Dryden observes,

> they wholly mistake criticism, who think its business is principally to find fault. Criticism, as it was first instituted by Aristotle, was meant a standard of judging well; the chiefest part of which is, to observe those excellencies which should delight a reasonable reader.
>
> (Scott 1808: 106)

and, in 1706, one finds the statement, 'How strangely some Words lose their Primitive Sense! By a Critick, was originally understood a good Judge; with us now-a-days, it signifies no more than a Fault-finder' (Boyer 1706: 5).

Indeed, examining the *Oxford English Dictionary* accounts of these terms is very informative. The first entry under 'critic' stresses the fault-finding nature of criticism. A critic is 'One who pronounces judgement on any thing or person; *esp.* one who passes severe or unfavourable judgement; a censurer, fault-finder, caviller' (OED online 'critic, n.1' 2020: n.pag.). Two wonderful examples follow from the seventeenth century: 'Take heed of Criticks, they bite (like fish) at any thing, especially at bookes' (from 1606), and 'Nor play the Critick, nor be apt to jeer' (from 1692). The same sense of negativity pervades the first definition of the term 'criticism': 'The action of criticizing, or passing judgement upon the qualities or merits of anything; *esp.* the passing of unfavourable judgement; fault-finding, censure' (OED online 'criticism' 2019: n.pag.). An apt example comes from 1683: 'Criticism or a censorious humour, condemning indifferently every thing.'

The entertaining, brutal condemnation of art certainly continues to be popular in the entertainment industry and the dance field well into the twenty-first century. Witness television star personality Simon Cowell's many brutal comments, like when he remarked to an auditionee for *American Idol* in 2007, 'You look a little odd, your dancing is terrible, the singing was horrendous, and you look like one of those creatures that live in the jungle with those massive eyes.'[1] That same year, meanwhile, the *New York Times* hired Alastair Macaulay, a well-known British theater and dance critic, as their chief dance critic. Until his retirement in 2018, he was known for his sharp and witty prose, merciless assessments and highly opinionated reflections on dance. One of the most scandal-worthy involved a review of the New York City Ballet's performance of George Balanchine's *The Nutcracker*, where he observed, 'Jenifer Ringer, as the Sugar Plum Fairy, looked as if she'd eaten one sugar plum too many; and Jared Angle, as the Cavalier, seems to have been sampling half the Sweet realm. They're among the few City Ballet principals who dance like adults, but without adult depth or complexity' (Macaulay 2010: n.pag.).

Readers have responded with outrage at these kinds of personal, often petty attacks on performers and sweeping condemnations of choreography. For instance, following Macaulay's review, many e-mailed the *Times* and posted on blogs to condemn his comments about Ringer's weight, in particular, as mean-spirited, hateful, gratuitous, scathing, embarrassing, insensitive and cruel. Ringer, who had spoken in the past about struggling with an eating disorder, responded by observing that,

> I do have, I guess, a more womanly type than the stereotypical ballerina, but that's one of the wonderful things about, actually, the New York City Ballet […] we have every body type out there, and they can all dance like crazy, they're all gorgeous. And I think […] that's what should be celebrated.
>
> (*The Today Show* 2010)

Media analyst Michael Kackman, meanwhile, calls this kind of criticism 'Brit-wit' (which is 'scathingly acidic') and 'snarkasm' (a combination of snarky and sarcasm, and/or snide and remark) (2010: 65). Kackman argues that there is a pervasiveness of judging as a cultural norm that involves personal insults and judgments. This is clearly seen in Reality TV, which he calls 'an apprenticeship in incivility' (2010: 65). From his analysis of judging in a wide variety of Reality shows (including *So You Think You Can Dance*), he concludes that, 'We are in the midst of a media-fueled popularization of bullies, a convergence of micro-violences perhaps comprising a will-to-humiliation' (2010: 66).

Indeed, dramatizing the unequal power relations that are primed to humiliate the dancers and creators is in overt display in Reality TV dance shows during judging and elimination scenes. These moments establish a relation of dominance, with the judges, partially hidden behind their authoritative, raised podiums, on one side and the standing, fully vulnerable, dancers on the other. As Anja Hirdman observes,

> The framing of these scenes consists of several elements including strict bodily and emotional regulations. The behaviour rule is to keep the body still, usually standing and facing the jury and not respond orally [...] And when one of the contestants is showing signs of distress or is about to cry, then but not until then, will the camera move on. In other words, when the participants are overwhelmed with emotions and have difficulty controlling them.
>
> (2011: 26)

The dancers are, in other words, expected to display primary, infantile emotions, 'such as tears of disappointment and powerlessness, or of tension as well as relief. The situation demands a very clear divide of power between the ones invested in authority and the ones who are not' (2011: 27–28).

Clearly, the larger context in which these scenes take place revolves around, and thrives on, spectacle, human interest, controversy and conflict. This is part of the 'brand' of such shows. However, the potential cruelty of this setup, and the very real harm it can cause performers is often not fully appreciated until it is challenged in some way. During an episode of *Dancing with the Stars* (Season 13, week 6 in 2011), a professional dancer dared to respond directly to the judges' comments in a manner that did not seem scripted, thereby making the deeper power hierarchy of the show more visible and linking to authoritarian pedagogical patterns found elsewhere in the dance field. Master British judge Len Goodman proclaimed of the rhumba just performed by professional dancer Maksim Chmerkovskiy and soccer star Hope Solo that it was her 'worst dance of the whole season in my opinion'. A bit later, he remarked that 'half the fault is yours' (motioning to Chmerkovskiy).[2] In the charged exchange that followed, Goodman justified his evaluation by invoking his fifty years in the business. Chmerkovskiy reacted instantly by interrupting with 'maybe it's time to get out'. Judge Carrie Ann Inaba pointed to Chmerkovskiy and twice stated, 'don't be disrespectful like that'. He responded with, 'Let's not be disrespectful to everybody, right, because everybody is putting a lot of effort [...] everybody has been dying and killing themselves only to hear you guys' little judgmental comments, you know what I mean, it's a little much.' During the following melee, Maks is barely heard to continue, 'I'm not being disrespectful, I'm just protecting my partner.' Afterwards, another of the professional dancers, Lacey Schwimmer, said during an interview that she'd like to occasionally talk back to the judges but just doesn't have the guts:

> Regardless of what Maks said or if he hurt people's feelings, he had the courage to stand up for him and his partner and I think that is amazing [...] A lot of us wish we would say stuff, but we never do. We're afraid of it.
>
> (quoted in Borzillo 2011: n.pag.)

She further admitted that when Judge Bruno Tonioli called her partner Chaz Bono a 'cute little penguin' that:

> It's hard to hear your friend bullied by three people we are supposed to respect and called names like animals. It's unnecessary, it's rude. I feel embarrassed to be standing there when he [Bono] doesn't deserve to be treated like that. I actually lost it backstage. I was crying because I was so hurt. It's awful.
>
> (n.pag.)

As an interesting aside, there has also been recent pushback against harsh critique in dance contexts where insulting others can be viewed as an art in its own right. In the Black, gay context of Ballroom culture, for instance, which in itself draws on a long history of African and African American cultural traditions, performers and judges often trash talk each other either through 'reading' or 'throwing shade'. In the film *Paris Is Burning*, legendary drag queen Dorian Corey states, 'To read is to insult imaginatively, in opposition to the blunt gay-bashing taunts of the straight world [...] Reading is gay-to-gay sparring' (quoted in Lewis 2016: n.pag.). Corey summarizes shade in the film in this way: 'Shade is I don't tell you you're ugly, but I don't have to tell you because you know you're ugly' (Livingston 1990: n.pag.). When done respectfully and within context, reading is considered performative and a part of Ballroom as a way to point out competitors' flaws and boost one's own score. This performativity of throwing shade is meant to be light hearted, similar to 'yo mama' jokes. But for some in the LGBTQ+ communities, shade is their only way to show affection and can be easier than showing love. In an honest and heartfelt dialogue on the meaning and role of throwing shade Darnell L. Moore reflects on the complicated cultural conditions that surround such 'play':

> Shade, as I see it, is incisive and witty jest. It is meant to be 'thrown', precisely targeted in another's direction. Shade is an exact, cutting and implicit response to another's exact, cutting and explicit foolishness. The best shade travels in stealth. Shade is also a posture, a cavalier attitude of attack that stings the person it hits precisely because they don't see it coming. Shade can be both offensive and defensive. Shade is some

thoughtful, smart-ass type of retaliation and comeback. But can shade ever be good? Maybe. Like you've mentioned earlier (and others before you, like the characters in *Paris Is Burning*, for example), shade may not always be laced with malice. And even if it is, it is very possible that you can throw shade at the very friend you would otherwise fight to protect. I don't know, however. I do know that I am often exhausted by the presence of negativity in general. I mean, we get enough arrows thrown at us all the time, so I am not sure that creating and throwing more negativity is useful.

(Moore and Davis 2016: n.pag.)

In this discussion, Wade Davis II responds by recognizing that, something he initially found comical started to

sadden me a bit, because the shade that is thrown or directed at someone usually comes from the same people or persons we should be embracing and loving, because they may need it most. What breaks my heart is that shade seems to come easier than love for some.

(2016: n.pag.)

In the concert dance realm, meanwhile, the linking of criticism with clear aesthetic preferences as pronounced by experts from on high, has led to identifying a largely unacknowledged 'canon criticism'. Dance scholar Ann Daly defines this as 'an approach that centers around the ideology and practice of connoisseurship' (2002: xxxiii). 'Canon criticism' refers to criticism by a highly select group of gatekeepers who hold their privileged positions for many years and praise works by particular choreographers as masterpieces, which then become part of the venerated 'canon' of Western theatrical dance. European critic Franz Cramer points to the connection between criticism and power when he observes that dance criticism is, 'always a negotiation between various parameters – *dance and its making, dance and its consumption first of all; the categories of taste, knowledge, privilege, and power –* that to my opinion make up for the present situation of dance criticism at least in Europe and in the Western world' (Cramer 2003: n.pag, emphasis in original).

One can see how 'canon criticism' has evolved from how some critics have positioned themselves as the ranking and recommending authorities who patrol the borders of great dance. For instance, Edwin Denby, who was a well-known and highly regarded critic from the mid 1930s to the 1960s, for the *Herald Tribune*, *Dance Magazine* and *The Nation*, among other publications, advocated that critics are, 'meant to function as watchdogs of the profession they review' (Denby 1998: 196). Clearly, there are certainly strong correlations historically between noted critics and the choreographers they championed. We can see this, for example, when John Martin, the prominent American dance critic for the *New York Times*, was a major advocate of Martha Graham, Doris Humphrey, Charles Weidman and Hanya Holm.

These became part of the established 'big four' of American dance history, over and above many other modern dancers working at the same period, at least in part due to Martin's extensive influence. Editors also can clearly play a role in establishing who is or is not perceived as significant, as when *Dance Observer*'s editor Louis Horst forbade critics from mentioning experiments by the Judson Dance Theatre in the publication because he could not see them as dance (George Jackson 204: 175).

When a select number of critics (and editors) play such a central role in identifying and hailing perceived masterworks (or the opposite), they become part of the larger ongoing narrative that instils unquestioning reverence for 'choreographic geniuses' and the pedagogical processes they employ. This is problematic, as demonstrated in earlier chapters, because it can justify unethical ways of training and creating dance works. In addition, reverence for masterworks can gloss over the ethical issues involved in producing and disseminating dance critiques, and understanding the significance of *who* is given authority to represent another person's performances or productions and to what end. This is a situation recognized by Mark Franko when he asks the following questions:

> Which critics or theorists have provided influential, indeed canonical, interpretations that have shaped our apprehension of what we see? What are the presuppositions of such influential texts – even if they appear as ephemera – and what other writings have been suppressed or gone unnoticed? What ideological credence has been bestowed on the 'great' critic, and with what ideological consequences for the art of dance? The history of dance and politics can often be read and deconstructed in the encounters between performance and the print discourse that marks its passage with a discursive afterlife.
>
> (2006: 7)

It is also a topic that Kate Mattingly tackles in her article, 'Digital dance criticism: Screens as choreographic apparatus' (2019), where she discusses how criticism is changing according to societal shifts and the use of online social media and press. Her intent is to 'highlight the influence of critics' work on readerships' values systems and artists' networks of support' (2019: n.pag.) and to challenge what she sees as an outmoded and skewed approach to dance criticism that unfairly marginalizes certain artists, especially people of colour. Ultimately her aim is to illuminate the digital sphere as a more democratic, just space, 'essential to countering the dismissals and hierarchies that privilege certain forms of assessment' and to provide access to more voices that consequently '[disrupt] the notion of a critic as sole authority' (2019: n.pag.).

To conclude this section: we need to take into account critics' education in dance as a whole and in a broad range of dance forms and genres. We also ought to better understand how people define their roles as critics or judges of dance and how this affects their writing or speaking. In the next section, I will dive more deeply into these topics, with the goal of helping readers navigate the different choices available to them to respond to dance work in a thoughtful and nuanced manner. Once again, I will draw attention to the relevance of virtue ethics, and especially relational ethics, for re-thinking how to approach critical assessment. The significance of virtue ethics, which focuses on the kind of person one wants to be, is brought home by the experience of critic Deborah Jowitt. A few years after Macaulay was hired at the *New York Times*, she found herself increasingly pressured to write more 'negative' reviews for the *Village Voice*. Jowitt, who had written about dance for the paper for over forty years, resigned in response. In reflecting on her decision, she stated, 'To comply with [her editor's] wishes, I would have to change not just the kind of writer I am, but the kind of person I am' (quoted in Dance USA 2011: n.pag.). She refused to do that, and instead launched her own blog on the arts website *DanceBeat*, which continues to go strong in 2021.

Ethical issues in critiquing dance

It is against these concerns that I now turn to look more closely at the kinds of ethical issues that arise when critiquing dance. My focus here is on questions of responsibility, truth and honesty, as well as fairness and the place of care and consideration in critique. This section addresses each of these topics with the goal of outlining a range of concerns for dance critics to consider. How critique is approached will inevitably vary depending on the critic's outlook and situation. These wide-ranging contexts include whether the critique is part of more standard print reviews, occurs within a competition setting (including for instance, televised competitive reality shows), is online or follows an informal showing of live choreography. Nonetheless, it is possible to be more aware of what is at stake in the process from an ethical perspective, and strive towards more humane practices that prioritize a productive outcome rather than causing undue and unnecessary suffering.

Who am I responsible to?

The first issue to address is that of responsibility, since different ways of thinking about your obligations in terms of critique shape perceptions of other aspects of the critical process. It is what Jennifer Fisher, a former critic for the *Los Angeles Times*, is getting at when she observes that as a critic 'you are the responsible watcher, not just an audience member, and you are responsible not just to give the reader a sense of what went on onstage, but to do it in a way that aligns with your values' (2011: n.pag.). Like Fisher, I consider responsibility to refer to the general state of being answerable or accountable for one's actions. The phrase 'ethical responsibility' refers to the specific ability to recognize, interpret and act upon multiple principles and values, according to the ethical standards within a given context. In many cases, the general obligations that can be outlined in terms of dance critique are varied, complex and overlapping, with aspects at times existing harmoniously and at other times in conflict with each other. In addition, the extent to which a person works within or for a large institution (vs. for a small organization or oneself) will greatly influence how they conceive of their accountability. This is especially true for ethical responsibility, since some institutions and organizations will have clearly articulated ethical guidelines a critic, judge or responder needs to follow. Others may not.

In terms of conventional print media, for instance, a dance critic's primary sense of responsibility is usually to the readership; other possibilities include the publication and its specific mission, editors and their preferences, and the critic themselves and their sense of professional integrity. There is often also a sense of obligation to doing justice to the dance being critiqued, to the field of dance as whole and to contributing to dance's evolution. As we will see, many critics see at least part of their role as documenting the experience of dance works for future generations and helping to improve the dance field in some manner. There may also be the question of concern for the dancers and/or choreographers and how the critique will affect them, although this is not a traditional worry in the field of journalism. Most dance critics believe that criticism 'isn't produced to instruct dancers how to correct or improve their work' (Siegel 2005: 1). In addition, traditional media/journalism sources will often have very clearly articulated ethical guidelines, that lay out the kinds of practices and behaviours they expect of their writers. The News Leaders Association, for instance, lays out the ethics codes and statements of values and principles of many of the major newspapers in the United States.[3] As I elaborate later in this chapter, these guidelines heavily influence how many critics conceive of their duties, and are therefore a valuable place to seek guidance on best practices.

In the case of competitive televised reality dance shows, judges' primary sense of responsibility is usually to the network: to meeting its objectives regarding the nature of the show and to garnering desired benchmark ratings in terms of viewership, in order to sell advertizing and make money. The extent to which the show is conceived as primarily entertainment, as opposed to say education, will definitely impact the nature of critique, as will the network's codes of professional conduct or ethical guidelines. Again, there could also be concerns regarding responsibility to the broader profession, in terms of upholding certain standards of the dance forms being assessed (such as different ballroom dance styles, for instance), and personal integrity, in terms of staying true to one's own criteria for evaluation, but the overall mission of commercial television does not always allow for these concerns to play out. In this context, moreover, presenting a close-up view of the emotional impact of assessment on the dance artists is a central part of the structure and goal of the shows, so considering these aspects is inevitably a top concern for the judges (unlike in print media, for instance). The degree to which these aspects influence a judge's word choices clearly varies with the show and the judge.

Many similarities exist in other realms where dance critique occurs, but it is clear that with distance from large media institutions and corporations comes greater flexibility in weighting the different responsibilities. For instance, a chore-ographer seeks feedback on a work in progress after an informal showing in the confines of their own studio or company: here the focus might be explicitly on assisting the dance artist in developing their work over and above any other possi-ble competing obligations. In other words, a choreographer may very well establish that the respondent's primary obligation is to help the creator (later in this chapter, I will discuss Liz Lerman's Critical Response Process, developed explicitly with this goal in mind). Or, a private citizen decides to post their reflections on a piece they viewed over the weekend on their blog: here they could prioritize their own personal tastes and maybe a sense of responsibility and that of a small circle of family and friends, rather than answering to any other overarching ethical criteria, a broader readership or the dance artists involved. While there remains a vibrant debate over freedom of speech on the internet, there is almost no oversight, allow-ing for individuals to express their views and freely pick and choose where their ethical responsibility lies. This creates opportunities for critiques to flourish largely unchecked, with the benefits and drawbacks that can accompany such freedom.

The place of truth, honesty and impartiality

By keeping in mind these different contexts in which dance critique occurs, and the varied ways that responsibility can be construed, we can better understand the ethical values (or virtues, to use the language of virtue ethics) of truth, honesty and fairness. This is certainly the case for traditional print criticism, which exists as an extension of journalism more generally, and takes seriously the responsibilities of a free press within a democratic society. Despite the recent attempts to discredit journalism, an emphasis on accuracy, facts, the truthful recounting of events and fairness are at the root of reputable reporting. I will discuss these concepts and why they are important before analyzing some of the problems that nevertheless can arise in their implementation.

The prominent dance critic Marcia Siegel, who has written for such publi-cations as the *Christian Science Monitor*, the *Boston Phoenix*, the *Soho Weekly News* and the *Hudson Review*, once shared with me that, 'independent criticism must exist if there's any difference between art and propaganda' (Siegel 2011: n.pag.). She was pointing here to a longstanding goal of journalism to provide an accurate and open-minded response to events without, in the words of the *Washington Post*'s 'Standards and Ethics' document, 'fear of any special interest, and with favor to none'.[4] Such a statement refers to the need for sources separate from government or other organizations potentially sponsoring or producing art, that can provide independent reporting. If such mechanisms neither exist or are heavily censored, then the result could be writings that simply reproduce the perspectives of those overseeing the events, rather than raise questions and engage in dialogue around the artwork. Independently produced art criticism is meant to explore our society through the lens of creators; critics should encourage scepticism, critical thought and discussion.

It is within this larger journalistic framing, I believe, that many dance critics operate, and that ideas regarding truth, honesty and fairness should first be examined. Starting with truth, using the *Washington Post* again as an example, there is a pledge to, 'tell the truth as nearly as the truth may be ascertained'.[4] For a dance critic, this can translate to recording, as accurately as possible, those aspects of the dance that are objectively verifiable. Such components might include descriptions of the venue, and details regarding the creators, the dancers, movement and aural and visual aspects of a dance event. The goal is to provide enough detail to vividly convey the dancing that transpired. As Banes indeed observed, description is a valuable aspect of dance criticism and is particularly important for live performances of limited duration that shift and vary. In her anthology of selected reviews *Watching the Dance Go By*, Siegel reflected at the time of writing (in the 1970s) on the lack of research and a robust literature in the area of dance history and importance of objective documentation in critiquing dance. She noted:

> The fact that dance has no institutionalized history imposes extra responsibilities on the critics. We are its reporters and sometimes its interpreters, but we are also its memory, its conscience. By that I don't mean that critics have the best memories, or possess any unusual moral qualities. I mean that they are professional observers, and that what they tell us is our only systematic account of an ongoing history.
>
> (1977: xiv)

Given the importance of description in the critical process, it is advisable to become educated both in general methods of movement analysis and familiar with codified vocabularies for different dance forms. Laban Movement Analysis, for instance, is a valuable tool for refining one's observational skills, since it is a nuanced system for examining how different parts of the body move in time and space. This system, developed by Rudolf van Laban in the early twentieth century, has been adapted over time to remain relevant for contemporary concerns. At the same time, it is not the only method, and familiarity with how different communities conceptualize and name movements is important to understanding each dance style's specialized language. Just as ballet has its own technical and codified vocabulary, so too do other forms, and being able to recognize and name steps and sequences is valuable, even if the critic may avoid such specialized jargon in their final critique in order to be accessible for a wide audience.

Another notable dimension to truthfulness, however, regards honesty in the sense of 'sincerity', and conveying a truthful account of your experience of a dance event. In this case, the focus shifts from accurately conveying objective facts, to providing a sincere explanation of your opinion of a work. Macaulay observes, 'A review will contain both objective information and subjective response. The objectivity is important as reportage (what music was used? how many dancers were there? and so on); the subjectivity is equally important because it indicates the work of art's power to affect our feeling' (2011: n.pag.). The subjective aspect arises, in other words, as a person delves more deeply into the interpretive and evaluative dimensions of the critical process, and forms associations and judgments shaping their opinion of a dance. The book *Dance Analysis: Theory and Practice*, edited by Janet Adshead, provides a great model and insight into how these critical operations work (also see Judith B. Alter's book *Dance-Based Dance Theory* in which she advocates for a dance-cantered basis for dance analysis). It emphasizes how an individual experiences certain features of the dance in a hermeneutic manner: meaning and assessment emerge within a clearly defined cultural, historical and artistic context. As the book states, 'Each dance is a unique treatment of certain subject matter by a choreographer and/or performers within specific and identifiable conventions and traditions' (1988: 84).

To be 'honest' in this sense, then, is about offering a trustworthy account of one's personal, yet deeply informed, response to a dance event. Siegel indicates this perspective when she reflects,

> I try to live an honest life – perhaps that satisfies some definition of ethical. Art cannot be judged by formulas. In fact, I don't try to be a judge. I try to give an account of what I've witnessed, what ideas, feelings, and associations it provoked that might be of interest to other people.
>
> (2011: n.pag.)

Choreographers can also appreciate this view when criticism reflects the kinds of depth and sensitivity to contextual factors surrounding the work's production. In his essay 'The perfect dance critic' (2002) choreographer Miguel Gutierrez professes that the perfect dance critic can, 'talk about individual pieces in relationship to the pieces that the choreographer has made before, and can write about how the piece fits in terms of the evolution of the work', and 'can make references to artists and ideas from other forms of performing and visual arts when trying to contextualize work' (n.pag.). To the degree that critics can successfully accomplish this task, and sincerely convey their conclusions, they can be seen to act in an honest manner.

This discussion of sincerity leads us to recognize the importance traditional dance criticism places on the connection between publications and their readership, and specifically the primary responsibility to provide fair and unbiased reporting as foundational to a free press, as outlined earlier. This is accomplished by frequently referring to *impartiality* in ethical guidelines, and making sure to avoid conflicts of interest. Using the *New York Times* as an example, their Ethical Journalism handbook asserts:

> The goal of *The New York Times* is to cover the news as impartially as possible [...] and to treat readers, news sources, advertisers and others fairly and openly, and to be seen to be doing so [...] *The Times* and members of its news department and editorial page staff share an interest in avoiding conflicts of interest or an appearance of a conflict.[5]

With specific regard to the arts and culture, there is an added emphasis on the need for independent and detached writing. Under the section Rules for Specialized Departments, the guidelines state:

> *The Times* has exceptional influence in such fields as theater, music, art, dance, publishing, fashion and the restaurant industry. We are constantly scrutinized for the slightest whiff of favoritism. Therefore staff members working in those areas have a special duty to guard against conflicts of interest or the appearance of conflict.[5]

The rules following this passage then state that contributors, including critics, may not develop, invest in, market or promote the creative endeavours of those they are likely to cover. For instance, one of the rules states that 'They may not comment, even informally, on works in progress before those works are reviewed.'

The importance of impartiality is taken seriously by many American dance critics, who believe it is important to providing an independent perspective and avoiding bias. Such a view has historical precedents in the work of the famous cultural critic Matthew Arnold, who wrote in his *Essays in Criticism*: 'I am bound by my own definition of criticism: *a disinterested endeavour to learn and propagate the best that is known and thought in the world*' (1865: 38–39, emphasis in original). In this view, the work itself should be the focal point, and the springboard for a person's response, and critics should steer clear of apparent favoritism garnered from, for instance, party invitations or free plane trips and hotel rooms paid by an artist or company, writer of programme essays, consultants, or advisors for events like summer schools. Siegel, for instance, states that

> the purpose of criticism is to provide a disinterested and informed commentary on work that's being done. I try to give an account of the work – what it looks like, how it operates, what effects it brings into play, and what the creators' intentions may be as discovered by one member of the audience.
>
> (Siegel 2011: n.pag.)

She is engaged in deciphering the dance and its 'lexicon' (Siegel 2001), as she has referred to those features that stand out in some way. Such a process becomes clear when Siegel argues that 'my best information is the dance' (Siegel 1998: 94) and that 'in many ways we learn from the dance what the dance is, and how to respond appropriately to it' (1998: 95).

The notion of impartiality applies to the extent to which a reviewer interacts with the creator of a piece they will be reviewing. Again, many American critics avoid intimate pre-premiere discussions with creators to prevent inappropriately skewing their responses. This is the result of a number of intersecting beliefs: a work's significance does not lie in the intention of the choreographer; the critic should be representing a typical audience member, who would not have insider knowledge of a production; and critiquing dance is an act that is inherently different than making dance and should be acknowledged and valued as such. 'Getting it,' a 2006 article by Jowitt, captures these views in a series of statements by celebrated critics. I quote them here in full as an excellent summary of these attitudes:

> [Joan] Acocella [of the *New Yorker*]: 'I do not see my job as requiring me to go to artists, find out their intentions, report their intentions to the reader, and then talk about how they fulfilled or didn't fulfill their intentions. There's actually a word for that approach; it's the intentional fallacy in criticism (that is, you judge [a work] on its intentions) [...] I see myself as a member of the audience, so whatever the artist's intentions are, many of them – maybe most of them – I won't be able to discern.'
>
> Jennifer Dunning of the *New York Times*: 'I don't think reviewers should have any inside knowledge; it seems to me very important to respond as an informed audience member. I hate the word *critic*; I like the word *reviewer* because I think that [what I write] is a second view, a re-view.'
>
> John Rockwell of the *Times*: 'Even if [critics] think they're deeply involved in the birth of a work, they have to be seeing it from the outside – and not just as the

audience's representative; the very nature of the perception of artwork places one at a distance from the creator, or indeed anybody else watching the artwork. To pretend otherwise is kind of futile.'

(2006: n.pag.)

Such views about impartiality, truth, honesty and fairness in the realm of traditional dance criticism thus lay out some important ethical considerations for you to consider when critiquing dance. However, as I indicate in the first part of this chapter, these attitudes have limitations. For example, critics may use the excuse of honesty to make snide or mean comments; claims of impartiality can be disingenuous and hide close friendships with particular dance artists or overlook deeply entrenched biases. What I will present next, therefore, are other principles and virtues that arise in examining the intersection of ethics and criticism that one might take into account to produce a more fully rounded, humane review.

Prioritizing fairness, respect and care

Edwin Denby once asked, 'Isn't "fair" another word for "mediocre"?' (quoted in McDonagh et al. 1969). Such a quip implies that being fair can lead to watered down, mediocre criticism, useless in its lack of honest evaluation and vivid perceptiveness. And for sure, there are definitely those who deprecate dance criticism that either relies too heavily on description, calling it boring and innocuous, or 'advocacy criticism', that seems to always find only positive things to say about a person's creative work or performing. Yet, there are important ways in which the notion of fairness relates to respect and care and can balance those tendencies that may lead to critiques that are unnecessarily harsh, destructive or unaware of the perceptual and language patterns that have historically worked against the interests of certain kinds of performers and performances. I will address these concerns now by looking at some of dance critics' less often articulated values and practices, which are nonetheless important in promoting best practices in the field.

One of these practices is to not ridicule or mock performers for physical features that are beyond their control. Jowitt observes:

In discussing dancers, writers will point out admirable achievement, great gifts, or flaws. But it bothers me when dancers are criticized for things they can't help – short stature, say, or short necks. It's one thing to explain why they may be miscast or cast against type, and another to fault them for something they were born with.

(2011: n.pag.)

Here is an example of fairness that relates to avoiding discrimination based on physical attributes. Jowitt is pointing out that people cannot necessarily alter certain aspects of their appearance, nor should they have to, if it has nothing to do with the dance's choreography or subject matter. To do otherwise is to act in a prejudiced manner, and be unnecessarily cruel.

Indeed, humiliating performers and mocking their appearance demonstrates a lack of respect and failure to treat dancers with dignity. It also fails to recognize the biases that inform, in particular, critics' ideas of 'beauty' and the ways that these are shaped by particular cultural and stylistic norms. So, when Cowell mocked the auditionee for looking 'weird' (as referenced earlier), and like 'creatures that live in the jungle with those massive eyes', he is not only unnecessarily humiliating the performer, he is also revealing an unstated bias that assumes the superiority of his idea of one culture over another, betraying a stereotyped judgment of who lives in a certain geographical terrain and has specific physical features as somehow inferior. He is using his position of power, in other words, to unnecessarily and unfairly humiliate a performer, in a manner that is fundamentally unfair – both overly harsh and prejudiced. Macaulay eventually had such a realization in the wake of the scandal following his remarks about Jenifer Ringer's appearance. He recognized that his comments were unnecessarily cruel and founded in problematic assumptions about the nature of the ideal female dancing body and beauty in ballet. He reflected later, 'In the long run, however, I'm glad that that furor happened […] it taught everyone – and not just me – not to talk that way about women's (or men's) bodies any more. Onward and upward' (quoted in Stahl 2018: n.pag.).

You also need to keep in mind that dancers are often carefully chosen for particular movement and performance qualities, and that these should be examined and taken seriously. Gutierrez notes this when he observes, 'The perfect dance critic understands that the dancer is an artist and not merely a tool of the choreographer's or director's work' (2002: n.pag.), and 'can articulate the qualities of individual dancer's energetic presence in the work' (2002: n.pag.). When a critic contemplates these unique performative qualities, moreover, it can open up the conversation to who may be considered a dancer, and what might be considered 'technique' and 'virtuosity' in ways that might otherwise be overlooked. Instead of a dancer only being a highly trained, thin, able-bodied young person, for instance, they could be older, have a disability or come from a non-dance background. Instead of 'technique' only referring to codified forms such as ballet, traditional modern dance, or theatrical jazz dance, it could apply to 'the ways in which dancers can access effectively and intelligently the numerous expressive possibilities that are available to them in their bodies' (2002: n.pag.). And rather than virtuosity only applying to multiple pirouettes in ballet, acrobatic feats or headspins in breaking, it 'can apply to the most idiosyncratic of weight shifts' (2002: n.pag.).

This leads to another important dimension of fairness (and honesty) that is not always sufficiently addressed: recognizing biases and limitations on the part of the critic. A certain level of ignorance, and the questions a work generates, can certainly be a generative starting point for a review or feedback. But inexperience and unfamiliarity can also lead to ill-informed, naïve and bigoted criticism, such as early twentieth-century reviews of dance performed by various African American artists that emphasized the dancers' 'primitive', 'natural' style in a manner that overlooked the sophistication and artistry involved in their work (Gottschild 2016). In 2005, the choreographer Tere O'Connor wrote a now celebrated letter that was then posted on the web in response to a review of his work by Joan Acocella in the *New Yorker*. He angrily observed that she wasn't able to accurately assess his work because of her aesthetic biases and inability to appropriately contextualize it:

> Through her lack of understanding and her inability to reach out and get informa-
> tion from artists, she joins a group of critics whom I will call 'the literalists'. These
> critics do not know how to read dances created outside the restricted confines of
> the narrative or musical frameworks from past centuries. What's more, they don't
> do the work of finding out what is actually going on in the minds of artists or what
> are the contexts in which these works are created.
>
> (quoted in Kim 2005: n.pag.)

This dimension means being more aware of one's biases and potentially levelling with a reader (or viewer) about one's possible limitations, biases or point of view. For a critic this might include anything from avoiding reviewing a performance one has slept through, never attended, or is predisposed to panning, to acknowl-edging close friendships with a choreographer they cover. More importantly, it also means recognizing one's aesthetic preferences and cultural position when reviewing unfamiliar work, and taking into consideration how that positionality might influence your feelings and responses. As Kirsten Bodensteiner states, 'A critic's background may influence their "moralistic assumptions", as might their age, gender, race and culture […] The era in which a critic lives and the culture or climate of their surroundings clearly help determine their tastes, and consequently their biases' (2000: 32). Being more reflexive is certainly something that Gutierrez seeks; he writes that:

> The perfect dance critic discusses the implications of the different cultural representa-
> tions of gender, race, sexual orientation or class in the work. The perfect dance critic
> acknowledges his own cultural position when addressing these issues, and how that
> cultural position may shape his feelings or responses.
>
> (2002: n.pag.)

Recognizing one's position does not mean denying the importance of assuming an independent, and impartial stance towards a work; rather it again provides some balance by illuminating the critic's standpoint, and how that shapes the critique. Indeed, this kind of recognition can provide an opportunity for opening up an important dialogue about the complex and multi-vocal ways in which meanings and values are ascribed to movement, rather than assuming the rightness and superiority of any singular perspective. It is what Mattingly advocates when she asserts, 'The role of the critic is not only to respond to artists' work, but also to set in motion the criteria through which audiences evaluate their performances' (2019: n.pag.). For Mattingly, it is part of the critic's work, in other words, to call attention to the very frameworks through which we look at dance and open up a discussion that is flexible and dialogic, rather than final, individual and authoritative. In her case, she sees this as a particular benefit of the digital sphere, which offers a greater sense of polyvocality by making visible reader responses through comments and providing opportunities to add opposing perspectives.

An example of considering varied frameworks through which we look at dance can be found in the work of Clare Croft. In her article 'Feminist dance criticism and ballet' (2014), she directs attention to how critics' language can both define and challenge prevailing problematic assumptions about female dancers in ballet repertoire. Rather than seeing female dancers as idealized bodies of 'Woman' and objects or instruments of the (traditionally male) choreographer's gaze, Croft argues that

> feminist criticism requires opening one's mind to the idea that multiple kinds of bodies and people with a range of approaches to performing gender are suitable for female leads, and that they deserve to be viewed as subjects capable of desire, action, and agency.
>
> (2014: 214)

Moreover, she argues that:

> The feminist dance critic then must attend to how dancers [...] in their occasional 'failure to repeat' idealized female norms, call attention to these norms' constructed nature and, on some occasions, subvert those norms. Such an approach to dance criticism requires a cultural studies approach to writing about dance – one that considers the relationships among codes of representation, institutional practices, and individual artists' material circumstances. Real people, not idealized bodies, dance onstage.
>
> (2014: 197–98)

In this way, then, a dance critic can bring attention to the issues at stake in discussing, for example, the way female dancers are traditionally perceived in dance performances, and aim to provide them more agency in the process.

An important dimension of being 'fair', then, is to be as complete as possible, within given word constraints, in gathering the kinds of information relevant to analyzing any particular dance event. Recognizing one's limitations can spur more indepth research into the circumstances in which a dance was created, the backgrounds of the dance style, dancers, choreographer and other possible collaborators, along with an awareness of cultural context and theoretical perspectives drawn from cultural studies. These include feminist theory, contemporary ethnography, queer theory, postcolonial theory and performance studies, among others. All of this material can provide a rich set of resources for making an informed critique that is thoughtful and well-supported. Jowitt states that she approaches her reviews with, 'An attempt to convey what the work in question is. And in terms of opinion, to state what is admirable about it, and to critique what is not without condescension or a destructive attitude' (2011: n.pag.).

Meanwhile, there are those who actively challenge the notion of having to stay distanced from the artists that one critiques, demonstrating that a solid distinction between critic and choreographer is not always possible *or* desirable. These writers believe that proximity with dance makers actually provides an important inroad into work – a perspective that recognizes that the world of concert dance is quite small where writers and performers have often been hard to separate in any strict sense – especially in small cities/communities where most everyone knows each other and people may hold multiple roles. Andy Horwitz, for instance, speaks of how *Culturebot*, an online New York-based publication he founded in 2003 devoted to critical thought about experimental performance,

> was, by definition, embedded. Our role was not to criticize from the outside, but to explicate an often opaque process, history & framework. We took as our mission a collegial relationship with artists, administrators and makers of all kinds, an obligation to make visible the workings of a hermetic world.
>
> (2012: n.pag.)

He continues to explain:

> [W]e are in the business of engaging community and building informed audiences, empowering ('emancipating', even) citizens to engage with performance work from a place of knowledge and autonomy, not consumerist passivity. We believe this approach is concomitant with the artist's process and desired outcomes.
>
> (2012: n.pag.)

145

Online forums such as this, in other words, may be committed to explicating the context in which contemporary art is created and received, in line with the needs of the contemporary dance community, in which roles are ever changing and the same person can be a curator, creator, performer or critic:

> Our contributors acknowledge their place as artists writing about their peers and seek to remove the barrier between critic and maker [...] we believe that criticism is a creative practice and critical discourse is essential for a vibrant and engaged cultural ecology.[6]

Indeed, approaching critique in a more holistic manner can signal respect for the work (and by extension, the artist), of showing regard for their efforts and taking them seriously. Jowitt sees her approach to dance criticism as 'A willingness to try to see into the work as deeply as possible [with] an effort to believe that this artist is serious and thoughtful and deserves your attention. In other words, a certain amount of respect' (Jowitt 2011: n.pag.). For her part, Siegel asserts, 'I believe devoting my time and talents to a public consideration of someone's work is an act of respect. This is the ultimate compliment anyone can promise to another person's work' (Siegel 2011: n.pag.). Fisher provides an even more extensive explanation when she observes: '"Do unto others as you would have them do unto you", is an interesting one for a critic. Like most people, I don't like being criticized negatively, but I learned a lot from taking critique seriously, from friends or teachers who helped me improve' (2011: n.pag.). As a result, she reflects:

> [A] critic is charged to represent the dance well. So that means 'listening' to what the dance has to tell you [...] As a critic, I would take description seriously; I would interpret freely, because it's my strength and helps people find layers in dance; I would note negative aspects without descending to being snarky or dismissive; temper my own sharply critical and often satirical or sardonic streak because it didn't serve the purpose of reviewing dance [...] They worked hard to do the performance, you work hard to write about it.
>
> (2011: n.pag.)

As Fisher observes, an important part of demonstrating respect is listening, and in this context, 'listening' is a means to indicate one's appreciation of the creator.

Taking this even further, I would like to demonstrate that active concern for a choreographer's welfare is also valuable to consider, in addition to a more generic notion of respect for 'the work'. In reflecting back on her time as a critic for the *Los*

Angeles Times, Fisher remembers, 'I also suffered with the idea of hurting choreographers, and that's what led me to a different style' (2011: n.pag.). She credits Deborah Jowitt for encouraging her to never write anything that she wouldn't want to say face-to-face to a choreographer – and that imagining talking to the choreographer made her think of the person, not just the critic's job insofar as power had been wielded in the past. Meanwhile, Joan Acocella, shared in an interview with me that 'You hurt. They are artists and they want your help' (Acocella 2011: n.pag.). How this sensitivity can manifest varies from investing time in researching from afar a particular choreographer's body of work to participating in ongoing dialogues that span years. This is an approach Lerman advocates. She observes that instances where she has developed long-term, one-on-one conversations with critics have yielded the most meaningful growth on both sides. She states, 'critics know a lot and are in an excellent position to help you see things you can't see' (2011b: n.pag.).

Artists, meanwhile, can help critics break out of their own confined perceptions of what they think the artist *should* be doing, and help them make the work they want to make. Lerman gives as an example a critic who thought her work should be more confrontational. Lerman was able to explain why this was not an approach she valued, and through conversation over several years both have become more informed, and helpful to each other's evolution (2011b: n.pag.). What this suggests is that while this goes against what many American critics may be taught through peer to peer exchange and believe to be appropriate in terms of managing conflicts of interest, it is not necessary or even desirable, for there to always be a strict separation between critic and artist. As a critic you can be in dialogue with a choreographer in a responsible manner that provides deeper insight into their interests and processes, and ultimately enriches your reviews of dance.

Liz Lerman's Critical Response Process (CRP), in particular, exemplifies how critique can centre beneficence and care for the creator and as such be a useful training tool for critics that can be deployed in a variety of contexts from the page to stage.[7] Lerman developed this approach largely due to her frustrations with the traditional critique formats. In 1993, she wrote:

> Several years ago, I finally acknowledged to myself how uncomfortable I was around most aspects of criticism. I had been involved in the process of creating art, seeing art and teaching art-making for a very long time, but I had not found peace with my many questions, and with the array of feelings brought up by both giving and receiving criticism. I found so-called 'feed-back sessions' to be often brutal and frequently not very helpful [...] I had trouble getting it, and I had trouble giving it.
>
> (Lerman 1993: n.pag.)

She continued,

> The more I worked as a choreographer, the fewer people I trusted to tell me about my work, since much of what I received in the form of criticism from others seemed to tell me more about their biases and expectations than about the particular dance of mine being discussed. It didn't seem to me to really be about helping me to make the best dance I could from my *own* imagination.
>
> (1993: n.pag.)

And Lerman found that, in turn, when she was in a position to critique others' work, the same thing tended to happen: 'If I didn't see my own ideas confirmed in the work of others, I found myself being very critical – my critical comments told me more about myself than about the nature of the work I was seeing' (1993: n.pag.).

As a result, she developed CRP as a method in which a facilitator assists the artist and responders by constructively offering a generative method of critique that is useful for both further developing and improving choreography, as well as allowing critics to become more aware of their biases, and depart from strict objectivity ideals that may prevent deeper understanding. CRP can be applied to full work or an excerpt, in relation to formal performances, informal presentations or in-class showings. Everyone is invited to be responsible for creating a safe space for productive communication, where each person is respected and the emphasis is on dialogue and building understanding. One of the greatest benefits of this approach is its sensitivity to the artist as a person and the ways in which responders can address the creator with thoughtfulness and caring – recognizing that often the most useful feedback is generated from a place of curiosity and openness and is received from a place of trust rather than defensiveness, anger and pain. The responder, in particular, 'engages in dialogue with the artist, with a commitment to the artist's intent to make excellent work'.[8] From experiencing the process first hand in many different contexts, I believe that the strategy works and frequently 'even the most disparate points of view can be taken into account through dialogue and response' (Lerman and Borstel 2003: 18).

There are four steps to the process: (1) statements of meaning, (2) artist as a questioner, (3) neutral questions, and (4) opinion time. Statements of meaning allow the artist to receive the elements that stood out as evocative, interesting, exciting and/or striking. Examples might include – 'I found the constant use of entrances and exits compelling because it made me think of the ways in which I am constantly rushing around in my life', or 'For me the moment when the dancers suddenly dropped to the ground was really powerful because I thought they had died and that connected to the title of the piece.' This kind of sharing creates an atmosphere that allows the creator to feel comfortable in discussing their work, and the audience in responding. Why? First, because showing work, especially in progress, can be a vulnerable act, and this step demonstrates respect on the part of the responders and allows the artist to feel protected from a rush to (negative) judgment. More importantly, it illuminates how work gains meaning for a particular community, which is of special import to the creator, who wants to make something that speaks to others. As Lerman says, 'the Critical Response Process begins with the philosophy that meaning is at the heart of an artist's work, and to start with meaning is to begin with the essence of the artistic act' (Lerman and Borstel 2003: 19).

People's varied responses in Step 1 bring attention to their different ways of seeing the work and the layers of possible interpretation. This point brings light to the observation I made earlier in this chapter, about the valuable ways that criticism can illuminate the varied frameworks with which people approach artwork. As Lerman illuminates, 'It is in that moment of group reflection that responders first become aware of the numerous ways people see art, and the array of value systems underlying their differing visions' (Lerman and Borstel 2003: 19). This awareness can both deepen their appreciation for the work and lead to greater tolerance of diverse viewpoints rather than promote a singular interpretation or evaluation. For the viewer who is a critic, the process can expose them to different perspectives that they can incorporate into their review of the dance.

The artist next oversees the questions they want addressed about what was just experienced, with the facilitator making sure that viewers' responses stay on topic. While the responder may express opinions – especially when asked – the aim is often to provide insight into the associations and thoughts the artwork generated rather than a pronouncement of why something was right or wrong. For instance, the artist might request a response regarding the experience of a certain choice of partnering at the end of the piece, or a response to a particular lighting choice; the responder would then provide as objective a description as possible of how they experienced that moment or choice. The artist can then store this information and later match it with their intentions for the piece. Having the artist ask questions first about the intent of their work means the respondents are now better able to frame the discussions around the needs of the artists. Lerman observes, 'Often we observe that the artist has the same questions as those watching. When the artist starts the dialogue, the opportunity for honesty increases' (Lerman and Borstel 2003: 20).

The third step involves the viewer's asking questions that are as neutral as possible, without opinions attached. This is often the most challenging step because of how people (especially professional critics) are accustomed to providing critique – in terms of judgment of something as 'good' or 'bad'. This is where the facilitator frequently needs to help rephrase comments. For instance, a person is led to ask,

'Can you explain your choices for costumes?' rather than 'The orange costumes are ugly, so why did you use them?' This provides the artist with insight into which of their choices were unclear or confusing to viewers without defensiveness getting in the way. Sometimes what is obvious to the artist is not to audiences; these gaps provide important guidance on elements the artist might give further attention to. This step also allows viewers into the mind of the artist and can actually build greater insight that leads to resolution of the viewers' questions and greater appreciation of the work. In other words, the dialogue does not necessarily reveal something missing from the work; it can itself be the missing piece for the viewer. In this case, the viewer walks away more knowledgeable, again demonstrating how meaning-making, at the heart of critique, can be a collective process as opposed to a one-way pronouncement.

The final step, Opinion Time, is the time when 'Responders state opinions, given permission from the artist; the artist has the option to say no.'[8] The usual formulation is 'I have an opinion about X, would you like to hear it?' Setting up the opinion in this way does a number of things – places control in the hands of the artist, cues the respondent to be thoughtful and respectful in what they plan to say, and as Lerman notes, 'For the artists, it affords a chance to readjust their focus to become receptive to a [...] new idea' (Lerman and Borstel 2003: 22). An example might be, 'I have an opinion about the transitions between the first two sections. Would you like to hear it?' or 'I have an opinion about the decision to have the dancers speak. Would you like to hear it?' If the artist is willing to hear the opinion, responders provide their evaluation of what might have been ineffective or problematic without offering a 'fix-it' or specific prescription to the artist. This provides the artist with agency and the choice to hear the opinion and then decide whether or not to see it as relevant to their vision for the work. The approach empowers the artist; the respondent is no longer the authority on what constitutes 'good' dance. As Lerman observes,

> artists can use these opinions to help place the work in a larger context. There are times when artists can hear all of these opinions and use them to weave his or her own solution. But artists may not want to hear from everyone, or everyone at that particular time. In this process, the artist can control this moment.
>
> (1993: n.pag.)

As Lerman points out, the next step often involves the choreographer getting back to work, hopefully motivated and excited rather than disillusioned and despairing (as is often the case, for instance, resulting from negative newspaper reviews). Ideally, the responders have gained new awareness of the artist's intentions and processes and the satisfaction of participating in the kind of meaning-making at the root of art's value. Lerman notes, 'If it has functioned well, the responders feel invested and engaged, and the artist has gained a fund of useful, even inspiring, information' (Lerman and Borstel 2003: 24). Many professional dance critics working in a traditional medium speak of the importance they place on the role of criticism to help audiences deepen their relationship to dance. In many ways, the CRP does just this as an inherent part of the process. While any formulaic approach can become stilted and lose its efficacy if overused, when applied in the appropriate manner, in whole or in adapted form, CRP seems a sensitive and caring approach to providing rich critique that benefits the artist and audience, and ensures that respect of persons is maintained throughout. Incorporating it in your education in providing critique could be very beneficial.

Conclusion of Part 1

In this discussion, I offer some insights into the ethical issues that lie at the heart of critiquing dance, especially in relation to written dance criticism, verbal critiques of dancing in reality TV shows and feedback sessions following informal choreographic showings. I consider such topics as responsibility, fairness, truth and honesty, some of which are more usually addressed in the context of journalistic ethics, along with respect and especially care, which can help to move critique to a place of greater humanity. I advocate for an approach that avoids humiliation of dancers and choreographers and recognizes the varied ethical issues at play, with an aim to engage in dialogue that enriches experiences of art from positions of mutual respect. This approach may not, ultimately, be as possible within the rigid constraints of particular media, such as a newspaper column of two hundred words or a sound bite in a televised dance competition. In many contexts, however, such as online forums, class settings and dance scholarship, this approach can be particularly fruitful. As Fisher reflects when she decided to stop working as a newspaper critic,

> I was tired of pronouncing as *the* L.A. Times critic. I needed a format that let me explore dance and not have to 'rank and recommend', which was always a major part of newspaper reviewing. I needed to stop figuring out how to tell people what I saw and just start to see again. I didn't want to have to decide what was good and what was bad; I wanted to write about what was interesting. Nearly everything was.
>
> (2011: n.pag., original emphasis)

151

The place of 'Ethical Criticism' in dance

The last part of this chapter more closely considers the nature of 'ethical criticism' in dance and whether criteria from the ethical realm should be imported to evaluate the aesthetic realm. The earlier conversation seems to make an obvious case for including ethics in assessments of dance, but there is debate within the history of the arts relating to this topic. It is worth examining this more closely. To do so, I will briefly consider the various positions and draw on the work of Noël Carroll and Eric Mullis to argue for the relevance and value of considering dance works' moral dimensions when it seems meaningful and appropriate. Banes herself recognized the important role played by ethics when she observed that the 'moral dimension' is one of critics' key criteria for deciding whether a work is good. It is also something Macaulay notes when he states, 'Criticism is about the application of criteria. Those criteria will often be ethical, moral, political' (2011: n.pag.). I will explore more fully why this is the case, while recognizing the limitations of only viewing work through one lens.

On one side of the spectrum is autonomism or aestheticism. As I explained earlier in this book, this is the idea that art and ethics are separate and autonomous realms. In terms of criticism, this view holds that criteria from the ethical realm should not be imported and used to assess art. For some autonomists, known as 'formalists', aesthetic experience revolves around appreciating the work's formal aspects, such as its purely visual or material aspects. In painting, for instance, formalism emphasizes compositional elements such as shape, line, colour, texture, brushwork and framing, rather than the work's meaning or historical and social context. In the case of dance, a formalist approach involves concerning oneself primarily with characteristics such as the use of space, timing and force; patterns and interrelations between the movement, lighting and music; and the dancer's technical ability to achieve certain lines and shapes. As Raewyn White observes,

> the formal and structural aspects of the dance under appraisal, and its aesthetic surfaces and effects, are seen to provide the context of critical attention, and the consideration of the social and cognitive import of the dance is correspondingly excluded. Integral to this aesthetic orientation is the assumption that accurate description of the aesthetic object is the primary means to an aesthetically sufficient response.
>
> (1989: 4)

On the other extreme, meanwhile, is a perspective that artwork should only be viewed in moral terms. This is a form of ethical criticism known as moralism or ethism, or 'the view that the aesthetic value of art should be determined by, or reduced to, its moral value' (Peek n.d.: n.pag.). Indeed, radical moralism asserts that an artwork's aesthetic value is determined solely by its moral value such that works of art are aesthetically bad if they have ethical flaws. Leo Tolstoy is often referenced as the most outspoken modern proponent of this view, as outlined in his publication *What Is Art?* (1897). Tolstoy argued that art should not be viewed as a source of pleasure or 'beauty' but a means of communicating feelings. He wrote, 'so the evolution of feelings takes place by means of art, replacing lower feelings, less kind and less needed for the good of humanity, by kinder feelings, more needed for that good. This is the purpose of art' (1995: 123–24). In this view, good art successfully inspires feelings of shared humanity, love and reverence for human dignity, while bad art corrupts and leads people astray from these ideals.

Each of these positions benefits dance criticism. A more formalist approach can bring much needed attention to those elements that are the building blocks of dance – the moving body in time and space, which I stated earlier, can easily be overlooked or undervalued either through ignorance or the haste to interpret and evaluate. A formalist approach may also be an understandable match for critiquing plotless, non-representational dance such as those by choreographers like Merce Cunningham of Lucinda Childs, certain tap dance pieces, 'nritta' in Bharatanat-yam, or the dance form 'threading' in breaking – attending to those aspects that the choreographer/dancer and conventions of the particular style value, such as rhythmic complexities or shifting spatial patterns. In addition, sometimes autono-mism can be a means of getting around the limitations imposed within totalitarian or authoritarian societies. A critic who may face pressure to denounce a particu-lar artwork based on its so-called 'degenerate' nature might employ a formalist approach to validate the work's aesthetic value and save the work from censorship.

Meanwhile, focusing critique on the ethical implications of a dance work can help shed light on the work's moral values and implied messages. This may be particularly appropriate for dances created with the clear intention to embody and impart specific messages related, say, to gender, sexuality, race, class, war and social justice. In other words, a critic writing about *The Green Table* by Kurt Joos might understandably concentrate on its anti-war message, or a reviewer writing about Adam McKinney's *HaMapah/The Map*, may spotlight the ways in which he addresses his queer, Black, Jewish, Native American identity – seeking to heal himself and communities' traumas. Emphasizing ethical dimensions can also bring out otherwise overlooked aspects of dances typically viewed through a formalist lens. For instance, Norman Bryson demonstrates how considering Vaslav Nijinsky's 1913 *Rite of Spring* through a feminist lens reveals the extent to which the ballet staged early twentieth-century anxieties of modernism through a ritual sacrifice of a young maiden. Bryson observes the severe limitations of a circular approach to dance, in which critics use the overarching narrative of the 'progressive liberation of dance movement from narrative function' (1997: 70) to analyze its objects in purely formalist terms. Instead, he advocates a cultural studies approach to dance history, where 'modernist dance can be taken as a reflection upon the undeniable changes of modernity, as these affected the body and the sense of the body's relation to its historically new environment' (1997: 73).

In general, however, neither extreme of autonomism or moralism is usually the most productive or insightful in terms of art critique. Assuming either position means overlooking an entire dimension of a work that can bring insight into how the art is put together and the feelings and meanings individual viewers can ascribe to it. In fact, a purely formal approach to some work can do more than miss out on diverse interpretations; it can overlook how it participates in spreading totalitarian propaganda, as when Leni Riefenstahl's film *Olympia* (1938) is praised for its editing and filming techniques without considering its political context. Likewise, a singularly moralistic perspective can reduce a work of art to a set of simplistic truisms or crude claims that miss out on the full experience of the artwork. This occurred when the celebrated *New Yorker* critic Arlene Croce dismissed Bill T. Jones' work *Still/Here* in her now infamous essay 'Discussing the undiscussable' (1994) based on her assumptions about its moral nature without having attended a single performance of the piece.[9] A reductive approach that strives to extract what an artwork 'means' is what philosopher Susan Sontag railed against in her famous essay 'Against interpretation' (1966), and it is important to keep in mind her warnings that approaches that impose pre-existing frameworks 'violate', 'impoverish' and 'alter' the work of art. She observed:

> The contemporary zeal for the project of interpretation is often prompted by an open aggressiveness [...] The old style of interpretation was insistent, but respectful; it erected another meaning on top of the literal one. The modern style of interpretation excavates, and as it excavates, destroys.
>
> (2001: 6)

What recent philosophers propose are more moderate forms of these approaches, including moderate moralism. Moderate moralism argues that 'some works of art may be evaluated morally (contra radical autonomism) and that sometimes the moral defects and/or merits of a work may figure in the aesthetic evaluation of the work' (Carroll 1996: 236). In his article 'Art and ethical criticism: An overview of recent directions of research' (2000), philosopher Noël Carroll provides an excellent overview of why such an approach is warranted. He argues, for instance, that a critic may assess a given work with respect to both its formal properties and its ethical dimension; that the two aren't mutually exclusive. He observes, moreover, that certain writers/artists create their work with the understanding that it possesses an ethical dimension, which they expect their audiences to consider. And other art may be shown to provide moral insights, whether the artist intended them to or not.

Carroll's main point is to demonstrate that ethical critics provide understanding into how art gives us knowledge of what an experience would be like by providing richly particularized details of life that engage the audience's imagination and emotions. He notes, 'There is also 'knowledge of what such and such is or would be like' (2000: 362). And this is the kind of knowledge that 'art excels in providing and that the best ethical critics look for, or at least should look for' (2000: 362). Indeed, Noel emphasizes how this kind of knowledge is especially relevant for moral reasoning, because it provides audiences with different alternatives when contemplating particular actions in their lives – for instance, confronting the results of murder by reading Fyodor Dostoevsky's *Crime and Punishment*. He further elaborates on how the 'educative value of art resides in its potential to cultivate our moral talents' (2000: 366) by encouraging viewers, readers or listeners to form moral evaluations of characters and situations (in the case of literature). He states, 'Where artworks cultivate our moral emotions by exercising and/or expanding them, the ethical critic can commend them' (2000: 367). As an example, he talks about how,

> In the best cases, artworks can also expand our emotional powers of discrimination by appealing to our imagination in such a way that we come to apprehend some objects, say AIDS victims, as worthy of emotions such as sorrow, where previously we had been oblivious or even hostile toward them.
>
> (2000: 367)

He sums up his view when he observes:

> For what art teaches us generally is not new maxims and concepts, but rather how to apply them to concrete cases, engaging and exercising our emotions and imagination, our powers of perceptual discrimination, moral understanding, and reflection, in ways that sustain and potentially enlarge our capacity for moral judgment.
>
> (2000: 368–69)

If Carroll argues for including moral aspects in critique, so too does Eric Mullis, a dancer and philosopher and author of 'Ought I make political dance' (2015). In this article, he draws on the work of Mark Franko and argues for an approach to dance performance and criticism that includes what he refers to as both a 'formalist' and 'contextualist' perspective in approaching dance. In this case a formalist perspective, along the lines I described earlier, 'stresses the perceptual immediacy of the dance experience, and, when relevant, relationships between dance movement and other aspects of the performance (such as narrative, music, and lighting) that contribute to or detract from a sense of formal unity' (2015: 72). The contextualist model, on the other hand, emphasizes how 'history and social context inflect dance making, performance, and reception, since it views dance as symbolic of broader social values, beliefs, and practices' (2015: 72). This view recognizes the inherently ideological nature of dance, and the fact that, 'gender, race, ethnicity, sexuality, age, and ability play into the appreciation of bodies both on and off the concert stage' (2015: 72).

For Mullis, a multivalent hermeneutic of the body and the function of dance in society call for a pluralist approach. Drawing on theorists such as Maurice Merleau-Ponty, Julia Kristeva and Michel Foucault, he observes that we can experience the body in a number of ways, including as a subject, as an object and in terms of social norms, among others. He states that this can happen as an audience member at a performance, where,

> At different moments in the same performance, I can see the dancer as a kinetic formal object that has the capacity to create choreographic forms, as a subject with a particular embodied history, and I can view him or her in terms of widely held cultural values such as physical beauty and ability.
>
> (2015: 73)

To this extent, formalist and contextualist approaches to critical reception are *both* justified in that they focus attention on different aspects of embodied experience. In addition, he points out that dance does many things in a society: it educates, entertains, inspires and strives for social change. Recognizing that dance is a pluralist social practice means approaching it from an equally pluralist perspective when thinking about its reception; both dance creators and recipients will make or experience work in a variety of ways, from the purely formal to the overtly political.

To conclude, morality holds an important place in dance critique. This is due to how artists may approach their work with conscious messages to impart and to the nature of dance works themselves as particularly oriented to ethical criticism because of their subject matter or their larger ethical/political context. Ultimately, Mullis observes the plurality of ways that people engage with dance work. Indeed, as Marcia Siegel points out, even when it may not be obvious in a critic's writing, underlying attitudes towards art and its relation to morality are nevertheless present. She observes:

> Beneath every critic's evident motives are his or her attitudes toward art and artists. This implies more than taste, although one's taste forms around these underlying

codes. It soon becomes clear, reading a critic, that he or she loves glitter and sleaze, or cringes from sex, or is a sucker for virtuosity. What is less clear, but more influential on the way a critic uses the journalistic platform, is the collection of art-moralistic assumptions from which he or she works. [...] Is movement to be considered an accessory to the dance, like a costume; a primary language with its own meaning; a vehicle for getting at verbal meaning? Should art be political or must it not concern itself with politics? Is the artist special; ordinary; oppressed; anointed; subversive?

(quoted in Bodensteiner 2000: 31)

Ultimately, in other words, whether a critic is conscious of it or not, their views about dance and ethics will influence their critiques.

Conclusion

In 2014, Canadian dance critic Philip Szporer observed, 'The gambit for the future resides in new platforms for reviews, platforms that elicit thoughtful comments from audience members speaking their minds that can sit comfortably alongside the views of established dance critics' (2014: 194). This is clearly more and more the case, as spaces for critique have opened up online through websites featuring dance criticism, such as fjordreview.com, criticaldance.org, theartsdesk.com and individual blogs by writers like Rachel Howard and Jess Ruhlin. As Mattingly observes, digital curation of dances and responses to them are shifting relationships between artists, performances and audiences. She argues:

As contemporary artists present work [...] advocating for moments that are challenging and creating durational performances, a new choreographic apparatus emerges that brings together websites, audiences, and frameworks for engaging with their performances. Contemporary performance is congruent with a digital sphere that engages with ideas, philosophies, and aesthetics from a broad range of critics, theorists, and practitioners.

(2019: n.pag.)

Within this new online sphere, there is a shift towards more dialogic and inclusive forms of discourse. While online forums have democratized the practice of critique in important ways, there are certain ongoing and fundamental issues to consider as you write about dance in relation to ethics. Macaulay, for instance, observes, 'A serious critic is always going to re-examine opinions on the connections between art and values' (2011: n.pag.). In other words, when considering a dance piece or experience, it is important to keep asking such probing questions as:

> How do you review a work of art whose ethics or morals seem to clash with your own? Have your ethics, morals and politics changed while you have been a critic and/or frequent dancegoer, and, if so, have works of art played a part in affecting this change? How important to you is it that a work of art expresses any moral, ethical or political point of view? Or, much more simply but crucially, how important to you is that a work of art is expressive? and if so, how do you respond to its expression?
>
> (2011: n.pag.)

These kinds of questions illuminate the close connection between movement and meaning and how ethical concerns participate in this symbiotic and ever-changing, ever-evolving relation.

Moreover, as I outline in this chapter, there are ongoing questions to ask about how to best serve the audience, the dancers, the choreographer, the field and one's conscience. I have laid out key issues to consider relating to the place of truth, honesty, and fairness, with a special concern for respect and care, in the process of providing critique. Everyone will have a different approach to these questions. There is no simple answer. This is especially true for the question of how much interaction a critic should have with the artists they are writing about. Each person will draw the line in a different place. However, recognizing the dialogic nature of critique is important, I will reiterate that respect for persons, beneficence and justice should be considered when offering critique. As the opening quote by cultural and educational policy educator Ralph Alexander Smith indicates, 'The ultimate aim of criticism in an open society is the criticism of life in the furtherance of humane values' (2006: 88).

NOTES

1. See https://www.youtube.com/watch?v=W61VK6JDUTw. Accessed 5 July 2021.
2. See https://www.dailymotion.com/video/xsqsxp. Accessed 5 July 2021.
3. https://members.newsleaders.org/resources-ethics. Accessed 19 July 2022.
4. See https://members.newsleaders.org/resources-ethics-wapo. Accessed 5 July 2021.
5. See https://www.nytimes.com/editorial-standards/ethical-journalism.html#rulesFor SpecializedDepartments. Accessed 5 July 2021.
6. See https://www.culturebot.org/about/. Accessed 5 July 2021.
7. In its emphasis on helping the creator develop their work there is an overlap with the role of the dance dramaturg. For more on this topic, see Phil Hansen and Darcey Callison (eds.) (2015), *Dance Dramaturgy: Modes of Agency, Awareness and Engagement*, Basingstoke: Palgrave Macmillan.

8. See https://lizlerman.com/critical-response-process/. Accessed 15 July 2022.
9. For an excellent analysis of the public debate that took place around the Arlene Croce essay over the nature of dance criticism, see the 1995 issue of *Dance Connection*, 13:2, pp. 20–26.

6

Ethical Issues in the Presenting World of Dance

We have inherited spaces and protocols for arts participation [...]
I propose a process to identify new guiding principles based on
community, dialogue, and empathy for the presentation of contem-
porary and experimental choreography.

(Steinwald 2014: 22)

The practice of presenting dance – namely, the act of hiring or arranging for a dance artist or company to perform at a particular place and time – is a highly collaborative and diverse industry that makes ethical decision making particularly challenging.[1] Those active in the field may variously be referred to (or refer to themselves) as presenters, producers, programmers, artistic directors, managers, Chief Executive Officers (CEOs) or curators, with a range of characteristics applied to each, depending on numerous factors from the personal to the institutional and geographic. The differences in how people conceive of their roles definitely impact their approach to ethical issues, however, for the purposes of this chapter, the realm of dance presenting writ large is the main focus.[2]

The chapter addresses dance presenting primarily as it relates to live concert dance (rather than, for instance, commercial dance or dance online or in other contexts), and particularly what is considered 'contemporary' and especially 'experimental' choreography within the United States. By these latter terms, I refer to a performance that is generally viewed within the concert dance world as 'of the now', 'innovative' and 'cutting edge', although what falls in that category depends on the presenter, and can range widely from more established modern dance companies to highly controversial performance art and include non-Western and hybrid dance styles. The notion of 'contemporary dance' (like the concept of dance presenting itself) is highly contested, fluid and ever shifting, and indeed its definitions depend on the very presenters who promote it (Kwan 2017).

This chapter considers the broader historical, cultural and economic forces that influence presenters of dance and how these especially impact equity and fairness, often negatively, and in a manner that in certain ways is beyond the control of any one organization or individual. What is at issue is how particular presenting ecosystems function in different cultural contexts and communities to favour certain kinds of artistic and ideological choices at the detriment of others. I will also address other ethical issues related to the integrated and mutually dependent nature of the field, centring on responsibility and trust. Dance presenters tend to act as gatekeepers and arbiters of taste and constantly weigh the perspectives of multiple stakeholders such as artists, audiences, patrons, funders and boards of directors. This makes ethical concerns around honesty, transparency, openness, responsiveness and empathy particularly relevant. In this chapter, I draw on relational ethics and care ethics as beneficial for making the presenting field more humane, especially for the treatment of artists and particularly since the COVID-19 pandemic shuttered performing arts venues and deeply affected the presenting field at all levels.

Understanding dance presenters and the dance presenting world

While most people have at least a passing familiarity with what is involved in being a dancer, choreographer, dance educator and even a dance critic, the work of dance presenters is much less clear. However, those in presenting roles are at the nexus of many intersecting parts of the dance world and are critical to making dance visible and available to the public. They work as facilitators between artist, art and audience. For this reason, I will begin by briefly examining the different factors presenters often need to consider in deciding whom to present and the stakeholders to whom they often feel responsible. Even more than dance critics, who often work alone, those who function in some form of presenting capacity constantly face a variety of competing needs and desires. As I will explain, their ethical obligations are varied and depend on their region, budget and institution size. This overview of the presenting world's ecology establishes a foundation for understanding certain key cultural and economic forces that influence the ethical choices presenters face.

So, first, what does a person who presents dance do? Most commonly a presenter works for an organization or has an established relationship with a festival, performance venue or presenting organization. They invite or otherwise hire artists and companies, either informally or through a contract, to perform and/or produce existing repertoire or new work as part of the venue's season, as part of a festival or for some other kind of event or specific purpose. Sometimes presenters act as dramaturgs and provide feedback on or otherwise edit the work in discussion with the artist, addressing form, pace, aural aspects, emotional arc and so on. Depending on the institutional context, a presenter will need to consider everything from practical concerns, such as the venue's size, technical specifications and budget limitations, to the organization's mission, any boards of directors and/or financial supporters and funding agencies' concerns, their target audience's tastes and their own aesthetic and ideological interests. Contingent on all these factors, a presenter may travel nationally or internationally in search of artists to present/produce, or may focus on presenting and supporting dance artists from a particular region. They may provide the entire fee for the artist or may co-present with partners or the artist to share costs. Australian arts presenter Brett Sheehy reflects on this complexity in 'Confessions of a gatekeeper' (2009); he states that festival directors 'need to be commissioners and nurturers of new works, collaborators with arts companies both here and overseas, producers and presenters of the arts, and diplomats in balancing the needs and wishes of local artists with the brief of presenting the finest international arts' (2009: n.pag.).

The wide range of contexts in which presenters may operate can include state-funded and operated theatres; artist-founded and run venues, events and choreo-graphic centres; performance programmes curated within museums; small, local and shoe-string efforts at presenting; artist or community curated events; grass-roots and volunteer-run Fringe Festivals; municipal culture houses that serve various neighbourhoods; artistic performances presented within refugee camps and prisons; university presenters who may be mandated to include student and professors' work along with other professional programming; and many more.

As indicated before, presenters of dance come with different titles and job descriptions, and from a range of backgrounds (often without formal training in live arts presenting), depending on the time period and specific context, and can often hold their positions for many years. For instance, presenters were tradition-ally called 'impresarios', a term that originated in the context of Italian opera in the mid eighteenth century. The impresario, usually a man, was the key figure in organizing a lyric season and assumed the financial risks of funding composers, the orchestra, singers, costumes and sets. In the twentieth century, such legendary figures as Sergei Diaghilev, Lincoln Kirstein and Sol Hurok, played a central role in the concert dance field, raising the money for, and organizing, performances and tours of ballet and modern dance through Europe, South and North America. These men were passionate about the arts, ambitious and skilled at raising money at a time when there was no government funding and support of the arts consisted of private patronage. More recent examples include Joseph Melillo, who was executive producer at the Brooklyn Academy of Music (BAM) from 1999 to 2018, and his successor David Binder, who has produced work on Broadway and off-Broadway along with international festivals.

Sam Miller was an especially influential person in the dance presenting world in the United States during the last several decades. His first jobs in dance were with ballet companies in Arizona and Pennsylvania. He then joined Pilobolus as Managing Director (1982–86), before working at Jacob's Pillow from 1986 to 1995 and then as the director of the New England Foundation for the Arts between 1995 and 2005. He also helped to establish with Pamela Tatge the Institute for Curatorial Practice in Performance (ICPP) at Wesleyan University in 2011, as a formal training programme in the realm of performing arts presenting. His particular talent was for building partnerships, international exchanges and attracting resources for bold new enterprises. He saw it as part of a presenter's responsibilities to care about how the work gets to the stage and sponsor its development, for instance through residencies, and to also support the dissemination of the work, through establishing mechanisms for exposure to different art markets. Among other influential programmes he initiated over his lifetime, for instance, was the National Dance Project in 1996. This has become the primary programme that supports the commissioning and touring of contemporary dance in the United States.

Paul Szilard, who managed international tours for companies like the Alvin Ailey American Dance Theater, observed in his autobiography *Under My Wings: My Life as an Impresario* (2002):

> It's a strange profession, isn't it? Not an artist, yet hopefully with an artist's taste, not even a critic, yet certainly with a critic's judgment. Indeed an impresario is a critic who puts his money where his opinion is, a man making his living not so much off the artist but through the artist. A man who presents, but first has to choose; a man who encourages, but first has to discern; a man who spreads a message that he first has to receive. And also a man who lives dangerously not only on his own wits, but on the wit of others. To some extent, like a critic, he is a parasite, but, even more than a critic, he has to be symbiotic with his host. He has to help others before he can help himself. And he also lives a hell of an interesting life. His eyes are constantly glinting, brightly searching for the new and unexpected.
>
> (2002: 11)

Szilard captures a particular conception of the presenter as an unusual specimen who exists apart from (but intimately connected to) artists and audiences, and through their prescient discernment or connoisseurship produces for audiences, that which is great, new and unexpected. Diaghilev, the role model for this conception, is famous for demanding of the artists he brought together: 'Étonne moi!' – 'Astonish me!' His efforts were behind the Ballets Russes becoming a modernizing force in the ballet world of the early twentieth century, and he has had lasting effects to this day for what it means to be a successful producer.

In many ways, this view of the presenter as a galvanizing force of excellence and discoverer of fresh talent continues to hold sway, even as the presenting world has expanded and diversified and many of those who present dance also assume roles as dancers, choreographers, critics, editors, educators and agents. For instance, the early twenty-first century has seen the rise of the term 'curator' in relation to dance presenting; this term is borrowed from the visual and media arts and museum context, demonstrating that realm's influence on dance. While 'curation' in the dance context can be traced to the 1970s, it is only post-2005 that its use has taken off in the North American contemporary concert dance context.

One of the important characteristics of curation is that it provides an intellectual frame for looking at a work or group of works and situating it in a larger context. Here, the *idea* of the exhibition or festival can take precedence over the individual pieces or artists/choreographers displayed or presented. Peter Taub, who curated performing arts at the Museum of Contemporary Art Chicago from 1996 to 2016, explains it this way: 'Curating is [...] scholarship, framing ideas, telling stories – showing the edge that exists between the thing curated and the rest of us' (quoted in Borrelli 2013: n.pag.). Insofar as presenters have increasingly been conceived as curators, like impresarios they can assume a major authoritative role in the producing process. In a March 2020 *Dance Magazine* article 'What do dance curators actually do?' author Nancy Wozny states, 'They spot raw talent, develop and shape careers, identify trends and create context around what they are presenting' (2020: n.pag.). In other words, by packaging art for audiences, curators play an important part in influencing the art world and public perception. And like impresarios, recent curators are often interested in innovation and surprise: in how a curated event has the potential to challenge established canons, for instance, and the primacy of individual artworks to draw new relationships based on a particular theme.

Notably, however, the curatorial role has also come to be seen by some as a response to the elitism, commodification, and taste-making aspects of traditional arts presenting – with an emphasis on the *guardianship* aspect of the term and need to care for and protect those in their custody. In this view the curator is conceived as an artist embedded in a particular community, working with a more grassroots approach and committed to furthering the needs and values of the varied constituents. For instance, Dena Davida, who founded Québec's first dance presentation organization Tangente in 1980 (along with the Festival International de Nouvelle Danse de Montréal in 1985 and laid the ground for Canada's first dance touring network CanDance), has argued that, 'the curator's imperative [is] to care for artists and audiences' and that, 'more than merely an intellectual framework, I believe (and hope) that curators are largely rooting their ethos in caring' (2021: n.pag.). More will be stated about this distinction later, but it demonstrates the extent to which different perspectives shape the field and impact the ethical dimensions we will discuss.

Today, then, in any one region of the United States (let alone globally), a complex ecology exists, with varying levels of dance presenting by people with varying titles and functioning within different contexts. For instance, in the state of Arizona, there are 'world-class' arts presenting organizations like ASU Gammage, which is part of Arizona State University. Its Senior Director of Programmes and Organizational Initiatives, Michael Reed, has worked closely and for a long time with Executive Director Colleen Jennings-Roggensack in planning seasons of nationally touring Broadway shows and national and international contemporary arts performances. They include contemporary dance as part of the 'ASU Gammage Beyond' series, and support new works and artist residencies, sometimes collaborating with ASU's dance programme, which also presents its own dance performances of faculty, student and guest artist work. Area cities also operate performance arts centres, such as the Scottsdale Center for the Performing Arts, Phoenix Center for the Arts, Tempe Center for the Arts and Mesa Arts Center. Each of these has executive or programming directors/coordinators who oversee annual seasons of performing arts, which may include a few dance companies. Then there are large, independent, non-profit organizations, such as The Herberger Theater Center in Phoenix, which house or provide space for dance performances and small companies like Conderdance, run by Artistic Director Carley Conder, which produces Breaking Ground, an annual dance and film festival of contemporary dance by usually regional performers. Finally, local dancer/choreographers and companies also self-produce – either in their own spaces, rented locations or public locales – as when performers Marlene Strang and Leanne Schmidt organized pop-up parking lot performances during the COVID-19 pandemic.

Even while this kind of complex, multi-tiered ecology exists in different regions across the country, New York City is a major pole of the contemporary concert dance presenting world, with a nexus of influential venues and organizations, all with their affiliated presenters, shaping the national field over the last few decades. Similar to regional stratification, these institutions and organizations vary in prestige – but those choreographers who 'make it' form a route, or ladder, from relative anonymity to acclaim not only within the state but also across the United States and potentially beyond. These include, but are not limited to smaller, more unrestricted and widely accessible venues like Movement Research and Dixon Place, to the more selective and rigorously curated spaces like Performance Space New York (formerly P.S. 122), The Kitchen, New York Live Arts (formerly Dance Theater Workshop), Baryshnikov Arts Center, The Chocolate Factory Theater and Danspace Project at St Mark's Church. Other spaces include The Park Avenue Armory and The Shed; plus established, high-status venues, such as The Joyce Theater and the Brooklyn Academy of Music (BAM). Annual festivals focusing on experimental dance have included the Crossing the Line Festival, with the support of the French Institute Alliance Française (FIAF) (active 2007–19), and the American Realness festival curated by Thomas Benjamin Snapp Pryor (active 2010–19). Several modern art museums have also presented contemporary dance performances – these include the Museum of Modern Art (MoMA), MoMA PS1 and the New Museum. Another influential presenter is Performa, founded and curated by RoseLee Goldberg, which has put on a biennial festival since 2005.

In addition, New York is the site of a massive yearly gathering organized by the Association of Performing Arts Presenters (APAP), the national service and advocacy organization that supports performing arts presenting, booking and touring. Basically, it is an industry convention and art marketplace. Usually held at a luxury hotel like the Hilton Midtown, the annual conference attracts national and international presenters to effectively 'shop' for performing arts, including dance, by meeting informally or formally with dance artists, their agents or managers, and viewing performances of dance at the earlier locations and places like City Center Studios, the Ailey Studios, Peridance Capezio Center and the Hilton itself. The satellite venues are rented and booked, usually by artists' management companies to host multi-artist showcases.[3] Attendees pay a registration fee to attend (in 2020, the full onsite fee was over one thousand dollars) and dance artists/companies pay to perform their work and gain access to other kinds of benefits. As a whole, it is a time for those on the presenting and managing side of dance to meet, listen to presentations, and share perspectives, and for artists and companies to promote themselves and hopefully get bookings for the future. For the 2022 APAP/NYC gathering, the event as listed on the site Events in America encourages people to 'Join more than 3,600 of your colleagues from all 50 US states and more than 36 countries for 5+ days of professional development, showcases, unmatched networking and the world's largest performing arts marketplace.'[4] And the announcement also observes that, 'This marketplace offers artists, managers, agents, producers and vendors an unparalleled opportunity to meet presenters, sponsors, partners and other professionals who collectively lead and fuel the presenting and touring field worldwide.'

As I will elaborate, these various venues and organizations, and the presenters and curators who work with them, are a major force in determining which artists are highlighted, and which are not, in the local, national and international dance field. They also shape the field's overall ethos and spoken and unspoken ethical guidelines governing interactions between stakeholders. Presenters in any one part of the country, in other words, will be influenced by their local ecology and to varying degrees by what is taking place in New York and internationally, as revealed during annual gatherings at APAP. This complex, dynamic system of interactions can affect how they work, the policies and protocols they develop, the contracts they use and even how they conceptualize their profession.

Meanwhile, broader societal and economic forces also deeply affect the presenting realm and related ethical considerations in the United States. These form a
backdrop to the entire presenting field, and as such, require some attention. The
first of these is the relatively limited public support and audience for live professional performing arts in the United States. According to a 2017 Survey of Public
Participation in the Arts, the country's premier instrument for tracking adult
patterns of arts engagement, in 2017, only 9.4% or 22.9 million Americans reported
attending at least one non-musical play in a 12-month period, 8.6% or 21 million
people reported attending at least one classical music event, and 2.2% or 5.3 million
reported attending at least one opera event (NEA 2018). In terms of dance specifically, the report has only 3.1% or 7.6 million reporting attending at least one ballet
performance and 6.3% or 15.2 million attending at least one dance performance
other than ballet. The statistics for dance have remained fairly steady since 2002's
findings of 6.3%, which was for a dance performance other than ballet, and 3.9%
for ballet performances; in the other areas, numbers have declined – from 12.3%
for non-musical plays in 2002, 11.6% for classical music, and 3.2% for opera.

Government support for the arts is also extremely limited in the United States.
The reasons for this are complex and varied, but for the purposes of this chapter,
it is particularly helpful to look at recent debates around federal government
assistance. During the 1980s and into the 1990s, the so-called Culture Wars
erupted, revealing a deep ambivalence over public arts funding, especially as
related to contemporary art. During that period several powerful Republican
lawmakers, including Alfonse D'Amato, Jesse Helms and Newt Gingrich
attacked a group of artists whose work they found offensive and unworthy of
taxpayer assistance. These included visual artists like Andres Serrano and Robert
Mapplethorpe, and performance artist Karen Finley, among others. The main
object of Republican condemnation, however, was the National Endowment for
the Arts (NEA), the principal government organization established in 1965 to
oversee public funding for the arts in the United States. (The first NEA grant of
$100,000 was actually to the American Ballet Theatre in December 1965.) On
the one side of the debate are those promoting the rights of artists and asserting the economic and educational benefits of the arts for society as a whole; on
the other side are those arguing against the use of tax dollars to promote what
they believe is an elitist, self-serving group of largely immoral artists producing
unethical work. For instance, on 18 May 1989, D'Amato adamantly voiced his
opinion on the Senate floor against then acting NEA chairman Hugh Southern
about the agency's perceived poor choices of using tax payers' dollars on artists
such as Serrano: 'If you want free speech, you want to draw dirty pictures, you
want to do anything you want, that is your business, but not with taxpayers'
money' (Congressional Record 1989: n.pag.). In July of that year, Jesse Helms

introduced legislation to ban funding of 'obscene or indecent art'; in September a Congressional committee added an anti-obscenity clause to NEA appropriations that would ban federal funds for art that,

> may be considered obscene, including but not limited to, depictions of sadomasochism, homoeroticism, the sexual exploitation of children, or individuals engaged in sex acts and which, when taken as a whole, do not have serious literary, artistic, political, or scientific value.
>
> (NEA Chronology 1993: n.pag.)

The Helms Amendment, formally adopted in October 1989, gave the NEA great power and latitude to define obscenity. It established an 'obscenity pledge', which required artists to promise they would not use government money to create works of an obscene nature. The NEA abolished the pledge in November 1990 but instituted a 'decency clause' which required award recipients to ensure that their works met certain standards of decency. The struggles between arts supporters and detractors of public funding and the role of the NEA reached their height in the mid 1990s, when both houses had a Republican majority. In 1994, Gingrich wrote the 'Contract with America' and promised to eliminate funding for the NEA over the next few years. The result was severe cuts to the NEA and the elimination of most direct support for artists. In 1996, the budget was cut by 39% from around $162 million to $99 million and most individual artist grants were eliminated – a move with serious ramifications to this day. This allocation remained more or less in place until the early 2000s; it has since gradually risen, but the underlying conflicts persist. As recently as 2017 under former President Trump the NEA faced the threat of elimination by Republican lawmakers echoing the sentiments of Gingrich, who has observed, 'Has the overall culture flourished in the 30 years of public funding of the arts and humanities? Or has it decayed? Many Americans would argue the latter case' (2001: n.pag.). According to Gingrich, Americans should not 'be forced to underwrite cultural dependents who add to our decay and undermine our values rather than enhance our lives' (2001: n.pag.). There are many Republican lawmakers, as well as members of the general public, who continue to share this view.

The scarcity of public funding for the arts in the United States contrasts sharply to countries in Europe and the Commonwealth, which also impacts the presenting world. A report from 2014 states that the United States spends 1/40th of what Germany does for the arts per capita. Germany's art funding in 2007 for instance, equated to around $20 per German citizen, in comparison to the 41 cents per American provided by the NEA (Gummow 2014). Other countries that rate high on per capita spending on the arts include France, Sweden, Australia, Finland, England and Northern Ireland (Hodgins 2019: n.pag.). In these countries, there is a deep-seated belief in the value of the arts and its positive contributions to society. For instance, from the Renaissance King François I to the Sun King, Louis XIV, and on through the post-World War II years, France has prided itself on extensive state support of the arts. There is a dedicated Ministry of Culture, founded in 1959, that is exclusively focused on arts and culture. The arts are regarded as a way to express the grandeur of the French nation, provide uplift for the soul and demonstrate the creativity of its citizens. In May 2020, when COVID threatened the livelihood of many performers, French President Emmanuel Macron promised to maintain the current systems of financing, including a robust system for supporting unemployed artists, stating, 'We thank all of those who've created and innovated during these difficult times' (quoted in Beardsley and Kheriji-Watts 2021: n.pag.). He continued, 'Culture is absolutely essential to our lives as citizens' (2021: n.pag.). Choreographer and dancer Liz Santoro moved to Paris in 2011 and commented on state financial assistance during the pandemic and the exceptional status of artists in France. 'I'm living inside a society where culture has been given a lot of value', she says. 'Coming from an American culture, it took a little while to adjust to that' (2011: n.pag.). This example demonstrates the extent to which each region and country in the world has developed particular ecologies of arts presenting that emerge from their social, political and economic structures, broader world views and cultural contexts.

More robust audiences and government support in other countries greatly affect the US art world generally and presenting world specifically. In terms of dance, it means that contemporary dance artists (like Santaro, and Trajal Harrell, a dancer and choreographer I discuss later) may decide to leave to find a more sustainable career in Europe, where they find more financial support and won't have to battle such limited audience appreciation and the potential for social and/or legal censorship. This also means that it can be less expensive for an American presenter to book a dance artist or company from abroad than from another part of the United States since that artist could receive financial support from their government to tour internationally. In addition to the already complex US dance ecosystem, then, these far-reaching social and economic factors influence dance presenters in both obvious and more subtle ways. It is to these outcomes that I now turn. I will first discuss the problematic ethical results of how the dance presenting world can function and then consider how the field has been striving for a more humane manner of operating.

Behind the dance presenting curtain 1: Problems with fairness

I am increasingly concerned about the system in which they make that work – the festivals, the organizations, the institutions, the

*individuals who create the structures in which the work is presented
and contextualized – who, in a spectacularly vertically integrated
closed ecosystem, determine both which artists get funded and who
gets presented and as such wield outsized influence in the aesthetic
and practical choices of artists.*

(Horwitz 2014: n.pag.)

It is important to recognize that many individual presenters are extremely dedicated to the admirable goal of presenting and work hard, in the words of arts leader Kenneth Foster, 'to connect art, artists and audiences and create transformative experiences for audiences' (2010: 10). Many artist–curators also work to strengthen local communities through culturally and aesthetically diverse performance programming. What is evident, however, from analyzing trends in contemporary dance presenting in the United States from approximately 2004 to 2021 is that, as a result of the various factors outlined before, a powerful presenting network exists that both formally and informally shapes perceptions of contemporary dance in the United States, with arguably inequitable results. This network illuminates a venue/festival track that has been shaping the dominant and elite discourse of contemporary dance, especially in New York City, on the national stages of major contemporary art institutions and, for some, within the international dance presenting marketplace. The result is a select group of gatekeepers promoting a fairly small group of artists with certain shared aesthetic preferences and characteristics related to ethnicity, race and sexuality. I now turn to examine this trend more closely, along with how it perpetuates the consequentialist tradition of seeing dances as masterpieces and choreographers as geniuses while sometimes disregarding dancers' as well as arts administrators' everyday vulnerabilities.

One of the major axes of this web travels between such institutions as The Institute of Contemporary Art in Boston (ICAB), the Walker Art Center in Minneapolis (WAC), the Wexner Center for the Arts in Columbus (WCA), the Museum of Contemporary Art in Chicago (MCAC), and to a lesser extent, the Roy and Edna Disney/Calarts Theater, based in Los Angeles (REDCAT), and the Portland Institute for Contemporary Art (PICA). During the earlier part of the twenty-first century, these institutions were part of a group known as the Contemporary Art Centers (CAC) network, which was an initiative of the National Dance Project (NDP), in turn a programme of the New England Foundation for the Arts (NEFA), known for offering grants to artists and organizations to support the creation and presentation of work. The programme's design began in 2004–05, and was implemented in 2006–07 with activity through 2012–13.[5] During those years, the CAC was 'comprised of performing arts curators throughout the U.S. who build collaborations and connections that support the work of innovative interdisciplinary artists and artist collaborators' (CAC website 2013, now no longer in existence). These curators represented eleven prominent institutions, and the traffic between them – especially the larger organizations – indicates the strong connections that have existed both formally and informally between the participating institutions and their curators.[6]

As explained on the CAC website at the time, this exclusive group decided whose work would be supported for CAC projects through a process of internal nomination rather than, for instance, an open call for submissions. The now defunct website declared: 'Artists and companies are selected for support for the commissioning, creative development, documentation, contextualization, and touring of interdisciplinary work through nomination by CAC members.' Along with a formal process of selecting projects for specific CAC support, the members also more informally displayed similar aesthetic tastes, prerogatives and ideologies by presenting many of the same dance artists as their counterparts even when they were not official recipients of CAC support, but with funding from the National Dance Project and NEFA, large foundations like the Doris Duke Charitable Foundation and the Andrew W. Mellon Foundation, and grants from the MAP Fund and Creative Capital (both of which actually receive support from both the Duke and Mellon foundations along with other foundations and individuals). As will be demonstrated, my research indicates that a similar pattern has been evident even since 2014 when the CAC ceased to exist as a formal entity.

Another of the major axes aligns a number of venues, festivals and individuals in New York City with certain overlapping aspects of the aesthetic/ideology of these institutions. Again, these presenters offer both formal support to select artists in the form of co-sponsorship, and informal support by recommending them to other presenters and funding bodies. These have included, among others, curators at The Kitchen, Danspace, New York Live Arts, Crossing the Line Festival, American Realness and many of the venues outlined here that are based in New York. Each of the spaces and festivals has its own unique history, and aspects that differentiate them within the contemporary dance landscape. At the same time, patterns of programming indicate there are certain shared aesthetic and ideological perspectives, as well as economic pressures, that draw these curators to the work of a select group of dance artists, and make them participators in their success, in today's contemporary dance art market.

As one of the most frequently presented dance artists, choreographer Trajal Harrell's career provides an instructive trope to navigate the last two decades of contemporary dance curation in the United States. On 1 and 2 October 2009, Harrell gave a solo performance at the New Museum in New York City. The work was the first of his now celebrated series *Twenty Looks or Paris Is Burning at the Judson Church* (*Twenty Looks*). This performance was co-presented by Danspace Project and Crossing the Line Festival and was one of a few select dance performance events at the New Museum held in 2009. The performance was curated by Eungie Joo and organized by Travis Chamberlain, the curator of performance and manager of public programmes at the New Museum. Telescoping out from this particular moment to examine the other primary US venues/festivals where Harrell has performed since 2004, one sees the various axes described earlier. For instance, in New York, he performed at the following: Danspace Project (2004, 2007, 2012); Dance Theater Workshop (2008, 2009); The Kitchen (2004, 2006, 2008, 2011); The Kitchen, co-presented with Crossing the Line (2014); American Realness (2011, 2013, 2017); New York Live Arts (formerly Dance Theater Workshop), 2012 and MoMA, 2016. In terms of the national scene, his work was presented by the Institute of Contemporary Arts/Boston (2010, 2011, 2014, 2016, 2018), Walker Art Center (2013, 2016), Museum of Contemporary Art, Chicago, 2019, Time-Based Art Festival (TBA), Portland Institute for Contemporary Art, 2013 and REDCAT (2014).

Looking a bit more closely, one can see how his work has been supported across these various institutions. For example, in January 2013, his work was presented at the American Realness Festival, followed by PS1 MoMA, in New York, and then at the ICA, Boston, and at the Walker Art Center, in Minneapolis. In terms of funding, the piece *The Untitled Still Life Collection*, was a collaborative work with visual artist Sarah Sze, first conceived in 2010 during a residency at ICA Boston. It was made possible by the CAC network, with major support from the Doris Duke Charitable Foundation. It was presented at ICA Boston in 2011 in conjunction with the 2011 ICA exhibit *Dance/Draw*. A revival took place in October 2014 at the ICA with dancer Christina Vasileiou as part of a 'Fiber' exhibit. As another example, Harrell's *Antigone Sr./Twenty Looks or Paris Is Burning at the Judson Church* (L) had its New York premiere at New York Live Arts in April 2012. The piece was commissioned by New York Live Arts' 'DTW Commissioning Fund' and was made possible, in part, by the National Endowment for the Arts. Additional funding was provided by, among others, The MAP Fund, then a programme of Creative Capital supported by the Doris Duke Charitable Foundation, with additional support from the Andrew W. Mellon Foundation.[7] After the premiere, this work was presented in various major national contemporary arts institutions. In April 2014, for instance, it was presented at REDCAT, without direct CAC funding, but in part with 'generous support from the New England Foundation for the Arts' National Dance Project' (REDCAT 2018: n.pag.).

Similar patterns can be found among the additional handful of other favoured US-based dance artists during the last fifteen or so years, including Miguel Gutierrez, nora chipaumire, Will Rawls, Faye Driscoll, Kyle Abraham and Rashaun Mitchell/ Silas Riener. In each case, since 2006 their work has been presented over ten times at a combination of New York venues such as Dance Theater Workshop and Danspace and national venues such as the Walker, Wexner, Museum of Modern

Art Chicago, ICA Boston, PICA, REDCAT and MoMA. Just looking at the period from 2014 to 2020, the following US-based dance artists were presented the most across these national venues along with Crossing the Line and American Realness festivals: Driscoll, Harrell, Rawls, Gutierrez, Ligia Lewis, chipaumire, Riener/Mitchell and Okwui Okpokwasili (Table 6.1). Moreover, with the exception of Riener/Mitchell, all of these artists received funding for their work from at least one of the following major granting organizations for contemporary dance over the same period: Doris Duke Charitable Foundation (DD), MAP Fund (MAP), Foundation for Contemporary Arts (FCA) and Creative Capital (CC) (Table 6.2).[8]

This research suggests that from simply a quantitative perspective, there is not a great deal of fairness in the presenting ecology of contemporary concert dance. Out of the thousands of choreographers who exist at any one time, only about a dozen are consistently promoted at a highly visible, national level. Just as an example, according to the May 2009 report of the US Bureau of Labor Statistics, there were approximately 1170 choreographers working for performing arts companies, 80 choreographers working for colleges and universities, and 180 independent choreographers. This means at the very least 1430 choreographers whose work was potentially eligible to be framed as 'contemporary dance' at the time that Trajal Harrell's *Twenty Looks* was presented at the New Museum, depending on how widely one wishes to open the aperture.[9] Now consider the total estimated number of choreographers given by the US Bureau for 2009: 14,700, which does not include the countless 'nonprofessional' dance makers who were working (US Bureau of Labor Statistics 2009). The potential problem with a system that consistently favours a dozen or so dance-makers at a national level becomes even more apparent.

A 2013 report prepared for the Brooklyn Commune Project voiced concern over this lack of fairness and access to funding. It pointed out that 'Even a cursory examination of the arts funding landscape reveals that there is a small cohort of curators, administrators and foundation programme officers who influence policy and funding initiatives' (Bartosik 2013: n.pag.). In this document, choreographer Kimberly Bartosik argues that the opaque relationship structures among this small group and the nomination-based model for awarding substantial grants 'create a pervasive sense of exclusion and inequity' (2013: n.pag.). She observes:

> This lack of transparency creates not only distrust but a sense of futility in many artists, as it creates the appearance that only a very few artists are supported, often repeatedly, while others are repeatedly turned down, or are never in contention to begin with […] Who are we missing by keeping these substantial grants within the nomination-based model and what is the long term cost to the health of the arts ecosystem when institutional opacity breeds a culture of distrust and futility?
>
> (2013: n.pag.)

Name	Total	WCA	PICA	ICAB	WAC	RED	MoMA	MCAC	CLF	AR
Faye Driscoll	11	2	1	3	3			2		
Trajal Harrell	10			2	1	1	1	1	2	2
Will Rawls	10		1	2	1		1	2	1	2
Miguel Gutierrez	9	1	1		1	1			1	4
Ligia Lewis	9				2	2		2		3
nora chipaumire	9	1		1	1	1			3	3
Silas Reiner	6	1		1	1	1		2		
Rashaun Mitchell	6	1			1	2		2		
Okwui Okpokwasili	5		1	1	1	1		1		

TABLE 6.1: Total performances at researched venues for the topmost frequently presented US-based performers between 2014 and 2020.

Name	Total	CC	DD	FCA	MAP
Okwui Okpokwasili	5	1	1	1	2
Faye Driscoll	3		1	1	1
Trajal Harrell	3		2	1	
Will Rawls	2			1	1
nora chipaumire	2		1	1	
Miguel Gutierrez	1		1		
Ligia Lewis	1			1	
Silas Reiner	0				
Rashaun Mitchell	0				

TABLE 6.2: Total awards given to the US-based dance artists most frequently presented by researched venues between 2014 and 2020.

Also at play here, notably, is the fallout of revoking direct NEA funding to artists in the mid 1990s and overall scarcity of financial support. Since then, artists have felt growing pressure to raise their own money through private foundation grants or crowdfunding to assist with presenting themselves or their companies. In a competitive and resource-scarce environment the burden of fundraising is put back onto the artist and artists who are good fundraisers, therefore, or who appeal to donors, can be more attractive to some presenters. Given the high expense of producing live dance, 'The economics demand presenters take advantage of whatever extra financial help they can get, whether from the artist's fundraising or from sharing the financial load of commissions, visas, travel, etc. with other venues, so they're largely all presenting the same artists' (Castro et al. 2020: 68). In other words, there are critical economic reasons driving the support of a select group of artists, above and beyond any particular desires of individual presenters.

The narrowly defined aesthetic/ideological orientation and profile of most of the favoured dance artists is an additional concern. In other words, there appears to be a lack of fairness in terms of the kinds of dance and the kinds of dance artists that are being presented. The narrow definition is in line with the 'curatorial turn' within the contemporary dance field and with shifts in the visual arts world. The resulting dominant aesthetic has been largely conceptual in nature, is closely tied to trends in Europe and takes a probing, curious, somewhat nostalgic look back to the 1960s and 1970s, when avant-garde arts in the United States were more closely interconnected, less institutionalized and beyond the mainstream. What has occurred is a convergence of paths between the powerful network of US presenters with a select group of international leaders, especially from Western Europe, who have favoured the conceptual turn. The European presenters who tend to promote and be in the market for this work come from the United Kingdom, France, Germany, Belgium, the Netherlands, Austria and Norway.

One way to understand the dominant aesthetic is to recognize an American fascination with European conceptualism. We can trace this by noting the support of French choreographer Jérôme Bel, considered one of Europe's most successful and prominent contemporary dance artists. Bel has been lauded in the United States since 2005, in a manner that directly correlates with the rise in a particular kind of curatorial discourse, its relation to trends in the visual arts and how such choreographers benefit from European funding. Bel was influenced in his own right by the Judson Dance Theater, a group of American experimentalists in the 1960s whose work was characterized by minimalism, use of everyday objects and pedestrian movement, and its critique of traditional ideas of dance/performance. He is known for pieces like *Shirtology*, where performers wear T-shirts that they take off/put on in various combinations. The performance's primary concern is 'with the way these things are decoded, read and experienced by the audience' (quoted in Etchells 1999: n.pag.), and *Pichet Klunchun and myself*, in which Bel and a traditional Thai dancer ask questions about each other's work and offer brief demonstrations. The piece sheds light on the cultural, economic and aesthetic assumptions that get in the way of performance generally, of intercultural exchange and of how people perceive dance.

From 2004 to 2020, Bel was presented multiple times within the venue/festival track outlined in this chapter. In 2005, he received a Bessie award, and, in 2007, was invited by Roselee Goldberg to be part of *Performa 07*. In a discussion, prior to the event Bel brings attention to the close relation between his way of working and the visual art world. He stated, 'I am so happy to be presented in the context of Performa 07 because I feel more connected to some visual artists than to other choreographers […] the people who first started to understand my work had a lot of knowledge in visual art' (quoted *Performa Magazine* 2007: n.pag.). In 2008, 2010, 2016 and 2019, he was presented by Crossing the Line, and at the Museum of Modern Art in 2012 and 2016. Throughout this period, Bel's work was also shown multiple times by the major national contemporary art institutions including the Portland Institute of Contemporary Art (PICA) (2008, 2010), ICA/Boston (2011), the Walker (2005, 2007, 2011, 2013, 2016), Wexner (2005, 2007, 2011), REDCAT (2007) and Diverseworks, Houston (2015).

Bel's funding streams, moreover, indicate the strong influence from European and European-linked sources, as an example of how a small group of choreographers find leverage in the American presenting ecosystem. His work has received support from Alliance Française, the French Ministry for Foreign Affairs, and Cultural Services of the French Embassy in New York, among others. It also received repeated support from the French US Exchange (FUSED) in Dance, which was created in 2004 to promote cultural exchange between the partnering countries. FUSED annually puts out a call for French and American-based projects, from which a committee selects several to fund. Between 2007 and 2014 FUSED supported a total of nine presentations of Bel's work in the venue/festival track in 2007, 2008, 2010 and 2014. For instance, in 2007, FUSED provided support for *Pichet Klunchun and Myself* to be presented at the Walker Art Center, Wexner Center for the Arts and at Dance Theater Workshop in New York.

The heavily conceptual orientation is also evident from the US-based choreographers although it focuses more explicitly on issues related to race, gender and sexuality. In particular, the dance artists mentioned earlier (i.e., Gutierrez, Rawls, chipaumire, Driscoll and Okpokwasili, etc.), often address topics concerning Latinx, Black and/or queer identity in their work, and most do so in a manner that tends towards minimalism, historical referencing, deconstruction and challenging mainstream social norms. Indeed, Harrell's *Twenty Looks* series is a prime example. According to Harrell, this piece seeks to answer the question: what would have happened if in 1963 someone from the New York voguing scene in Harlem had come down to the Judson Church in Greenwich Village to perform alongside the early postmodernists? In the original solo version of the piece Harrell, who is African American, combines voguing movement with minimal pedestrian movement in a way that highlights Black, queer performance. In their publicity, presenters emphasize connections to the Judson Dance Theater and that issues related to identity politics drive these works. For example, the publicity for *Twenty Looks* at the ICA, Boston, in 2010 characteristically stated: 'Like Yvonne Rainer or Trisha Brown, Harrell debates the very nature of performance – the role of seduction, glamour, and spectacle in dance and in the ways we present ourselves in everyday life' (ICA/Boston 2014: n.pag.). Similarly, REDCAT's publicity referred to *Antigone Sr./Twenty Looks or Paris Is Burning at the Judson Church (L)* in 2014 as 'a genre-bending exploration of race, gender, sexuality, culture and history' (REDCAT 2014: n.pag.).

There are some exceptions to this kind of programming in the United States, but the dominant aesthetic and ideological orientation of the most supported 'experimental dance' has been conceptually oriented work by European choreographers or US dance artists – especially New York-based artists – exploring Latinx, African/African American and/or queer identity. Others either relate in some way to these topics or represent the postmodern dance movement of the 1960s and its followers, along with connections between visual art and performance. In other words, although Kyle Abraham's work, which has also received a great deal of support from presenters (and funders), is much more dance-oriented in a more traditional sense of engaging/fusing diverse codified dance styles, one of his main goals as an African American choreographer is to, 'make work that highlights my community [...] work that sheds light on issues that have always been important to me and to people that look like me'.[10] Meanwhile, more established artists who have repeatedly appeared during the last two decades as performers at the main New York and national venues tend to include those directly associated with the Judson Dance Theater, like Lucinda Childs, Simone Forti, Yvonne Rainer, Steve Paxton and Trisha Brown, as well as postmodernists from the later generation, especially Bill T. Jones and Ralph Lemon.[11]

The dance events presented at MoMA between 2014 and 2016 provide a distilled snapshot of the close connections between these various intersecting threads. These included work by Forti, Rainer, Harrell, Bel and two other European-based dance artists – Alexandra Bachzetsis and Eszeter Salamon. The events were organized by curators from MoMA's Department of Media and Performance Art. Harrell's was part of a two-year artist's residency and Bel's event took place on the occasion of FIAF's Crossing the Line Festival 2016, which included a special focus on Bel, with performances at The Joyce Theater and The Kitchen. During this same period Lemon, the Trisha Brown Dance Company, Paxton, Harrell and Bel were all presented at the Walker Art Center.

What this means, ultimately, is that dance presenters can easily, whether intentionally or not, act as gatekeeps in a dominant 'star system', 'winner takes all' approach that perpetuates a problematic discourse related to masterpieces and geniuses. Indeed, the wording surrounding the work these privileged artists create tends towards the 'best in contemporary dance'. For instance, ICA, Boston has as part of its mission to 'present outstanding contemporary art in all media'.[12] When promoting a performance by nora chipaumire in 2019 they highlight a quote from the *New Yorker* calling her 'defiantly charismatic' and 'a kind of rock star of dance'.[13] The work, *#PUNK 100% POP *N!&GA,* is said to be 'raw and visceral'.[14] The same season's publicity calls Faye Driscoll 'One of the most fascinating and astonishing choreographers working today' and proclaims her work a profoundly 'moving elegy about loss, the substance of mourning, and the labor of grief.'[15] In both cases, lengthy biographies are provided that list accolades from prominent critics, who as noted in the previous chapter also play a crucial role in this gatekeeping ecology, along with prominent awards the artists received (such as from the MAP fund, Doris Duke foundation, etc.) and other locations of their performances (e.g., Wexner, Walker, MCA/Chicago, etc.), demonstrating how the entire system works to support and perpetuate itself. This reinforces the observation made by Arthur Danto in his famous essay 'The artworld' that it is the community of art professionals associated with powerful institutions that largely determine what is considered great art and non-art in today's art market (1964).

Placing a select group of artists on pedestals and seeing their work as the 'best' can, as I stated in earlier chapters, lead to overlooking or dismissing instances of unethical or problematic behaviour. Presenters can treat big name artists as untouchable 'rock stars' who need to be catered to, and never questioned regarding, for instance, the treatment of performers in rehearsals or performances, or staff that must work with them in producing their work (see Kimitch 2021). Two high profile examples include Marina Abramović's 2011 production for a Museum of Contemporary Art in Los Angeles gala, and Deborah Hay's 2012 *Blues* for MoMA curated by Ralph Lemon. In both cases, brave participating performers stepped forward to highlight ideological and economic injustices lurking behind alleged progressive programming and aesthetics. In the case of Abramović's piece, dancer Sara Wookey protested the low pay and minimal safety precautions within the presenting of *Nude with Skeleton* for a gala performance at MoCA (Museum of Contemporary Art, Los Angeles). She explained in a now famous 'Open letter to artists' that what she experienced as an auditionee for the production, was 'extremely problematic, exploitative, and potentially abusive' (2011: n.pag.). She detailed:

> I was expected to lie naked and speechless on a slowly rotating table, starting from before guests arrived and lasting until after they left (a total of nearly four hours). I was expected to ignore (by staying in what Abramović refers to as 'performance mode') any potential physical or verbal harassment while performing. I was expected to commit to fifteen hours of rehearsal time, and sign a Non-Disclosure Agreement stating that if I spoke to anyone about what happened in the audition I was liable for being sued by Bounce Events, Marketing, Inc., the event's producer, for a sum of $1 million dollars plus attorney fees.

179

I was to be paid $150. During the audition, there was no mention of safeguards, signs, or signals for performers in distress, and when I asked about what protection would be provided I was told it could not be guaranteed.

(Wookey 2011: n.pag.)

As Wookey observed, all of these factors failed to take into consideration her professionalism and extensive career as a performer; they were signs of an inability to provide dancers with basic rights to safe working conditions and a living wage for their labour. Instead, they relied on a legacy of dancers being willing to sacrifice themselves for the sake of the genius creator, rather than standing up for what they are rightfully owed both by a famous artist and institution. As she said, 'If there is any group of cultural workers that deserves basic standards of labor, it is us performers working in museums, whose medium is our own bodies and deserve humane treatment and respect' (2011: n.pag.; see also Wookey's 2015 publication *Who Cares? Dance in the Gallery & Museum*).

With *Blues*, dancer Kathy Wasik observed, 'The lines Deborah drew in the piece and in the process of creating the work raise troubling questions surrounding race, gender, power, and money' (2012: n.pag.). Wasik argued that the work's aesthetic framing (which failed to address power issues) and Hay's elevated status as a choreographer – 'She was Deborah Hay. Who was I to distrust her' (2012: n.pag.) – were disempowering: 'I felt stripped of my voice and my individuality' (2012: n.pag.). In this piece, Hay worked with two casts largely segregated by skin colour. The casts received different renumeration, were treated differently during the process and given different freedoms within the improvisational score. Wasik observes, 'After the performance – in a discussion among the performers, Deborah, and Ralph – dancers from both casts admitted to having felt a lack of security that afternoon and throughout the process' (2012: n.pag.).

These individual dancers draw rare attention to how, despite its seeming progressive ideological leanings, the current presenting (including curatorial) discourse can sometimes retain the hierarchical and authoritarian elements of the 'genius' creative artist tradition and the presenting structures that support them. Their comments also reveal that while the Judson Dance Theatre choreographers at one time might have operated in radically progressive, egalitarian ways on the margins of the dance establishment, their work is now being staged by mainstream institutions, which significantly reconfigures its meaning. Cultural historian Beatrice von Bismarck illuminates how these recent re-stagings of avant-garde artwork originally created in the 1960s and 1970s have become commodified and much less radical within today's neoliberal, globalized art market. Through her research, she demonstrates that 'hand in hand with the alterations of the temporal and material conditions of the exhibits go a number of capitalizations, which affect the artistic works, but also the participating artists, the curators and the exhibition itself' (von Bismarck 2018).

Ultimately, it is important to recognize both the potentially disingenuous nature of 'radical' contemporary dance, and that certain (though certainly not all) aspects of today's curatorial discourse may reproduce the very systems of oppression and inequality that it purports to critique. Horwitz has noted this potential in a scathing critique of the American Realness festival in which he called out the falseness of its claims of transgression, and the extent to which the festival not only reinforced the dominant institutional discourse of contemporary art but also in so doing lost touch with the 'reality' of its own highly privileged positioning. He observed, 'AR attempts to create a simulacrum of difference and transgression comprised of the signifiers of otherness and disenfranchisement while in fact being entirely of the system it purports to critique' (2014: n.pag.).

Behind the dance presenting curtain 2: Dance worker vulnerability

If one of the major ethical issues facing the dance presenting field relates to the insularity and lack of fairness outlined here, another serious problem concerns the extreme vulnerability of those in the US operating in the existing system as revealed by the COVID pandemic.[16] As the APAP report 'Building ethical and equitable partnerships in the performing arts', states, 'In the immediate wake of the shutdown, we witnessed a field-wide battery of artist engagement cancellations. The economic pressures on all parties – regardless of the size of the artist group, institution, or company – were sudden and unsparing' (2020: 2). The closures and cancellations brought to the foreground power imbalances, especially between large institutions and individual artists, which have been passionately voiced. The artist-driven document 'Creating new futures: Phase 1' illustrates how numerous independent dance artists felt disenfranchised, helpless, and exposed during this time and calls for changes in ethical guidelines for the presenting world.

'Creating new futures: Phase 1; Working guidelines for ethics & equity in presenting dance & performance' points out numerous problems with the dance presenting ecosystem and how those problems were exacerbated by the decisions that certain presenters and their institutions made following COVID-19 shutdowns. This document began to take shape in March 2020 through conversations on Facebook and other social media platforms and through freelance artists' open letters to presenters. Multiple individuals collaborated on this document, which includes testimonials from artists, perspectives from programmers, and alternative contract-related strategies for the future of the dance presenting world.

This document as a whole is 'an attempt to start transparent conversations in order to form principles and guidelines for how to act in this environment, and how to ethically share risk' (Castro et al. 2020: 22).

The situation that this document is critiquing is this: COVID-19 restrictions and the decisions of a large number of presenters led to mass cancellations of arts events, causing artsworkers to lose all their work seemingly overnight (Castro et al. 2020: 21). While some presenting organizations honoured their agreements and paid artists their wages, many presenters cancelled or postponed their events without any payment to their artists and did so in an insensitive, unconcerned manner. One of the testimonials reads: '*cancelled* [...] nope, that's not all i need you to say to me [...] in a text or email message [...] what all has been cancelled? that's not how this works. that's not how it *should* work' (Castro et al. 2020: 42, emphasis in original). These organizations relied primarily on 'force majeure' clauses in their contracts, which frees both parties from liability in the event of extraordinary circumstances beyond the control of both parties. In this case, the extraordinary event was the COVID-19 pandemic and its related government mandated shutdowns and restrictions (2020: 149).

The foundational idea that much of the document relies upon is that the performance ecology heavily relies on freelance artworkers' labour. Freelance artists often have a precarious income and little to no safeguards such as savings or other sources of income. The hierarchy of power that exists – with the presenter as the gatekeeper who chooses what artists to commission and engage with – mirrors the reality of resource access and financial security. While a presenter likely holds a salaried, full-time, stable job, an artist's wages are often inconsistent and constantly threatened by problems like physical injury, low funding and cancelled contracts (2020: 145–46). (Though it should be noted that there are exceptions for choreographers supported by college and university dance programmes, such as Rashaun Mitchell, who is currently on faculty at New York University and is the Associate Chair of the dance programme at Tisch School of the Arts.)

Also, the large institutions in charge of presenting dance often have access to extensive knowledge and infrastructure through which they create contracts and letters of agreement, an advantage not available to freelance workers (2020: 111). Overall, presenting organizations and individual presenters do not evenly share the risks associated with presenting dance with freelance dancers, who cannot access the same knowledge or financial security. For instance, often artists do not know how to read and assess contracts. When contracts change, or artists are not paid what the contract stated, they are afraid to speak out or do not know what recourse they have; nor do they the financial means to hire a lawyer. In the situation COVID-19 created, when presenting organizations abruptly and sometimes inconsiderately cancelled events, they forced dancers and other artsworkers to take on an unequal share of the financial burdens associated with losing out on presentation opportunities. Artist manager Laura Colby has claimed, 'it is always the artist who suffers the most financially' (2020: 146).

A lack of transparency stems from this power imbalance and unequal risk sharing: artists are at the mercy of those presenting them. Even when relationships between presenters and artists are good, artists often find themselves in a position where they must navigate a lack of information about an organization's internal workings while also negotiating for treatment and payment that they believe they are entitled to. For example, a longstanding complaint regarding presenters is that they do not return emails or phone calls (2020: 64). While it may be true that presenters are inundated with messages from artists asking to be presented, and may have massive job responsibilities (working for instance simultaneously as general managers and artistic directors), the fact that presenters seem to ignore artists – which comes off as a power move – strikes some as ironic, given that presenters would have no job if it weren't for artists (2020: 65). Also, artists do not have complete access to information that directly impacts the livelihood of workers – from how presenters make decisions to how grants are allocated – which makes negotiating wages and other conditions or expectations difficult. COVID-19 exacerbated the presenting world's opaqueness; working with artists in a productive way became increasingly difficult when programmers were faced with the possibility of lost funding and furloughs and layoffs (2020: 102–06). Although the uncertainties of the future generally make planning difficult, the lack of transparency concerning the presenting organization's processes prevents dance artists from making informed decisions regarding their future contracts and relationships with presenters.

The authors also argue that the presenting ecology suffers from a lack of accountability on the part of the presenter. Despite the fact that large organizations are more secure than smaller organizations – they enjoy general stability, can rely on earned income, and are able to quickly allocate new resources – they have shown themselves to be much less willing to make impactful change than current issues dictate (2020: 107). Most notably, some of the wealthiest museums in the United States have been cutting staff and laying off entire education departments because of the pandemic, and larger performance organizations have not been paying the fees for their cancelled engagements (2020: 122). This contrasts with the smaller organizations that tend to be the most vulnerable to drastic economic changes but have done an overall better job in listening, learning and responding to artists (2020: 102–06). In general, the authors argue that institutions resist critique and change and that artists who speak out against injustices fear negative implications for their careers (2020: 106). This has most notably resulted in artists' overall reluctance to challenge inequalities within these presenting institutions. Regarding the COVID-19 situation in particular, the burden of transitioning away from in-person performances fell almost solely upon artists, both financially and creatively. The function of presenting organizations is to present artists, but cancellation – the 'status quo' response – left artists feeling somewhat abandoned by their presenters in the new landscape of a pandemic. Dance artists struggled to figure out how to accommodate re-bookings into their already planned lives, while also adapting to possible virtual presentations and screendance creations (2020: 87–89). The contributors observe that organizations profit off of the work of artists and owe it to artists to be a source of support when needed.

The authors of 'Creating new futures: Phase 1' also express frustration over feeling like there is a tokenization of artists of colour, queer artists and artists of other marginalized identities who receive funding and employment within presenting institutions (2020: 111; for more on this issue see DeFrantz and McGregor 2015; Gan and Oke 2020). This claim does not weigh-in the clear ongoing pattern of extensive support and privileging of such artists in the US contemporary dance field as outlined earlier in this chapter. However, it is important to acknowledge the lived experience of these artists and the complex ways in which their concerns intersect with the presenting institutions and broader audience values with which they engage. Even though, for instance, Guttierez has been one of the most programmed dance artists for the last two decades, he is also one of the most vocal in discussing his discontent. In a widely viewed 21 March 2020 Instagram Post he wrote:

> Real talk. All my remaining spring gigs and one summer gig are cancelled (postponed). More pending. I'm not alone. In NONE of the cancellation emails does anyone mention a partial payment of the fee or acknowledge the commitment and the economic implication of losing the income.
>
> (quoted in Castro et al. 2020: 22)

What is clear from such a statement is that the presenting world in its entirety can and should do a better job in treating dance artists equitably and humanely. As Sam Miller observed, 'what artists do is difficult, they put themselves out there […] you need to create a community that supports them by creating environments that meet their needs' (2012: n.pag.). What will be emphasized now, is that freelance artists aren't the only ones who need to be more closely attended to – administrators, including presenters (who may very well also be practicing artists), are also suffering.

Establishing stronger guidelines for equity through collaboration and care

There is no such thing as a one-person show.
(APAP Equitable Partnership Working Group 2020)

Economic instability and financial precarity are not new to the presenting world. Attempts to address these factors through shifts in thinking and practice with regard to ethical considerations are ongoing. The 2008 economic collapse caused the United States presenting sector to rethink its 'business model' in favour of an 'ecological model' concerned with sustainment and resiliency. Around that time, Kenneth Foster made a call in a position paper titled 'Thriving in an uncertain world: Arts presenting change and the new realities' for a 'an entirely new approach to the way that we function' that would clearly connect sustainability, survival, and ethics (2010: 4). Foster was inspired by Robyn Archer, a prominent festival director, who at APAP in January 2009 laid out her vision of 'resiliency thinking' (influenced in turn by a book of the same name by fellow Australian Brian Walker, an internationally renowned scientist working on ecological sustainability). In his paper, Foster argued that, 'Sustaining the environment is about sustaining life, just as sustaining cultural and cultural production is also about sustaining life' (2010: 13). For Foster, the nature of this sustenance is relational and experiential, and lies in a shared goal among presenters to provide 'joy [...] to the community within an ethical and humanistic context' (2010: 18).

The COVID pandemic and the #MeToo and Black Lives Matter movements have further inspired the writing of ethical guidelines and protocols for the presenting world. APAP's 'Building ethical and equitable partnerships in the performing arts', along with 'Creating new futures: Phase 1', Dance/USA's 'Equitable contracting for dance touring: A new resource on supporting equitable partnerships' and other resources all offer recommendations for improving how the presenting field operates. In what follows, I will present several of these recommendations as a way to outline the kinds of ethical considerations that dance presenters are addressing. I will show a strong correlation with relational and care ethics, which emphasizes collaboration and working together in order to find solutions that help everyone to thrive. As, 'Building ethical and equitable partnerships in the performing arts', observes, '*This is a commitment to cultivating a new culture* where artist, agent, presenter, and producer partnerships evolve as long-term relationships as opposed to strictly transactional ones. This new culture requires a different approach to contracting, and of finding ways to balance legal frameworks and requirements with partnerships and human considerations' (2020: 3, original emphasis).

Many of the ethical influences I referenced in earlier chapters are relevant for the presenting realm. Relational ethics and care ethics, in particular, are germane to the integrated and networked nature of the presenting field. Relational ethics focuses on how we should live together. It recognizes relational interdependency, and the need to cultivate skills of attention, response, respect and adaptation. Care ethics in particular directs attention to cultivating just and caring relationships that benefit all those involved, but especially the 'cared for' who are in a less powerful, more vulnerable position. Such thinking can be seen in the appeals in 'Building Ethical and Equitable Partnerships in the Performing Arts', which observes:

> When considering how to move forward as colleagues, it is vital that we move forward with information and mutual understanding in true partnership with compassion, care and empathy.
>
> We must listen and *hear* each other. We must remember how to communicate with one another. And we must value having a conversation before making a decision.
>
> (2020: 3, emphasis in original)

Actually, these words echo those of Sam Miller in my interview with him, when he emphasized the importance of how people treat people – respect for difference, tolerance and recognizing that 'we're all in it together' (2012: n.pag.).

In addition, in his article 'Commensurate with experience' (2021), Benjamin Kimitch points out that 'artists and the administrators they encounter at institutions have more in common than either cares to admit' (2021: n.pag.). Not only are the vast majority of administrators also artists, but they too experience their own share of heartache, whether it be exhaustion from overwork, poor pay, insufficient support in the face of adverse reactions by the public or ill-treatment by established artists. As he states, 'It is a curious arrangement where the artists who work within the institution largely suffer at the hands of featured artists or those at the top' (2021: n.pag.). Kimitch challenges the continued discourse separating artist, audience and institution, instead recognizing that 'it is essentially the same people engaging across these identities' (2021: n.pag.). He also observes that when a cohort of artists was put in control at Performance Space New York in fall 2019, where he was working at the time, the work environment worsened rather than improved. He notes: 'Certain members of the cohort spoke of undoing hierarchies, but in practice indictments were handed down that reaffirmed the division between the artists' agenda and what they believed the workers in the institution represented' (2021: n.pag.). And even more troubling: 'The cohort's artist-identities protected them from accountability and existing norms of workplace conduct and respect' (2021: n.pag.). There was little real consideration for the well-being of others, and in 'their effort to reimagine institutional power, the cohort created a new, more elusive, repressive hierarchy' (2021: n.pag.). In order to address this kind of unequal and inhumane situation, he calls for a greater consideration of staff well-being, and: 'To acknowledge what we share. To care for each other' (2021: n.pag.).

Along with this emphasis on paying more attention to *care* in the presenting world, a desire for clear guiding principles and more standardized decision-making procedures and contracts demonstrates the impact of deontological ethical traditions. Rather than leaving situations unclear, and allowing organizations to function in ad hoc or closeted ways, these documents' recommendations mirror, in many ways, the ethical guidelines in place for institutional research involving human subjects (see Chapter 4) that stress accountability and clear parameters in terms of respect for persons, beneficence and justice. In working to make transactional interactions more ethical, in other words, presenters are being asked to assume greater responsibility for making their processes more accessible, transparent, complete and fair and to develop systems that hold themselves accountable.

Indeed, the overall consensus is that all parties involved in the presentation ecology – artists, presenters and funders – should prioritize transparency. Internal policies, processes and efforts should be made clearer and more accessible so that all those affected may make more informed decisions about their commitments. Along with this, contracts should communicate the varied commitments, agreements and expectations between the artist and presenter – signed and in advance – to be honoured in good faith. In practice, those taking on the role of the funder should commit to compensating or fulfilling payment to artists and presenters in the highest possible capacity and artists should commit to compensating any employees or associates in the highest possible capacity as well, even in cases of forced cancellation or force majeure. While acting with integrity, openness and honesty is a continuous choice for everyone involved, a quality contract sets the stage for every subsequent decision in the presenting process.

In fact, most of the solutions proposed by the various documents' writers and compilers target future strategies to implement in contract negotiations to ensure contracts cover the entire process and all the labour and additional concerns involved in being presented. For instance, the Dance/USA joint working group recommends revising 'Performance' Agreements to 'Engagement' Agreements, to include 'the period of preparation, communication and activity between the Artist, AMPP and Presenter, which includes but is not limited to contracting, advancing technical and residency activity details and ultimately completing a final performance' (Dance/USA 2021: 3). This is because the majority of traditional industry agreements fail to 'recognize the ongoing labor and financial investments from the Artist and AMPP that is necessary' (2021: 3) to realize a performance.

Similarly, 'Creating new futures: Phase 1' recommends that one way to help protect freelance artists' livelihoods is through a two-part contract: one contract covers the creation period and one contract covers the performance period. Both contracts should include set fees that are paid at scheduled times during the engagement. This ensures that an artist is paid for their work prior to the engagement event, even if that engagement is cancelled or postponed (2021: 159). A similar proposed strategy, which could be used in addition to a two-part contract is to include a 'timed' force majeure clause. This would specify how much payment an artist receives based on the timing of a force majeure incident. For example, if a leaky roof causes a theatre to become unusable the night before a performance, an artist can still be compensated for their work and any expenses incurred in preparation for the event due to the expectations outlined in their contract. With each segment of time that passes, a presenting company incurs expenses that should be paid out to the artist (2021: 160). To continue along the line of cancellation, any clause or phrase that is similar to a 'cancel at will' clause, which gives a party the power to cancel a contract for any reason, is highly discouraged because of the power imbalance such clauses introduce. Both presenters and artists should be creative and cooperate when thinking of ways to prevent or minimize future work stoppage, cancellation or postponement and implement strategies into expectations that are written out in contracts (2021: 118).

Indeed, post-COVID-19 it would be valuable for contracts to make room for the possibility of engagements in a digital space in lieu of, alongside, or integrated with traditional in-person arts presentation. Contracts should also address any compensation for the labour associated with creating virtual-based art, since creating, presenting and publicizing art digitally require distinct forms of labour and commitment. In addition, special riders might be considered for events that include and prioritize community engagement or other kinds of issues not directly related to the 'performance'. As I outlined in the chapter on the creative process, some artists are strongly committed to socially engaged work and/or political activism. Where appropriate, and in discussion with presenters, a rider can be a place to articulate expectations. These may ultimately not be acceptable to either party, but discussion about the rider would provide an opportunity, early in the process, to share perspectives so as to avoid potential problems and unmet expectations down the road. For instance, if an artist believes the presenting organization should participate in specific green, eco-friendly initiatives as part of their time in residence, the details could be worked out in advance on what this might look like, from printing programmes on recycled paper, to collecting them after the performance for reuse, or handling everything digitally.

Democratizing presenting

This chapter has outlined that one of the greatest challenges facing the realm of dance presenting is how to make the playing field fairer and create room for more dance artists: more diverse dance artists representing different stylistic heritages and different interests, with different profiles and from different regions of not only the United States but also globally. The challenges are great, given the constant economic constraints and reliance on a money economy along with an overall lack of broad appeal of live concert dance, especially dance that may push the boundaries of what people expect dance to be. This is not to mention the continued 'star system'/'winner takes all' approach, valorization of 'newness', allure of the New York dance scene, investment in tightly curated performances and overall insular nature of the elite contemporary dance world. Nonetheless, many presenters have been striving to find ways to address these concerns, and COVID-19 has provided new opportunities for exploring digital platforms and non-traditional venues. I describe several of these here, as examples of experiments in opening the gates to more dance artists.

One method is to delegate and expand the gate keeping role so that more people take up the mantle, hopefully broadening the profile of artists who are presented. This often happens through hiring guest curators to oversee select events. For instance, since 2009–10, Danspace Project has run a Platforms series, which are multi-week series of performances and events organized by guest curators. The Platforms were conceived as 'exhibitions that unfold over time' and act as 'inquiries into artistic, choreographic and curatorial concerns'.[17] The tilt towards the visual art world, organizing themes such as 'Judson Now' (the topic of the 2012 series) and range of guest curators, including Lemon (2010), Harrell (2011), Rawls (2016) and Okpokwasili (2020), all indicate a continued investment in the dominant aesthetic. At the same time, Platforms provides an opportunity for artists to assume more control over how their work, and that of those they admire, is seen. Judy Hussie-Taylor, the longtime Executive Director and Chief Curator of Danspace Project observes, 'From the first Platform in 2010 curated by Ralph Lemon, through the present Platform curated by Ishmael Houston-Jones and Will Rawls, artists, curators and writers have activated intergenerational networks to contribute to our reimagining of how we contextualize and present time-based art today.'[18]

Meanwhile, large institutions may hire guest curators to oversee special programmes. For instance, the Walker hires guests to curate their annual 'Choreographers' Evening' that celebrates Minnesota's dance and performance communities. This event began in 1972 as a showcase of work by independent choreographers; each evening features about ten works, lasting around three to six minutes in length. Guest curators have included a diverse range of dance artists such as Pramila Vasudevan (2018), Megan Mayer (2017), Rosy Simas (2016), Justin Jones (2015), Kenna-Camara Cottman (2014), Chris Schlichting (2011), Aparna Ramaswamy and Patrick Scully (2008), Emily Johnson (2007), and Sandra Agustin (2006) and others. In 2020, a call went out for a 'Choreographers' Evening Special Edition' titled 'Body prayers' to be presented virtually and in-person 4–5 June 2021. Guest curator and African-centred Healing Artist DejaJolle sought

'BIPOC Minnesota dancemakers working in all forms' for pop-up performances and six selected choreographic works to be filmed and presented virtually.[19] All these cases have indicated an effort to increase visibility and diversify offerings; at the same time an audition process and curatorial oversight remain in place limiting who is presented and who remains marginalized according to the guest curator's aesthetic and ideological preferences.

Another strategy is to expand opportunities by offering more accessible opportunities to present, develop and discuss new work, and more varied venues for performances. During her tenure as Artistic Executive Director at Velocity, between 2011 and 2018, Tonya Lockyer did just this for Seattle's centre dedicated to contemporary dance. Under her leadership open-mic performance nights titled 'Sh*t Gold' occurred, for artists experimenting in any genre. People who wanted to show something signed up the day of the event, and could bring food to share. Through Velocity's 'Speakeasy Series', community-led events also took place, including show and tells, performance lectures, conversations and panel discussions. They were free or by suggested donation and open to the public; and people were invited to propose their own project. Lockyer also developed the *Made in Seattle* incubator to work one-on-one with artists to help them realize their artistic and organizational goals, successfully bringing national visibility, funding and touring to many Seattle choreographers. She also produced performances around the city, including at St Mark's Cathedral, the Waterfront, the old Greyhound Station, the Moore Theater and Seattle Art Fair.

Indeed, Lockyer has been very committed to facilitating programmes that are community co-created or co-curated. In this sense, she arguably realized the recommendations of Archer, who encouraged performing arts leaders to be aware of the interdependent context in which they operate, entailing close cultural participation and interactive experiences. In his 2010 paper mentioned earlier in this chapter, he wrote, 'The organizations that survive will unquestionably be the ones that recognize these changes and are willing to reinvent their organizations for a new world and its new audiences' (2010: 9). In my interview with Lockyer in 2015, she spoke of Velocity as 'a grass roots organization that is really listening to all the stakeholders and is a place that is dynamic with many communities'. She also observed that she does not think about Velocity as a physical space or centre. She is interested in systems, and how the internet is changing the way we think about systems, and vice versa, and notes, 'I really think of Velocity as a dynamic system that has many portals and networks and it's the people who activate it, and it's not just that building, and it lives way outside the architecture of that space, including into the virtual world' (Lockyer 2015: n.pag.).

Recognition of the vitality of the internet and digital platforms as an important dimension and addition to regular 'live' performing, has never been as visible as during the COVID pandemic. During 2020–21, an increasing number of opportunities have become available for dance artists to present their work online, either in pre-recorded or 'live' form, or some combination of the two. One young dance maker based in Los Angeles, Jacob Jonas, who was already actively involved in screen dance, was quick to pivot in this direction, showing just how effective the online forum can be to bring attention to little known dance artists making outstanding work. In 2021 Jonas' The Company produced Films.Dance in partnership with *Somewhere Magazine*, and engaged 150 artists from twenty-five countries culminating in fifteen short dance films. It was co-presented by the Younes and Soraya Nazarian Center for the Performing Arts, Joan W. and Irving B. Harris Theater for Music and Dance, and Wallis Annenberg Center for the Performing Arts. Beginning 25 January 2021, and every Monday for 15 weeks, one film was premiered for free on the web at Films.Dance, on Instagram on the @films.dance account, and the Films.Dance Facebook page. The work was filmed in locations such as Brazil, Canada, China, Germany, Nigeria and Spain, and featured a diverse group of artists from a range of backgrounds, dance genres and abilities.

There are also artist-run initiatives and collectives that seek to transform the presenting landscape by finding new locations to show work, engage different processes and explore different methods of payment. The organization homeLa, for example, is a platform for experimental dance that calls itself a 'nomadic performance project' because it presents work in different homes around Southern California. Since 2013, it has presented works by more than 120 interdisciplinary artists in twenty homes. Artist collectives such as AUNTS and SALTA, meanwhile, apply non-hierarchical, collaborative strategies to curation and exist at least in part in a barter economy. The New York-based AUNTS was founded in 2005 and produces work in a variety of spaces including rooftops and boats, providing space, time, food and artist stipend for each event. In an interview in 2012 in *Time Out*, one of the organizers at the time, Laurie Berg, reflected, 'I think that one of the most important things is that it's always a place for the community [...] and not about our overarching ideas. To me, that becomes choreography, as opposed to an open-forum event and structure' (quoted in Kourlas 2012: n.pag.). Inspired by groups like AUNTS, the Oakland-based dance collective SALTA (a Latin word meaning 'to leap' or 'to jump') came together in 2012 and until 2016 curated a free monthly performance series taking place at different venues in collaboration with various spaces, communities and performances. They experimented with a range of curatorial approaches including 'chain curation' (where they invite an artist who invites another artist, who invites, another, etc.), guest curators, events based on themes and co-curated events with other groups. The performances occurred in donated spaces such as store-fronts, warehouses, galleries, cafes and yoga studios. Admission to the shows was a non-monetary donation to a free bar and boutique, where everyone could eat, drink and shop for free so that no money was exchanged.

Similar kinds of attempts are happening internationally. In Canada, for instance, the not-for-profit Toronto Dance Community Love-In (TO Love-In) has especially taken the concept of care ethics to heart. Established in 2009, it 'welcomes all bodies with an artistic and physical practice to join us in creating a space of inclusivity, generosity, respect and LOVE'.[20] Along with workshops, 'The Lovers' (as the organizers are known) launched an annual performance series *PS: We Are All Here*, in 2013, that presented local and international artists. As an example, in 2017 it was curated by Robyn Breen, Tina Fushell and Kate Nankervis and featured over a dozen artists sharing experimental contemporary dance. The series was billed as, 'making space for artists and their chaotic, immersive, messy, pleasurable, lo-fi, inquisitive' work.[21] The organization is interested in supporting 'democratic pedagogy' and 'anti-competition' and strives to remove barriers to accessing events by providing people with alternatives to paying for performances.

These are just a handful of examples that demonstrate movements to open the gates to more dance artists from varied backgrounds. Certainly, there are fringe festivals throughout the world that are extremely open, volunteer run and grass roots. Other options include having slots available on a series that are decided by lottery, or allowing audiences/communities more input on possible events by providing opportunities for online feedback in advance of decision making. The latter, in particular, honours the role of the audience, which may not always be fully considered. As Sheehy notes, 'One of the key reasons I believe people have stopped listening to some gatekeepers is because, on occasion, we have kept the audience out of the equation, underestimating them, and sometimes insulting their intelligence' (2009: n.pag.). He observes:

> Some artistic directors, curators and producers actually assert that audiences don't matter. That whether people attend our presentations or not is immaterial. 'A discussion of audiences attending arts events is infantile' one colleague has said. This, to me, is patronizing in the extreme, repugnantly elitist and alienating.
>
> (2009: n.pag.)

In contrast, Sheehy calls for including the audience in the conversation around the arts. More and more presenters are finding ways to do this, and to connect with diverse communities within a complex, interconnected network of relations that challenge a more vertical, top-down paradigm. Richard Evans, in his 2010 article 'Entering upon novelty: Policy and funding issues for a new era in the arts' offers a detailed outline of organizations 'structured for sustainability'

(2010: n.pag.). A few of his recommendations include: 'A mission that focuses on community impacts and value; Acknowledging and embracing the creative capacities in the community; Loose organizational boundaries, porous to the community, that blur distinctions between organizations and emphasize commonalities; Engagement of audiences as active participants in process as well as product' (2010: n.pag.).

Conclusion

To work nights and weekends. Many. To not be allowed a bad day.

To deal with everyone's bad days.

(Conquet 2020: n.pag.)

As should be evident from this discussion, the complexity of dance presenters' jobs, and the multiple stakeholders and interests they must balance, make an education in moral reasoning especially valuable. Ethical conflicts are unavoidable and ongoing within such a dynamic environment and can best be approached by having received training in ethics and techniques such as Nonviolent Communication, as discussed in earlier chapters, to understand the underlying needs requiring attention, as well as relational ethics and deontological ethics. For presenters, it is important to understand and have a sense of one's own values and priorities, as well as the ethical guiding principles and codes co-created by one's institution or group – a topic that will be covered in depth in the next and final chapter of this book, and is important for assuring that constructive institution-wide change can take place. Consider and plan for possible conflicts when first conceiving a performance series or event, and strive to clearly define the ethical dilemma(s) if/when it is faced. When a problem arises, gather information rather than reacting reflexively; consult those involved, and individually and/or collectively rank conflicting ethical issues. Creatively and thoughtfully seek an option that satisfies all parties if possible. Once a decision has been reached communicate the reasoning behind it to those affected and possibly beyond. Reflect and make changes in your planning for the future. The job is endless, and exhausting, and rewarding, as the Melbourne-based independent curator, consultant and art leader Angela Conquet so poignantly captures in her poetic 'And then, do you remember, and now … Farewell to an arts organ/isation' (2020: n.pag.), when she writes, 'To give up. Whenever no longer possible. But not too often. Not possible.'

Perhaps more than in any other case in the book, the positive traits associated with being a more humane presenter relate to improvisation and collaboration, and the ability to move adeptly, sensitively and generously with others towards a particular desired mission. It means being open, patient, listening closely and asking questions. And it entails approaching others with a caring and inquisitive stance. Echoing the earlier words of Dina Davida, Tonya Lockyer observes, 'To curate really means to care for, to *care-for*, this person's process' (Hytone 2015, original emphasis). And she elaborates in relation to commissioning new work, 'I don't think of it as a piece [...] It's a project. It's a collaboration, and [...] that's a much more non-linear way of working [...] When I'm working with artists I really feel like I'm investing in another human being over time and I have questions that I'm also curious about.'

This idea of investing in others as human beings, whether colleagues, audience members, funders or artists, has certainly been the focus of much recent efforts by those like Davida, Lockyer and many others internationally committed to furthering the professional field of dance presenting. This is evident from the proliferation of books, journals and classes on live arts curation that increasingly stresses this dimension of the field (see Davida et al. 2019; Malzacher et al. 2010). In the inaugural issue of the journal TURBA, which will be a journal published through Berghahn for global practices in live arts curation, the mission statement stresses, 'Within the live arts, the term "curation" is used in a manner that is largely, but not entirely, analogous to its use in the visual arts. The Latin root of the word "curation" is *curare*, meaning "to take care of" or "to heal"' (Mission Statement 2022: 2). This attitude will be particularly important as the presenting world recovers from the pandemic closures. As the 'Statement of values and code of ethics of the Association of Performing Arts Presenters' recognizes:

> Organizations are, at base, people, and it is up to the people working in the performing arts field – board members, executive leaders, staff, and artists – to demonstrate their ongoing commitment to the core values of integrity, honesty, fairness, openness, respect, and responsibility.
>
> (APAP n.d.: n.pag.)

NOTES

1. Some of the material in this chapter is drawn from two previously published articles: Naomi Melanie Jackson (2014), 'Ecology, dance presenting, and social justice', in Guy Cools and Pascal Gielen (eds), *The Ethics of Art: Ecological Turns in the Performing Arts*, Amsterdam: Valiz, pp. 197–226; and Naomi M. Jackson (2019), 'Curatorial discourse and equity: Tensions in contemporary dance presenting in the United States', in Dena Davida, Marc Pronovost, Véronique Hudon and Jane Gabriels (eds), *Curating Live Arts: Critical*

Perspectives, Essays, and Conversations on Theory and Practice, New York: Berghahn Books, pp. 101–13.

2. For instance, there are some who might see the vocation of a curator completely distinct from a programmer, based on their particular experience and outlook. While the different terms do have different histories and associations, as will become clearer throughout the chapter, the overall concern here relates to the realm of presenting dance as a whole, and the ethical issues raised regardless of the specific moniker associated with a person's job.

3. Note that Performance Space New York, the Kitchen, NYLA, The Shed, Danspace Project, etc. do not usually explicitly participate in APAP. Rather, they present work at that time, sometimes showcases, that are available for APAP attendees to see. This trend of 'satellite' festivals and venues started with Under the Radar (a theatre festival) in 2004 and has grown exponentially. American Realness was a satellite festival catering to a very niche market of 'contemporary' dance curator/programmers from the United States and internationally.

4. See APAP-NYC – Association of Performing Arts Professionals – 2022. Events in America, https://eventsinamerica.com/events/apap-nyc-association-of-performing-arts-profession-als-4/business/other-miscellaneous/fwyzyovmptcsnecq. Accessed 27 June 2021.

5. It was while Sam Miller was the director of NEFA between 1995 and 2005, that he founded the National Dance Project (NDP), the Contemporary Art Centers (CAC) and Centers for Creative Research (CCR) initiatives. He also came up with the idea for FACE (French American Cultural Exchange) in 2004 and later established the Institute for Curatorial Practice in Performance (ICPP) at Wesleyan University in 2011.

6. The institutions that were part of the CAC included: Asia Society (New York, NY), Contemporary Arts Center (New Orleans, LA), DiverseWorks (Houston, TX), MASS MoCA (North Adams, MA), Museum of Contemporary Art (Chicago, IL), Portland Institute for Contemporary Art (PICA) (Portland OR), REDCAT (Los Angeles, CA), Walker Art Center (Minneapolis, MN), Wexner Center for the Arts (Columbus, OH) and Yerba Buena Center for the Arts (San Francisco, CA).

7. See https://newyorklivearts.org/event/antigone-sr-twenty-looks-or-paris-is-burning-at-the-judson-church-l/. Accessed 27 June 2021.

8. The research also indicated that the top individual funding recipients during the period 2014–20 from these organizations were the following: Okwui Okpokwasili, jumatatu m. poe, Emily Johnson, Michelle Ellsworth and Rosy Simas.

9. In the May 2009 statistics 'choreographers' are tracked according to numerous categories, including: Elementary and Secondary Schools (50), Junior Colleges (60), Colleges, Universities, and Professional Schools (80), Other Schools and Instruction (12490), Performing Arts Companies (1170), Spectator Sports (40), Promoters of Performing Arts, Sports, and Similar Events (40), Independent Artists, Writers, and Performers (180), Amusement Parks and Arcades (40). This data is listed on the downloadable excel sheet titled nat4d_dl.xls for May 2009 under the tab 'National industry-specific and by ownership': https://www.bls.gov/oes/tables.htm. Accessed 29 June 2021.

10. See http://aimbykyleabraham.org. Accessed 27 June 2021.
11. This tendency is reinforced by those dance artists who were heavily influenced by the Judson Dance Theatre and are now in positions of authority at institutions including magazines, universities and art centres, where they promote the work of this period.
12. See https://www.icaboston.org/about/mission. Accessed 27 June 2021.
13. See https://www.icaboston.org/events/nora-chipaumire-punk-100-pop-nga. Accessed 27 June 2021.
14. See https://www.icaboston.org/events/nora-chipaumire-punk-100-pop-nga. Accessed 27 June 2021.
15. See https://www.icaboston.org/articles/icaboston-announces-schedule-performances-2019–2020. Accessed 27 June 2021.
16. It should be noted once again that responses to COVID-19 vary greatly according to country. In Canada, for instance, the Canada Council for the Arts and many provincial arts councils provided funding to cover artists' fees, and as soon as possible most Canadian theatres invited artists back into their spaces for residencies long before live performances were possible.
17. See https://danspaceproject.org/programs/. Accessed 27 June 2021.
18. See https://danspaceproject.org/2016/11/17/introduction/. Accessed 27 June 2021.
19. See https://walkerart.org/calendar/2020/open-call-for-body-prayers-choreographers-evening-special-edition. Accessed 30 June 2021.
20. See https://www.universe.com/users/toronto-dance-community-love-in-YXZWJM. Accessed 27 June 2021.
21. See https://www.universe.com/events/ps-we-are-all-here-2017-tickets-71GXRP. Accessed 27 June 2021.

7

'Care'-fully Negotiating Change: Moving Towards a More Humane Dance Culture

Deep, transformative change occurs when there is trust and respectful connection with others.

(Greg Latemore 2016: 114)

Live dance is fundamentally about movement – what Anna Halprin called 'breath made visible' (Groover 2010: n.pag.). And movement is about change, namely the shifting of the body, even if it is the cells dancing in apparent stillness. Yet the dance field, so full of skilled movers sensitive to every nuance of their muscles and tendons, sometimes remains a prisoner to rigid structures and ways of thinking and behaving that impede adapting and moving towards a more humane dance culture. In this final chapter, I consider the problems that arise in major paradigm shifts and large-scale institutional changes in the dance field. What can these problems tell us about how to address both internal and external impulses for change? How might the field of ethics shed light on how to preserve empathy and continue to treat people with dignity through times of transformation, especially when they are extremely stressful? The chapter draws inspiration from studies in ethical change management and leadership more generally and long-terms collaborative projects, such as Teija Löytönen's multi-year Dance Mosaic project in Finland, Becky Dyer's Arizona Dance Educator's Action Research Project and my own work with the American Ballet Theatre Jacqueline Kennedy Onassis School (JKO School). I will urge adopting a model of transforming servant leadership, sensitive facilitation and ethics institutionalization that includes ethics training and co-created principles and/or codes of ethics. Throughout, I invoke virtue ethics, an embodied ethics of care and deontological ethics to stress the importance of values and procedural fairness in addressing change in a humane manner.

Toxic transitions

The concert dance field is famous for its cyclical nature of breathless adulation of one generation followed by the harsh repudiation by another. One set of dance artists develops its own preferred aesthetic with an accompanying ideology about what certain movements and behaviours signify, which a particular community experiences as deeply meaningful. Then comes a time when a new generation or group no longer resonates with this crystallization of forms and values. The resulting clash usually has horrible and damaging results for at least some involved. Differences become not alternative perspectives on dancing but rigid claims regarding 'good' and 'bad' human beings and debates over the soul of the dance and art field as a whole. This takes place in both the professional dance realm and the educational context, and can lead to a great deal of unnecessary misery for those involved.

One famous example is of a transition from classical to modern ballet, as embodied by the premiere of Vaslav Nijinsky's *L'Apres-Midi d'un Faune* (1912) in Paris, with Nijinsky in the role of the Faun. This work signified a visible change from the norms of classical ballet as developed during the nineteenth century. In place of the graceful ballet vocabulary were stiff-armed, angular, two-dimensional poses and jerky heel-toe walking back and forth along the stage (in contrast to the graceful toe-heel convention found in traditional ballet). At the end of the twelve-minute ballet, the faun character lies down on a scarf on the top of a hill-like structure, contracts his pelvic area and opens his mouth. The piece is very slow moving with a lot of held positions and offered a stark aesthetic contrast to previous dances the audience would have experienced. The response was extreme and swift. Detractors and admirers focused not only on form but immediately on the work's moral value and significance for the art world as a whole.

Among the detractors, for instance, was the critic Gaston Calmette, the owner and editor of *Le Figaro*, an important French newspaper. He published a scathing attack on what he viewed as an immoral work. He wrote:

> Anyone who mentions the words 'art' and 'imagination' in the same breath as this production must be laughing at us. This is neither a pretty pastoral nor a work of profound meaning. We are shown a lecherous faun, whose movements are filthy and bestial in their eroticism, and whose gestures are as crude as they are indecent. That is all [...] Decent people will never accept such animal realism.
>
> (quoted in Buckle 1971: 242)

Calmette even went so far as to remark that the work was 'doomed to oblivion', demonstrating the extent to which he was not only drawing a connection between the aesthetic dimensions of the work, but the moral, and that having decided that the work was truly 'evil' it should have no place in the annals of dance or art history.

Advocates were equally extreme in making connections between art, morality and the piece's broader significance. The sculptor August Rodin, who supposedly stood up in his box to shout 'Bravo, Bravo!' in contrast to the simultaneous booing and hissing, saw the work as natural, beautiful and good. In a letter, that was published a day later in *Le Figaro* in defence of the work, he claimed:

> Nijinsky has never been so remarkable as in his latest role. No more jumps – nothing but half-conscious animal gestures and poses. He lies down, leans on his elbow, walks with bent knees, draws himself up, advancing and retreating, sometimes slowly, sometimes with jerky angular movements [...] His beauty is that of antique frescoes and sculpture [...] I wish that such a noble endeavour should be understood as a whole.
>
> (quoted in Buckle 1971: 243–44)

To Rodin, the minimal, more angular and pedestrian movement read as more realistic and appropriate for a faun who is half human and half beast; it also connected to the much-admired era of classical Greek art, seen as a timeless source of beauty in Western culture. Ultimately, in direct contrast with Calmette, Rodin felt the work deserved repeated performing, as a 'noble' endeavour worthy of the art world's admiration. He hoped that 'the Théâtre du Châtelet would arrange others [performances] to which all our artists might come for inspiration to communicate in beauty' (Buckle 1971: 244).

Another celebrated example of clashing aesthetics and changing values can be found in the premiere of works by Paul Taylor in a 1957 concert at the 92nd Street YM-YWHA in New York. This evening signified a moment when modernist and what would later be categorized as postmodernist approaches came into direct contact. During the evening titled 'Seven New Dances', Taylor presented pieces that included standing, sitting, kneeling and pedestrian style walking. 'The material in all of them was static postures', Taylor later recalled. 'Not poses, just natural postures like standing and shifting weight from one leg to another, slumping a shoulder, and so forth. There were other categories of posture we used – sitting, squatting, shiftings of the head, things like that' (Kriegsman 1982: n.p.). In response, Louis Horst published his now famous 'blank review' in the *Dance Observer*, consisting of the title of the concert, a blank space and his initials. The implication, of course, was that the evening was simply not worth reviewing: this was not dance and had no value whatsoever.

While an alternative assessment of this concert is not readily available, Jill Johnston's advocacy for the new postmodernist work clearly outlines the alternative, enthusiastic perspective. Johnston was the dance critic for the *Village Voice* starting in 1959. Her opinions are clearly laid out in her collection *Marmalade Me.*

She unapologetically panned the era of emotion-driven modern dance represented by Martha Graham, Doris Humphrey and José Limon. For instance, she wrote about Pearl Lang, 'The subject matter is joyous or sad. There is nothing left to the imagination of the observer, who must blindly ignore the vulgarity and ego and trappings if he be sucked into the swamp of distended emotion' (Johnston 1998: 87). In contrast, she lauds Merce Cunningham for having 'brought us back to the reality that dance concerns dancing' (1998: 88). She elaborates,

> many things 'happen' in the lift of an arm, an expression, a sudden fall, an excruciating stillness, which implies much more than a simple defined emotion. Which in the end, is more powerful, more human and exacting, than the sledgehammer technique of a doubled-over grief or a chest-expanded joy.
>
> (1998: 88)

As the London-based dance writer Sanjoy Roy points out, here again, a direct connection soon emerges between a dance style and a particular set of values, which are deeply imbued with moral judgment. He observes:

> as you read through these articles [in *Marmalade Me*] it becomes clear that her focus on the 'factual', the 'thing itself', is anything but an objectivist, matter-of-fact stance, but saturated with utopian aspirations and visions – not the world as it is, *but as it should be.*
>
> (Roy 1998: n.p. emphasis added)

For Johnston and others like her, the pieces by the Judson Dance Theatre choreographers in the 1960s and 1970s in particular were about truth, freedom and democracy. She is delighted, for instance, by Steve Paxton's *Satisfyin' Lover* with 'thirty-two any old lovely people in their old clothes from our any old lives [...] He likes people for the way they are and believes in their physicality (their shape and way of moving) for what it is' (Johnston 1998: 267).

Previous chapters in this book have examined the potential negative repercussions of unnuanced, extremist thumbs up/thumbs down assessments for dancers in educational contexts and for choreographers through the act of criticism. Harsh critiques have their place in stimulating thought and generating dialogue but can sometimes harm individuals, while adulation can launch dance artists to an untouchable, god-like status, which allows no room for more subtle ethical analysis of any wrongdoing. Less clear are the implications of this way of addressing paradigm changes for organizations where groups of people must continue working together day in and day out for extended periods. If the damaging effects may be less obvious in contexts where a single student or dancer can simply leave a studio, school or company that is causing them distress, or avoid performing at a particular venue with a curator they disagree with, the problems become more evident when one is stuck in a large organization with few other options. In that case, the sad toll of a very damaging process plays out for all to witness.

I have had the unfortunate opportunity to experience first-hand this uncompromising, painful and often unproductive approach to changes in the dance field as a faculty member in a dance programme in higher education. The first unfolded shortly after 1996 when a new chair was hired from outside the programme. This person championed a release-based postmodern aesthetic and sought to promote it through the kinds of faculty and guest artists she hired. Accompanying her preference for this aesthetic – all very well in and of itself – was clear favouritism toward the advocates of this form and its belief system and a clear disrespect for those who were more aligned with a modernist set of practices and values and who happened to be older. Her displays of contempt for the latter included rolling her eyes and cutting people off mid-sentence in faculty meetings. This could escalate into nasty exchanges, which I luckily cannot recall verbatim, but definitely involved anger and raised voices. As a young, newly hired untenured faculty member I recall being both rather bemused and increasingly uncomfortable as both camps strove to entice me to their side. The situation got so heated that first a psychologist was brought in to try and find some kind of resolution, and then a professional mediator. Nothing worked. Eventually a terrible situation arose (that could have itself been avoided) that catalyzed a sequence of events leading to both coerced and voluntary retirements and the chair being removed from the leadership position. It was a metaphorical bloodbath, which occurred over a couple of years and has left scars to this day for those who were involved – basically the entire dance faculty and staff at the time.

This situation, unfortunately, was not unique. Since my initial hire in 1995, I have observed a fairly recognizable pattern that is usually related to changes in immediate leadership, and/or top-down directives for change coming from the higher administration (which in turn, may relate to larger paradigm shifts in higher education and/or the broader culture). For instance, around 2008, there was another major shift. The university hired another outside person to lead the dance area; their preference was for the European conceptualist aesthetic described in the last chapter. This time, while there was initially more collaboration among the faculty on the design of a new curriculum, the implementation, when it came, was swift and rigidly controlled. Once again, the leadership polarized faculty into 'for' and 'against', and any critique of the changes was framed as resistance and punished. These forms of punishment could include everything from subtle forms of disrespect in meetings, such as ignoring or dismissing suggestions, to failing to support the individual faculty in their requests during the academic year. Perhaps most hurtful of all was turning faculty on each other and alienating those perceived as 'resistors' from their peers such that they felt isolated and vulnerable. Ultimately these problems were partially resolved when the leader was fired, although once again, the damage to faculty and staff relations persisted for years, with some schisms remaining to this day between individuals who had once been close colleagues.

Perhaps more than anything these experiences have taught me that while aesthetic and ideological shifts are already problematically handled within the broader dance field, with allegiances and counter allegiances constantly forming, within large institutions the underlying issues closely relate to leadership and how change is managed throughout an organization, especially by those with power. In other words, shifting views of dance and its meaning are inevitable and part of the ebb and flow of living systems; what we need is a much better way to analyze the nature of group change and facilitate and navigate it collectively in a more constructive and humane manner.

Analyzing organizational change

Much of the existing literature on ethics and organizational change pertains to business. But we can easily adapt it to educational and other institutional contexts while also recognizing what dance itself, as a realm of kinaesthetic intelligence and empathy, can bring to the topic. This section draws on this research – especially in the realm of 'ethical change management', an area of specialized study that has emerged during the last couple of decades – to more closely examine the barriers to productive change and possible solutions. I will be arguing, in line with Gregory Jin, Ronald Drozdenko and Sara DeLoughy (2013) that an ethical approach is one that adopts a 'humanistic, democratic, enabling, open and trusting organizational environment, rather than a mechanistic firm, which is characterized by authoritarianism, control, enclosure and coercive bureaucracy' (2013: 17). The former is open to positive change, with a transforming servant leadership approach and an environment conducive to participative empowerment, while the latter can not only shut down the change process but harm those involved.

To start, some definitions are helpful. 'Change is the planned or unplanned response of an organization to some internal or external pressure' (Long and Spurlock 2008: 30). Change can involve a simple policy or procedural change, a personnel shift, engagements of new technology, or major organizational change. Suzanna Long and David Spurlock (2008) identify developmental, transitional and transformational changes. Developmental changes are those that merely refine existing managerial structures and styles without prompting significant upheaval. Transitional and transformational change, however, involve greater levels of change and come with higher levels of uncertainty. Change management, then, is defined as the methods and manners in which an organization 'describes and implements change within both its internal and external processes. This includes preparing and supporting employees, establishing the necessary steps for change, and monitoring pre- and post-change activities to ensure successful implementation' (ASQ n.d.: n.pag.). *Ethical* change management strives to root strategies for change in ethical ideals related to dignity, beneficence and justice. As Greg Latemore observes, 'If the heart of change is transformation, then the heart of an ethical approach to change is respect for the dignity of human systems' (2016: 114).

Before I consider more closely what an ethical approach consists of, it will be helpful to summarize unethical approaches to change. Perusing the research shows that the various features of unethical change are clearly in evidence in the scenarios that opened this chapter. These relate to problems with leadership, the harmful ways in which people can treat each other, and how 'resistance' is conceived and addressed in a destructive manner. It also has a great deal to do with how webs of power constrain individuals in diverse, multifaceted ways that can severely limit productive change by disconnecting them from the process or spurring them to actively work against it.

Beginning with leadership, my direct experience and the research literature both show the detrimental effects of the following behaviour: Leaders assume a position of absolute authority and run roughshod over others without taking time to learn the organization's history or listen closely and authentically to the concerns of the diverse stakeholders who make up its community (Schyns and Schilling 2013). Instead, they make demands and implement mandates, leaving little room for critical engagement and debate. Such leaders may or may not have a vision, but they do not bother to communicate a clear and well-reasoned argument for why change is needed in the first place, or why people should invest in the 'new' vision from a place of individual and collective growth. Poor leaders respond to others in an aggressive and/or manipulative manner – not unlike the abusive teachers and artistic directors we met in earlier chapters – for example by taking employees aside and having coercive 'off the record' conversations to try and convince them to follow their bidding. Perhaps worst of all, poor leaders have rigid black and white thinking when it comes to change – creating 'us' and 'them' categories for those they perceive as 'for' change or 'against' it – and distributing rewards and punishments based on those categories that vary from behavioural signs of encouragement (such as smiling and nodding in meetings) to monetary compensation and raises. For promoting a new aesthetic and ideology in the dance world examples described earlier, this means demonizing the older aesthetic and framing individual practitioners as 'bad people' who should be censured and punished for resisting change.

Within this leadership model, interpersonal relationships can easily turn sour and extremely unproductive. In such an environment, individuals' natural differences are brought to the foreground and exploited. Rather than approaching each other with respect and tolerance, stakeholders can manifest a range of attitudes and behaviours, from imitating the leader's 'us' vs. 'them' thinking, to striving to stay neutral, to remaining silent and/or disconnecting mentally from the change process. How power functions in this context shapes people's responses. Those with less job security and lower standing in the organization will likely choose to either actively support change (to show allegiance to the leadership and/or because they believe in the cause), strive to stay neutral (to avoid alienating anyone) or remain silent (also to avoid alienating anyone). Those with more power and job security may rush to support and imitate the leadership (again to demonstrate fidelity and/or shared values), try to actively resist change (by speaking out or working behind the scenes to build counter proposals), or check out of the process (by not actively making any changes out of the belief that the phase will pass or because they genuinely think it is wrong). The latter position of silent resistance will also be chosen when it is clear that showing *any* sign of active dissent will be met not only with group censure (what is currently termed 'cancel culture' in which a group or mob thrusts someone out of social or professional circles for perceived wrong-doing) but possible termination of employment. At this point, the entire organizational community is in disarray and rife with stress, distrust, ill will, hurt feelings, low motivation, anxiety and fear. As I've personally experienced, this is clearly not a constructive or humane environment in which to work, let alone to affect the kinds of positive, lasting or meaningful transformation I have outlined earlier.

In contrast, I advocate for a different approach to leadership and change management, along with a more nuanced understanding of how change occurs in unexpected, dynamic ways that can provide both greater insight and hope that old patterns need not be repeated. The leadership model I promote is influenced by ideas related to 'transforming or transformational servant leadership' (TSL) and combines the 'principles of servant leadership focused on benefits to followers with transformational leadership focused on the leader's influence on motivation and organizational performance' (Stauffer and Maxwell 2020: 108). David Stauffer and Delois Maxwell argue the benefits of this approach in their article 'Transforming servant leadership, organizational culture, change, sustainability, and courageous leadership' (2020). As they explain, 'servant leadership', a term first coined in 1970 by Robert Greenleaf, is about embracing a stewardship approach to leadership rather than a dictatorial style. Some of the most common characteristics include a focus on listening, an ability to empathize with others, an aim to heal suffering from broken spirits and emotional hurts, self-awareness, a commitment to people's growth and the drive to build community inside and outside the organization. In *The Servant as Leader* Greenleaf wrote:

> It begins with the natural feeling that one wants to serve, to serve *first*. Then conscious choice brings one to aspire to lead. The best test is: do those served grow as persons; do they, while being served, become healthier, wiser, freer, more autonomous?
>
> (quoted in Spears 1996: n.pag., original emphasis).

By placing the term 'transforming' in front of 'servant leader' these authors reference conceptualizations of leaders as 'change agents' consciously seeking to influence organizational culture. James MacGregor Burns (1978) first introduced the concept of 'transforming leadership', defining it as a leadership approach that causes change in individuals and social systems. In its ideal form, it creates positive change by enhancing the morale, motivation and performance of those affected. Bernard M. Bass extended Burns's work by using the term 'transformational' rather than 'transforming' and examining in detail how such an approach operates. Four key elements of transformational leadership consist of (1) Individualized Consideration – attending to each stakeholder's needs and demonstrating empathy, support, respect, and mentorship; (2) Intellectual Stimulation – challenging assumptions, taking risks, soliciting others' ideas, encouraging creativity, and nurturing those who think independently; (3) Inspirational Motivation – the leader articulates a vision that is inspiring to others, challenging them to achieve high standards and providing meaning for the tasks at hand: Purpose and meaning provide the energy that drives a group forward; and (4) Idealized Influence – the transformational leader is a role model for ethical behaviour and instils pride and gains the respect and trust of others (Bass and Riggio 2014).

Combining 'servant leadership' with 'transformational leadership' mitigates the abuses of power that might occur in the latter model. In other words, while both emphasize the importance of appreciating and valuing people, listening, mentoring and empowering others, there are differences. Studies have observed, for instance, that 'transformational leadership lends itself toward self-promotion due to its close association with charismatic and impressive management' and that it can lack 'accountability measures to avoid a dictatorial and oppressive leadership approach' (Stauffer and Maxwell 2020: 109). Another issue that has been noted is an unhealthy leader–follower dependency in which, contrary to the aims of the model to grow stakeholders' independence, the leaders' narcissistic tendencies feed into the followers' dependency needs, making room for manipulation. Since the transformational leader is more vested in getting stakeholders to engage in and support organizational objectives, they may lose sight of these interpersonal issues. In contrast, the servant leader's focus on service to the people with whom they work provides an important recalibration that directly impacts ethical change.

Actually, if we look more closely at studies specifically on ethical leadership, we can see the strong influence of both virtue ethics and deontological traditions including Kantian ethics. Virtue ethics is evident in the close attention to the recommended kinds of values and traits that good leaders manifest, such as confidence, courage, self-control, empathy, honesty, inner integrity and trustworthiness. Care and relational ethics are also manifest in leaders' continued emphasis on attending to the needs and concerns of those around them (stakeholder sensitivity), rich and respectful communication and facing transformation from a place of dialogue and collaboration rather than autocratically (Latemore 2016). Or, as author and activist adrienne maree brown has so succinctly put it in *Emergent Strategy: Shaping Change, Changing Worlds*, 'Relationships are everything' (2017: 28). The importance of deontological approaches, meanwhile, lies in a Kantian respect for individuals and their autonomy and freedom of choice and the importance of being consistent in one's actions. Matthew Hisrich argues that leaders modelling ethical behaviour and decisions adopt a deontological ethical approach where decision making is based on adherence to moral principles rather than outcomes, and oversee and implement procedural fairness, 'understood as equal treatment for all' (Hisrich 2018: 97). Consistent demonstration of these behaviours establishes the trust needed for successful and productive change.

Clearly, however, leadership is not the only factor that can create a more humane work environment. Hisrich in particular notes that, 'The combination of ethical leadership working in tandem with change management strategies directed toward ethics institutionalization is the means by which practitioners can establish an ethical work culture' (2018: 108). The main strategy involves institutionalization of ethics in the organization's culture. There are a variety of change management mechanisms that fall under the theme of ethics institutionalization. These include ethics training for stakeholders, the co-creating and implementing of ethics statements and codes, and co-creating systems of accountability. The ethics training ideally is in-depth and thoughtful (rather than simplistic and dogmatic), similar to what is offered within institutions of higher education regarding research with human subjects, but tailored to the needs of the organization. Methods of stakeholder assessment should also be developed that are relational rather than performance-driven and, for instance, feature more individually tailored expectations rather than comparative expectations of performance and rewards or punishments for meeting competitive goals. Informal mechanisms should also be designed to convey organizational core values.

Organizational justice (drawing on the deontological tradition in ethics), in particular, helps assure successful and ethical change management. Was the way something was handled fair? This relates not only to the outcome, but to *how* the decision was made, communicated, implemented and, perhaps most importantly, perceived. There are three forms of organizational justice: distributive, procedural and interactional. The first, distributive justice, relates to employees' perceptions of the fairness of the outcomes they receive, namely if they believe they are being paid or treated equally and/or appropriately in relation to others in the organization. Procedural justice centres on how decisions are made, and whether the procedures and mechanisms used to make decisions, set goals or investigate and address a grievance are fair. Consistency of application, unbiased decisions, accuracy of information, avenues for appeal, input from those who have been affected and the maintenance of the co-created, established ethical standards across the organization are valued here. Finally, interactional justice focuses on the interpersonal behaviour of those involved in carrying out decisions. Did they consistently treat people with dignity and respect? Did they provide sufficient and complete explanations in executing procedures or determining outcomes?

In 'Guiding principles for ethical change management', Pamela A. Kennett-Hensel and Dinah M. Payne propose a code for ethical change management that takes many of these factors into consideration. It considers the different phases from planning to implementation and review/revision of the change process and centres consistency, honesty, respect, autonomy, integrity, justice, inclusivity and two-way communication. They emphasize that the workforce should be involved in planning and implementing changes. They write,

> Motivating employees to participate in the change and incentivizing them to do so is critical. Punitive approaches in change management are cancerous, and it, therefore, is critical for managers to understand what the workforce values and leverage this value system [...] Lastly, once change is implemented, all stakeholders will be involved in the assessment of change and work towards continuous improvement.
>
> (2018: 39)

As I have personally witnessed, such an approach can help to both mitigate fragmentation and the damaging silos of 'us' and 'them' within an organization and build unification, which is so important to morale and motivation.

Finally, it is important to keep in mind that change processes are far from linear, fixed, predictable or organized in how they unfold. Successful change arises from the ongoing, dynamic, push and pull (rather like a Jive or swing dance) co-construction of meanings by all those involved – it is non-linear and iterative, involving repetition and experimentation. As Robyn Thomas and Cynthia Hardy observe, organizations are, 'unfolding enactments, constituted by local communicative interactions among its members. Whether and how new arrangements constituting change ensue depends upon the meanings that emerge from itera-tive negotiations involving multiple organizational members' (2011: 18). In their fascinating article, 'Reframing resistance to organizational change' they demon-strate that roles are far from fixed, and that organizational change is 'accom-plished through complex, messy, day-to-day working practices' (2011: 19). People can assume different and flexible positions, and so-called 'resistance' should not be framed as inherently negative but can provide important alternative perspec-tives that, if listened to, allow forward motion for the community as a whole as the meaning-making process assumes a new level of integrating different voices. Recognizing the 'unexpected' nature of change is inspiring, since it indicates that even when momentum seems stalled, something might still occur to turn the situ-ation around, perhaps with an even better outcome than initially planned.

Dancing examples of wide-scale ethical change

So, where are the dance examples of ethical leadership and change management? Detailed analyses of dance-related organizations and broad scale change are scarce, and much remains to be done in this area. Instead, what I offer here are a few exam-ples of carefully facilitated change processes in the dance field that illuminate the role of guided collaborative movement-based inquiry in transforming organiza-tional dance culture as well as the ongoing need for an ethics of care – especially an embodied ethics of care. I draw these examples from three separate collaborative processes overseen by Teija Löytönen in Finland, Becky Dyer in Arizona and myself in relation to the JKO School of the American Ballet Theatre. All three address changes within educational contexts, with some focused more on public education and others more on pre-professional and professional dance training. Including both European and American studies provides an important insight into contextual sensitivity, although many of the broad conclusions are similar, in terms of the ethi-cal considerations that arose and how they were addressed. These examples demon-strate that what dance artists and educators can contribute to our understanding of leadership and change is particularly holistic, meaning, as Jane Alexandre empha-sizes in her book *Dance Leadership: Theory into Practice* (2017), they consider the 'health of the whole, with no sacrifice of any one part for another' (2017: 191).

Teija Löytönen's research interests include studying dance teachers' everyday experiences of life in institutions, and the connections between emotions, values and morality. In March 2008, she began a two-year research study titled 'Moving mosaic – collaborative inquiry as a way of identifying and transforming the culture of dance teaching'. As part of the project dance teachers and principals from three different dance schools in southern Finland formed a collaborative group to inquire into the culture of dance teaching. One of the main motivations for the inquiry consisted of changes in the legislation of basic art education in Finland, and by extension, extensive changes in the nature and demands of dance teachers' work. A new Act on Basic Art Education in Finland had impelled considerable change in the culture of dance teaching with a new set of national requirements for dance curricula and increased credentials in terms of dance teachers' educational backgrounds. Also, the increasing number of programmes and broadening spectrum of dance education was challenging the cultural conventions of teaching dance as an art form. In earlier studies Löytönen had found that some dance teachers were experiencing the new challenges as a threat to their identity, while for others the changes meant a professional challenge for promoting growth. Even more importantly, perhaps, 'in this extensive reformation the dance teachers have quite often felt isolated without adequate support to manage the new requirements' (Dyer and Löytönen 2012: 124).

The three-year study unfolded as follows: Löytönen invited three dance schools – the Vantaa Dance Institute, the Dance Institute Sonja Tammela in Lappeenranta and the Nurmijärvi Dance Institute – to participate in the project. She had previously interacted with the schools as a consultant and spent over a year of planning with the principals and confirming that dance teachers who represented different areas of expertise and different dance genres were interested in sharing their knowledge and comparing ways of managing everyday challenges. Initial meetings provided an overall outline of the project, with more specific aims and ways of working discussed at a first joint seminar when all the dance teachers and principals collaboratively planned the inquiry process. Over the following two years (March 2008–March 2010) five subgroups formed on specific topics of their own choosing, and met to observe each other's classes and student performances and share teaching materials. The groups also convened to explore co-teaching approaches, develop teaching materials and deliberate over different aspects of their professional practice. The participants also met in joint seminars to discuss the issues that were emerging from their work together. They additionally arranged open seminars for other members of the Finnish dance education community; these took place in May 2009 and April 2010. Along with the dance teachers, Löytönen presented her observations, focusing on the ways the 'peer groups made meaning of their professional practice. Hence, my presentations were a kind of meta-analysis of our inquiry process' (Dyer and Löytönen 2012: 130).

Löytönen explains that the overall purpose of the project was twofold: 'first to pursue practical collaboration and support amongst the dance teachers; and second, to bring forth some core but unarticulated undercurrents within the present-day culture of dance teaching' (Dyer and Löytönen 2012: 125). What is important to understand, is that in this study, the objective was not to advance or brainstorm specific interventions or outcomes to address particular changes. Rather, it 'aimed to enhance self-understanding as well as to provide a means for collegial reflexivity within the complex and rapidly changing circumstances of dance education in Finland' (Dyer and Löytönen 2012: 125). Perhaps most importantly, Löytönen wanted to explore how to empower dance teachers themselves by developing a process that would allow them the means for feeling less lonely and isolated, and more self-directed in sharing their knowledge and expertise rather than relying on an external consultant when addressing challenges in their everyday work spaces.

One of the most important guiding principles for the collaborative inquiry was the metaphor of a 'moving mosaic' as described by Andy Hargreaves, in his book *Changing Teachers, Changing Times: Teachers' Work and Culture in the Postmodern Age* (1994). In this work, Hargreaves argues that organizations that thrive in conditions of constant change are those that show 'flexibility, adaptability, creativity, opportunism, collaboration, continuous improvement, a positive orientation towards problem-solving and commitment to maximizing their capacity to learn about their environment and themselves' (1994: 63). He recognizes that teachers belong to different informal groups that form dynamic collegial networks and that for these to function in adaptive ways they need collaborative opportunities to share experiences and ideas, and question beliefs and perspectives. As Löytönen observes, 'Through this informal and open form, I wanted to give space and authority to the dance teachers themselves in designing their collaboration' (Dyer and Löytönen 2012: 125).

Löytönen found that bringing teachers and principals together in a largely self-directed collaborative process of inquiry was successful in its aims, although sensitive facilitation also played an important role. She observes, for instance, that, 'This kind of thinking together with colleagues opened new perspectives to the dance teachers own teaching and sometimes made their taken-for-granted assumptions and habits of practice visible' (Dyer and Löytönen 2012: 129). It was also importantly a place for recognizing and exploring conflicting views from multiple perspectives: a valuable opportunity unencumbered by pressure to resolve problems or take prompt action. In terms of her own role, she observed that while the issues evolved quite naturally, the group needed some support and encouragement, and that she was able to observe things that the members missed. From her vantage point as both an insider familiar with the educators and outsider (she is neither a professional dancer nor a choreographer), Löytönen was in a unique position to guide the process. In particular, as someone trained in discourse analysis, she listened closely to the teachers and reflected back to them patterns of communication and how they conceptualized and experienced their efforts. In this way, she also assisted them in identifying and exploring their feelings, and connected them to values that in turn provided a pathway for making changes in their institutions.

Similar benefits of a sensitively facilitated collaborative approach to group transformation can be found in the work of Becky Dyer, which places a special emphasis on the roles of kinesthetic empathy and promotes an embodied ethics of care. Dyer is a dance education specialist and certified somatic movement therapist interested in collaborative inquiry and especially participatory action research (PAR). In fall 2008, she organized the Arizona Dance Educator's Action Research Project with a group of secondary dance educators in public and private high schools in Arizona. The initial purpose of the project, which continues to be active in 2021, was to create a supportive community and means for the teachers to reflect on their practices. But 'the teachers quickly realized their interests in instigating change and transforming their practices' (Dyer and Löytönen 2012: 127). As Dyer explains it, they desired to find ways to better meet the challenges they faced in their classrooms and schools. These included difficulties both they and their students confronted, including, 'disrespect, intolerance, racism, classism, exclusion, violence and students' personal struggles due to peer pressure, low self-esteem, and lack of adequate guidance, support and positive role models in their lives' (Dyer and Löytönen 2012: 127). Indeed, the goal became one of positive social transformation, by 'fostering positive change within their classrooms through experiences that encouraged students to reflect upon their social and moral choices and responsibilities' (Dyer and Löytönen 2012: 127).

Dyer brings to the project a strong commitment to PAR, which is an approach to research that emphasizes participation and action by members of communities affected by it. The focus is on collective inquiry, grounded in lived experience and history, but is clearly geared towards action and social transformation. As Dyer reflects, with PAR, 'critical inquiry moves the community towards the implementation of desired actions through collaborative processes of discovering needs, creating goals and constructing and realizing plans of action' (Dyer and Löytönen 2012: 132). In this way, PAR is interested in personal and collective transformation and linking reflection and critical engagement to change. She states, 'It is a move from the way things are to the way things could be' (2012: 132), which closely resonates with the concern of ethics, and an interest in improving society.

Another strong set of influences on Dyer derive from her advanced studies of embodiment, somatics and movement therapy in conversation with her personal experience as an educator in both high school and university settings. Social and cultural somatics is a field of study that examines the relationship between our inner embodied experiences and the broader systems of beliefs, values, and behaviours that shape our lives. The assumption is that the individual 'soma' of lived experience, is deeply intertwined with the social/cultural context that surrounds it – the social context and experiences in the world shape the soma or 'self' and vice versa. Through moving and reflecting, especially through guided experiences, we can become aware of our social bodies and 'transform internalized, relational, structural and cultural conditions that impede wellness' (Swann 2021: n.p.). Dyer draws on a rich palette of understanding that includes training in Laban Movement Analysis, dance therapy, somatic psychotherapy and body-mind centring and finding embodied means and movement-based ways of doing the work of reflective inquiry and change-making. One of the most impactful has been the Dynamic Embodiment Somatic Movement Therapy work developed by Martha Eddy, which has applications in conflict resolution and peace building. Some of these dance strategies are outlined in Eddy's article 'Dancing solutions to conflict: Field-tested somatic dance for peace' (2016), where she shares elements of the curriculum she has developed to enhance human tolerance, connection and understanding within communities.

Dyer has brought this expertise to her participation alongside the other teachers in their monthly gatherings. She has shared theoretical and conceptual frameworks, for instance, related to critical pedagogy and PAR, and occasionally leads the teachers through embodied experiences in order to facilitate their thinking and curricular development. She reflects, 'Bringing their thoughts into a physical state of awareness and responsiveness allowed the teachers to gain greater understanding of their own constructed viewpoints and those of others' (Dyer and Löytönen 2012: 140). She notes that this was particularly valuable when the teachers were grappling with contrasting or conflicting perspectives, either within themselves, or in the group. For instance, in one activity she invited the teachers to assume seemingly opposing perspectives, each on different sides of the room, then physically improvise towards the middle, to experience what it was like to hold 'both perspectives in relation' (Dyer and Löytönen 2012: 140). In other instances, she guided them in improvisations where they explored different perspectives, observing the feelings and thoughts that emerged as they spoke and moved from each point of view. Dyer and the teachers utilized LMA and the Laban/Bartenieff framework to accomplish this, along with rich visceral descriptions to investigate and make sense of the places of tension and/or harmony within themselves, interpersonally and as a community. Dyer explains, 'I also encouraged them to become aware of how the nature of their dialogue might be reflected in their movement patterns and attributes, sense of inner-connectivity, awareness and responsiveness to others, and relationship to the world beyond themselves' (Dyer and Löytönen 2012: 140). Over time this improvisational framework has revealed a middle space that holds their diverse points of view in a relational, respectful dialogue for which everyone assumes a sense of responsibility.

For Dyer, one of the biggest take-aways from the experience has been rethinking what it means to be a facilitator for the group. She has observed that it takes great sensitivity and is not about imposing her own interests and agendas, or wielding her power to persuade the teachers in either overt or subtle ways. Although previously a high school teacher herself, she is currently a professor at Arizona State University, which as a Research 1 institution, holds an elevated status within the educational ecology of the state. In her position, Dyer has access to many resources unavailable to the high school teachers, who are often the only dance specialists in their school. Dyer also has the time and mandate to conduct extensive research as part of her job – allowing the kind of in-depth investigations of different research paradigms and somatics modalities described here. Dyer recognized that to be true to the values and priorities of PAR and social somatics it was critical for her to prioritize teachers' articulated needs and goals. Since these were very much about creating a nurturing environment that would allow for their personal growth through their relations with each other, it led Dyer to, 'realize my role in working with members of the group [was] to construct an ethical community of self-care that encouraged caring about the interests of others' (Dyer and Löytönen 2012: 135). Indeed, it also allowed Dyer to embrace the 'meaningful opportunity within this capacity for my own self-care, growth and professional development' (2012: 136). As she observes, it has meant that she, 'can engage, along with the participants, in my own as well as their processes of growth and change' (2012: 136).

Together, both Dyer and Löytönen came to realize that their approaches individually and together have reflected the characteristics of an ethics of care, especially an *embodied* ethics of kinesthetic empathy and care. Between 2009 and 2012, the two were in conversation about their separate projects, leading to the joint authorship of the article 'Engaging dialogue: Co-creating communities of collaborative inquiry' (2012). At the end of this article, they observe that collaborations are fragile, and subject to periods of disruption and places of tension due to strong personalities, prescribed roles and expectations, diversity in perspectives and other kinds of situational forces. It is crucial, therefore, to not only focus on knowledge creation from a more intellectual, content-driven perspective, but to find ways to facilitate respect for different perspectives, and engage with others with somatic awareness and a sense of relational responsibility. They assert: 'holding the inquiry together, at its core, is caring. Embodied sensitivity and care-based ethical relations towards self and others is a prerequisite for an inquiry stance that is self-reflective, appreciative, socially conscious and meaningful. Hence, we propose that 'care'-ful attendance to complex incidents and to difference as well as negotiating conflicting views are foundational to collaborative communities' (Dyer and Löytönen 2012: 143). It is through such a care-based approach that positive personal, institutional and broader social transformation can occur.

It should be noted that their work resonates with the study in leadership and dance undertaken by David Zeitner, Nicholas Rowe and Brad Jackson in their

213

article 'Embodied and embodiary leadership: Experiential learning in dance and leadership education'. In this study the authors observe that leadership scholarship has increasingly considered how the 'arts may be applied to support explorations into creative ways of thinking and being within organizations' (2015: 170). In their work, they reflect on how experiences of creating and performing dance can 'imbue organizations with a motivated engagement in transformation, towards organizational goals that are continuously emergent' (2015: 170). They argue that the experience of discovering, exploring and engaging the moving body in the highly social process of making dance, regardless of the dance style, offers participants various organizational schemas to explore and reflect upon. In particular improvisation, as well as collective problem solving during the creative process, assist with leadership development and organizational behaviour, as does the haptic aspect of dance, in which people physically touch each other and receive direct sensory information about how others feel. For the authors, 'The moving body provides clear opportunities for collaborative, innovative and expressive ways of organizing people in transformative action' (2015: 180).

The final example of how large-scale change might be approached within a dance context comes from my own on-going efforts in collaboration with faculty and staff at the American Ballet Theatre Jacqueline Kennedy Onassis School based in New York City. Beginning in 2020, I spoke with the school's leadership about developing a code of ethics as one important step in their desire to change the school's culture and make sure that it was a place welcoming to all of its diverse stakeholders. This was taking place during the COVID-19 pandemic, when everyone was scattered around the globe and the school's classes were online. I had come to their attention through my research on ethics, along with dance and human rights, and through various remote sessions we began discussions about how best to address their hopes and concerns. Unlike the previous examples outlined above that were more open-ended and investigative in nature, this was a situation in which I was being sought out as a specialist to help realize a specific goal within a flexible, though finite time line. At the same time, since my experience is more as an academic researcher, scholar and educator, than as a seasoned business consultant, there are many ways in which my approach and observations overlap with those of Dyer and Löytönen.

For instance, from the beginning we worked collaboratively to figure out how to best proceed. I listened to the varied motivations for developing a code of ethics and offered some suggestions on how I might best be of service. We settled on starting with two online interactive presentations over Zoom, of an hour and a half each. During these, I introduced some of the core concepts of Nonviolent Communication, laid out some of the key principles for ethical engagement with human subjects drawn from the research realm and offered my views on why ethics as a discipline can be so helpful to addressing pre-professional dance training's legacy of abusive and discriminatory attitudes and practices. There were opportunities both during the sessions and through an anonymous questionnaire for participating staff and artistic faculty members to comment on the material. People were also encouraged to report on issues that they felt the school did not handle ethically – initially allowing them to define that term themselves, since my aim was also to expose them to the complexity and variety of ethical theories. Examples of concerns included how, for instance, different cohorts of students were sometimes treated, and how to respectfully and compassionately handle the dismissal of students no longer meeting the school's expectations. There was also a great deal of interest in how to offer caring and quality instruction online.

Rather than striving to immediately answer these concerns myself, my instinct instead was to stay focused on knowledge acquisition around ethics, community building and finding ways, similar to Dyer and Löytönen, to empower the faculty and staff to collaborate on finding their own resolutions to such challenges. I was aware that I lacked detailed understanding of the specifics of their institution let alone the specialized knowledge that would be helpful in addressing many of the specific concerns. For instance, I am not a specialist in online teaching, nor am I an experienced studio-based pre-professional dance technique instructor. To that end, I instead focused on listening closely to their varied perspectives and worked towards creating a document that would reflect the kinds of ethical principles collectively supported by the participants and which could be a guide for future deliberations, policy changes, decision-making and shifts in behaviour towards each other and students.

The next step involved my drafting a document that included two parts: a statement of shared aspirational ethical principles and a professional code of ethics. This was my recommendation, based on my extensive experience in writing reports and by-laws within the context of higher education and my familiarity with the effectiveness of having one or two people take the lead. Moreover, I did not approach this as a rigid final product, but a living document that would function as a springboard for collective discussion and refinement. Informing this document were the school's mission statement and various existing policies and codes of behaviour, as well as all the discussions I had been privy to up to that point. I also consulted codes of ethics of professional organizations both within and beyond the dance world, and contacted places such as the National Ballet School of Canada, which is known for its progressive pedagogical outlook and the National Ballet of Canada, which has a Code of Conduct and Ethics for its professional company.[1] I also consulted the Staff Code of Conduct for The Royal Ballet School in London, which although not explicitly related to ethics, clearly concerns itself with ethical issues such as treating all students with respect and dignity.[2] Finally, I kept in mind the wording in union contracts for the major dance companies in the United States.

Ultimately, I chose to structure the shared principles largely in line with the major guiding principles recommended by the Belmont Report (respect for persons, beneficence and justice). In this context, they became (1) Respect for People's Rights and Dignity; (2) Concern for Wellness; (3) Commitment to Fairness and Justice, plus an additional category: (4) Belief in Integrity and Responsibility (Code 2021). For each of these, I drafted aspirational statements influenced by all of the research outlined here, meaning that 'their intent is to guide and inspire members of the School in an active and ongoing effort to embrace and practice the very highest ethical ideals of the profession'. One of the inspirations for such a perspective was Aristotle's notion that pursuing the ethical life is a lifelong endeavour, one of constant movement. Another was that ethics is complex, and that it is more valuable and inspirational to articulate shared values in an open-ended manner, than to simply list do's and don'ts, which can feel dogmatic and restrictive, especially to those in a creative field such as dance.

At the same time, the second part of the document, the Code of Ethics, brought more specificity and clarity regarding ethical conduct, in order to hold people accountable for their actions – something some among the leadership continually requested. This section drew on many of the same guiding principles as the earlier one, but turned them into directives for behaviour. For instance, while the first ethical principle acknowledges that 'Members of the JKO community respect the dignity and worth of all people' the first expected behaviour in the Code of Conduct states that Faculty, Staff, Parents/Guardians, Volunteers, and any other supporters of the ABT School will: 'Treat all students with dignity and respect' (Code 2021). Some of the most detailed directives in this section drew on language found in AGMA contracts for dance companies, which forbid a range of physical, sexual and emotional harassment or behaviour that create an intimidating or hostile environment. Others came directly out of my conversations with various stakeholders at the school.

In my estimation, it was after the document was drafted that the greatest transformation took place in the JKO School community. During two meetings, members of the staff and artistic faculty were divided into small break out rooms on Zoom where they were tasked with going through the document line by line, word for word. Everything, I let them know, was open for discussion, including the document's structure and the inclusion of the two parts. These groups were organized as cross-sections of the school, distributing representation of different positions within the institution's hierarchy. While there were some technical glitches as we sought to figure out such things as group editing using Google docs, the engagement was lively, detail-oriented and intensive. The groups debated terminology and concepts and strove to find language that truly reflected their values and beliefs. Between the sessions, individuals sought out additional resources to enhance their positions, and offered more feedback on the document. In each meeting, following the small group discussions, we re-assembled as a whole, and went through each comment – providing an opportunity to voice different positions and seeking solutions that satisfied the entire community. In some of those cases, we were able to resolve the issue in the moment, while in others, I followed up later and sought language that would reflect the collective inclination. The final version was circulated for any remaining comments before the school adopted it.

The main changes I have observed to date concern the degree of enthusiasm for engaging with ethics as a field of enquiry and the extent to which the process has affected employee interactions and empowered stakeholders to address ethical issues. While this is not a research project, and there remains much work to do in following up on how this document is actualized in different aspects of the school's operations, at this point in the process, I have witnessed some of these changes first-hand. Various participants have also reported their own impressions of the success of the process. I observed how some people who were initially sceptical became fully supportive of holding ethics-related discussions. I have also been informed that the discussions have impacted people's interactions: in particular, stakeholders have expressed appreciation for clearer guidelines about expectations for behaviour and the clear statement of consequences for failing to comply with this code or with other official school policies. Finally, there is a great deal of pride that the JKO School is taking a leadership role within the field of pre-professional dance training as a whole, in establishing a document that states its ethical principles and code of ethics. As one participant observed, 'This is an exciting opportunity to act as a leader in making the dance field more aware and educated about ethics' (personal communication).

These three examples highlight the value of approaching change with ethics in mind. In particular, they consider the importance of sensitive leadership, engaging in flexible and democratic processes, and designing and implementing co-created principles and/or codes and methods of accountability. Sometimes it is beneficial to have external facilitation and stewardship by someone who is both an insider and outsider to the field and is skilled in honouring and balancing diverse perspectives, with the wisdom and skills needed to help a group craft and implement its vision. And sometimes, it is valuable to engage embodied means to move through ideas and feelings, and appreciate the ability to hold complex and contradictory impulses within and between ourselves. As Alexandre observes, this involves, 'acknowledgement of the multivalency of the body, and of dance practice; and a mandate to embrace complexity in dance leadership theory and practice' (2017: 191).

While I have yet to fully utilize such movement-based approaches in my own consulting, my experience of this approach in other settings involving groups of performing artists has been that it can be very generative. If employed carefully and authentically, forms of structured improvisation in particular immediately position people in a playful and creative frame of mind, which honours both individual agency and collective ingenuity (see Albright 2004; Goldman 2010; Wetzel and Renterghem 2015). It can also be valuable to engage Indigenous and ritual practices in communities that regard them as grounding and inspiring (see Kenny and Fraser 2012). For instance, maybe it is fruitful to start a meeting with an embodied prayer to the land or to one's ancestors. Or to integrate a talking or peace circle, whereby people take turns handling an object to hold the sacred intention of the circle, passing it around to indicate whose turn it is to speak/dance. Each group should consider what approaches may be valuable in its change process and use the most generative to move forward together in body-mind-spirit in a respectful and tolerant manner.

Moving towards a more humane dance culture

At the human scale, in order to create a world that works for more people, for more life, we have to collaborate on the process of dreaming and visioning and implementing that world. We have to recognize that a multitude of realities have, do, and will exist.

(brown 2017: 158)

This book began with the question of why we should study ethical issues in relation to concert dance. It should be clear by now that one of the main reasons is that the field of ethics provides theoretical platforms for understanding people's moral decisions and illuminates the values and principles guiding their actions, such that changes can be made to improve the dance world. In particular, the field of normative ethics reveals the frequent engagement of quasi-consequentialist arguments to justify a great deal of behaviour – namely, that the ends justify the means, or great dance is worth any sacrifice because of its impact – in a system that often values mutually supportive, sacrosanct products (rather than processes) – namely, genius choreographers, virtuosic dancers, choreographic masterpieces, major presenting venues and elite institutions. What is missing, is attention to virtue ethics and deontological traditions, which bring attention to the importance of character and values and of rules, duties and obligations that go beyond the individual or the result and provide a more impartial sense of fairness and justice to acts in and of themselves. In particular, relational ethics and care ethics, along

218

with social contract theory, provide detailed considerations of how to interact in a more caring and collective way to counteract some of the historical cruelty and abuse that has occurred within the dance field, especially at the pre-professional and professional levels.

Throughout the book, I have called for all of us to embody and practice kindness, humility, generosity, patience, forgiveness, hope, curiosity and mutual respect. And I encourage all in the field to work together to develop empathic processes for relating to each other, whether between peers and colleagues or with students or other stakeholders with whom one is in contact. To be sure, signs of such activity are also being seen within the sphere of social dance, as people have stepped forward to develop codes, best practices and means of fostering a culture of consent (see Riva 2017; McMains 2021). These actions will help to counteract the varying degrees of objectification, disrespect, domination, humiliation, degradation, coercion, deception, betrayal, exploitation, manipulation, discrimination, negligence, aggression, sexual harassment and cruelty that have existed and remain active in the dance world, across the entertainment, concert and vernacular dance realms. As I outlined in each chapter, working independently and collaboratively to determine our values, principles, rights and responsibilities, in any particular studio, school, programme or company will provide greater clarity and a sense of shared responsibility for the changes that we want to see.

In relation to the arc of a dance artist's life, I have sought to indicate why this approach is valuable and suggest how to achieve transformation. I advocate for dance artists to reflect on what it means to be a decent human being, especially a caring individual, as one pursues a career in dance – whether as a performer, teacher, critic, presenter or member of a dance institution in some other capacity. This not only recognizes the 'human' in 'dancer' to counteract traditions that alternately dehumanize or idolize dance artists, but recognizes that dance artists, educators, critics, curators and administrators do not function outside the bounds of civil society, nor should they be allowed to. It is important to seek interconnections and interdependency and to move away from self-centred views of the lone genius, and/or star performers and master teachers who are beyond critique. Care ethics, and ethical traditions from other cultures that stress establishing respectful relationships between self and other, self and the environment, self and ancestors, are all relevant here.

At the same time, hopefully, readers will recognize that I do not advocate removing or denouncing resistance, disagreement or conflict. Shutting out or shutting down questioning voices, as stated earlier in this chapter, is a sure way to cause resentment, let alone invoke an authoritarian and oppressive environment, regardless of the content of the discussion. Certainly, change can take place within both dictatorship or collectivist models, but it will not be humanistic in nature.

When people feel pressured to think and behave in certain ways, whether by a single leader or group of peers, they will not usually do so from a place of good will. They will seek either subtle or more obvious ways to display their discontent, follow along out of fear, shut down or turn to self-harm. We have seen this in the context of traditional dance classrooms where controlling teachers, companies and institutions micro-manage everything from what people can wear, to when they can eat or drink or go to the bathroom. Such behaviour strips people of their individual autonomy and can lead to a range of emotional and physical abuse and resulting trauma – enough to lead highly talented dancers to leave the profession due to the heavy toll on their health and well-being.

Rather, freedom of speech and respectfully expressed oppositional positions provide an important opportunity to find even more satisfying new paths to humane attitudes and behaviours that embrace 'more people and more life' as adrienne maree brown advocates. As the choreographer Victoria Marks has observed, resistance can often be a form of active participation – how one participates when no other options seem viable and where there are not yet words to explain what stands in the way (Marks and Schwadron 2022). In particular, open, thoughtful and informed debate, even if heated at times, offers multiple perspectives that can broaden people's views. We need to be able to listen to others, to offer our opinions and do so without fear of reprisal or dire consequences such as losing one's job or reputation. Almost (if not) all ideas might offend someone regardless of our intentions, so rather than censoring others it is important to find ways to dialogue using reason, compassion and respect, and strive to be curious rather than judgmental about others' motivations and experiences. As *Index on Censorship* magazine editor, Rachael Jolley, observes, free speech is crucial for change:

> Free speech has always been important throughout history because it has been used to fight for change. When we talk about rights today they wouldn't have been achieved without free speech. Think about a time from the past – women not being allowed the vote, or terrible working conditions in the mines – free speech is important as it helped change these things.
>
> (2016: n.pag.)

In terms of the dance field, we need to be able to listen and move together with positive intention, seeking to understand the complex ways in which people make constantly shifting meanings of their embodied experiences. Rather than getting caught up in the destructive cycle of denouncing or blaming those in the past or who practice different styles of dance, I invite you to find out more and ask questions about why people value how they move or teach or write about or present dance. As observed by practitioners of Nonviolent Communication discussed earlier in the book, people share basic needs and values, including the need to feel connection with others, safety, physical well-being, meaning, play and autonomy. While the dance form will vary, and the aesthetic choices seem different, it is possible to connect at this other level – our collective humanity – and as such make constructive changes. As brown notes, 'the combination of adaptation with intention, wherein the orientation and movement towards life, towards longing, is made graceful in the act of adaptation. This is the process of changing while staying in touch with our deeper purpose and longing' (2017: 70).

To this end, dance history can be a terrific playground for learning about complexity. Choose any period, style, individual or piece and you will find a variety of possible interpretations – some of which exist in harmony and some in seeming contradiction. For instance, ballet can be associated with Western royalty and upper-class values, due to its origins in the courts of Europe during the Renaissance. However, it has also been an expression of working-class rebellion, as during the Cultural Revolution in China (Wilkinson 1974). In Cuba, ballet was also adapted by Alicia Alonso as a postcolonial reformulation of a European legacy in which Cuban dancers brought distinctively nationalist accents to their performances (Tome 2011). Meanwhile, in *The Oxford Handbook of Jewishness and Dance*, authors such as Marion Kant and Liora Bing-Heidecker, have noted how ballet has been interpreted as embodying Jewish identity (2022). This is just a brief example – every style will have its richly diverse historical and geographic landscape, in which even dancers in the same company might have wildly different feelings and meanings associated with what they do – from revelling in a pointed toe as the completion of a perfect line, to preferring an un-pointed foot as an expression of naturalness and lack of artificiality. Understanding and appreciating the diversity of perspectives can help us tolerate differences in the present moment without falling into complete relativism.

Indeed, as indicated by these examples, this same complexity exists in relation to the highly contested and often polarizing debates around race in the dance field. Rather than approaching racial categories in reductive, essentializing terms, it is helpful to recall that different racial categories are human constructions. Race is not founded on objective and identifiable biological differences – the Human Genome Project has shown there are no 'races', only a single human race – but on a cluster of characteristics that groups and cultures consider significant. Notions of who constitutes white, black, brown, etc. has, and will, vary historically and geographically, and depends on a variety of factors – sometimes related to physical characteristics like skin colour, but also often related to socio-political and economic factors. Sometimes distinctions between and within racial identities originate from within communities and other times they are imposed from without – often simultaneously. This means that notions of whiteness, blackness, brownness,

Jewishness, Asianness, Indigeneity and Latinidad, etc., are all in motion and highly contested, as much as our ideas of dance, and should be viewed with just as much nuance – and scepticism – especially when they are mobilized in order to separate people and blame and shame each other.

To provide just one brief example, consider Jewish dance artists and how to address their relationship to Jewish culture and religion, and how that further intersects with their dance choices – there is no single answer. Rather, as Rebecca Rossen notes in *Dancing Jewish: Jewish Identity in American Modern and Postmodern Dance* (2014), 'Jewishness is not a matter of essences but rather a repertory of images, themes, and frames that signify "Jewish"' (2014: 3). In this perspective, 'dancing Jewish', involves examining the 'artistic, ideological, political, and racial implications of this term over time', and recognizing that it 'embraces the fluidity and complexity of Jewish identity' (2014: 2–3). Jewish dance artists come from varied geographical/ethnic backgrounds, including Ashkenazi (primarily from Eastern Europe), Sephardic (primarily descendants from Spain), Mizrahim (primarily from the Middle East and North Africa), Ethiopian (from Ethiopia) and Indian (including Cochin Jews, Bene Israeli and Baghdadi). There are also many different religious orientations among Jews, from Ultra-Orthodox to Conservative, Reform, Reconstructionist, Humanistic and atheist – which also can vary greatly depending on place and individual. The same concerns political orientation – Jews can be found across the political spectrum, with some supporting more conservative causes, and others more liberal. In Israel alone, a fifteen-minute ride can take you from an environment in which you are surrounded by men with long beards, black coats and *shtreimelen* (large fur hats), to one with hipsters sporting body tattoos and piercings.

How Jews, and by extension Jewish artists, are identified along racial lines from outside of the community and how they self-identify is just as varied. At many points in history and within particular regions, Jews have been seen as 'other' and placed alongside disenfranchised groups. For instance, in Spain 'blood purity' statutes from the fifteenth through the eighteenth centuries condemned non-Christians – Jews and Muslims, Africans, Native Americans and Roma – to exile and oppression. *Raza* ('race') while invisible, because it was carried in the blood, signified the Blackness of religious difference in contrast to the whiteness of Christian virtue. During the Nazi period, Jews were also aligned with other *Untermenschen* ('subhumans') based on a racist doctrine asserting the superiority of the Aryan race over Jews, understood as 'Semitic' people, along with others such as Roma, people of African descent and to a varied extent, peoples of Slavic decent. As a consequence, Jewish dancers were sent to the gas chambers regardless of their personal views, the degree to which they were assimilated into German society and whether or not they even considered their Jewish identify significant in their lives; being born Jewish was enough to get one murdered. As the Italian writer and chemist Primo Levi so famously observed,

> If it hadn't been for the racial laws and the concentration camp, I'd probably no longer be a Jew, except for my last name. Instead, this dual experience, the racial laws and the concentration camp, stamped me the way you stamp a steel plate. At this point I'm a Jew, they've sewn the star of David on me and not only on my clothes.[3]

In the United States, Jews have also experienced a precarious status in relation to racial categorization. In the earlier part of the twentieth century, Jews were often regarded as something other than 'white' – as playwright Alfred Uhry was told growing up in Atlanta in the 1940s, 'We're not white; we're Jewish' (quoted in Schechter 2016: n.pag.). Many scholars agree that at some point during the post-war period Jews, particularly of Ashkenazi decent, became accepted and treated as white. This occurred for a variety of reasons, as Dave Schechter outlines in his article 'Are Jews white? It's Complicated' (2016: n.pag.), including Jews' success-ful assimilation into and contribution to mainstream American life, and a shift in perceptions of Jews from victims to powerful defenders of a nation. At this point in time in 2021, Jews are often labelled and stereotyped as white, even though some identify as such, while others do not, with quite a few feeling conflicted about how to address such a politically charged question (Kampeas 2020). All of this does not, however, stop Jews from being increasingly vilified – by the extreme right, as corrupt influences requiring extermination (as with the Tree of Life synagogue mass shooting in Pittsburgh in 2018) or, by the extreme left, as uniquely privileged and actively contributing to white supremacy either at home in the USA or, espe-cially, through the uniquely targeted state of Israel (Hirsh 2017).

What this means is that 'dancing Jewish' comes in many forms and flavours, each requiring a nuanced and contextually sensitive approach. Jewish dance artists have, for instance, sometimes sought an 'authentically' Jewish movement based in everyday nineteenth century Eastern European *shtetl* life, or among the various traditional practices and customs of particular cultural backgrounds found in, for instance, Yemen or Ethiopia. Others have found alignment with what they iden-tify as Jewish values in such diverse styles as ballet, postmodern dance, Flamenco and hip hop. Many Jewish dancers in the twentieth and twenty-first centuries have had no conscious or sustained interest in their Jewishness or its relation to their dancing, preferring instead to simply identify as a dancer or choreographer of the style of choice. At times, such identification is simply an aesthetic preference; at others, when a pattern can be discerned, such decisions may relate to broader cultural trends in which Jewishness is being constructed. For instance, Ninotchka Bennahum (2018) and Douglas Rosenberg (2022) have demonstrated that many

American postmodern dancers' progressive movements towards democratizing concert dance and making it more accessible to diverse communities can be linked to traditional Jewish values and ideals, especially as related to *tikkun olam*, or repair of the world.

Such a complex situation is the case for every group associated with a racialized category, indicating the value of being educated in broader historical movements along with specific dance histories when striving for less discrimination, more inclusivity and greater racial justice within the concert dance field. This is not to mention the added complexity gained by approaching these topics through an intersectional lens, which reveals how factors such as gender, sexuality, class, and nationality further contribute to the diverse ways in which individuals and groups experience dance styles and dancing in different settings. Just as 'us' vs. 'them' thinking has not served the dance field well when it comes to aesthetic differences, neither does it foster good will in relation to distinctions along rigidly patrolled racialized lines. Working towards change means being sensitive to Walt Whitman's claim 'I am large, I contain multitudes' and avoiding the temptation to simplify, reduce and otherwise pigeonhole oneself or one's colleagues, coworkers, students or audience members. Rather, in line with this book's ongoing argument, movements for a more equitable dance culture can be well served by ethical approaches that nurture caring relationships and co-create fair processes and structures for all people to thrive.

Final moving thoughts

Working out the terms of moral justification is an unending task.

(Scanlon 1998: 361)

During the process of teaching my course on dance and ethics at least one student inevitably asks how to navigate all the different ethical positions with their varied strengths and weaknesses, and how to address moral dilemmas when matters can become so complicated. As Steve Wilkens comments, 'Open-endedness can make us a little crazy because we crave certainty. Especially in the realm of ethics, where so much is on the line' (2011: 213). Yet, as he continues to argue, simply turning off all the questions that arise and returning to the status quo is not helpful if the norm is leading to harm and abuse. Nor is choosing cynicism and the idea that one should disavow any engagement and simply belittle anyone foolhardy enough to take a stand on ethical matters. For Wilkens, these are easy but cheap and disingenuous solutions, which miss the constructive purpose of deliberating on all the options available in any particular context and choosing those aspects from each position that may be intentionally integrated into our own worldviews. This very process, in and of itself, allows each one of us to become more conscious of the values that matter to us, permits us to articulate such values to those around us as a form of responsible public accountability and can become an important guide for future action.

Approaching moral questions with the kinesthetic intelligence and empathy accessible through dance further enhances the process. Whether a highly trained professional, or someone who simply loves to move, tapping into the body's sensitivity allows us to also try out, experiment with and find answers that feel right. With this in mind, I finish with one final moving example – the inspiring work of S. Ama Wray. Wray has developed an approach she names Embodiology® – an approach to improvisation prompting participants to key into body-mind sensations which affirm that intelligence is obtained through intersensory stimulation of the body. This approach uses principles drawn primarily from Indigenous performance methodologies, specifically West African performance traditions, to innovate, and enhance 'wellbeing, vitality and empathy.'[4] In talking about this approach to improvisation Wray says, 'You will be a fire, you will light the space. As well as you will be lit by others in the space' (2017: n.pag.). As she says, it is a 'multi- poly- cross-integration of many forms of beingness' (2014: n.pag.). Just as she dances and speaks with ease as she facilitates improvisational sessions with others, I invite you to consider the issues raised in this book and the tiny or expansive, vibratory or smooth, solo or collective, steps you might take to move the dance world in a more respectful and caring direction promoting dignity and respect for all.

NOTES

1. https://national.ballet.ca/Code-of-Conduct-and-Ethics. Accessed 19 July 2022.
2. See https://royalballetschool.org.uk/wp-content/uploads/2015/12/Staff-Code-of-Conduct-Dec-2015.pdf. Accessed 5 July 2021.
3. Primo Levi, interview with Ferdinando Camon, in Massimo Giuliani, *Centaur in Auschwitz: Reflections on Primo Levi's Thinking* (Lanham: Lexington Books, 2003), 51.
4. https://www.embodiology.com. Accessed 19 July 2022.

References

Acocella, Joan (2011), telephone interview with author, 5 August.

Adshead, Janet (ed.) (1988), *Dance Analysis: Theory and Practice*, London: Dance Books.

Albright, Ann Cooper (2004), 'Living the gap: Improvisation as political practice', *Proceedings International Dance Conference, Ethics and Politics Embodied in Dance*, Theatre Academy, Helsinki, p. 59. http://citeseerx.ist.psu.edu/viewdoc/download?-doi=10.1.1.453.792&rep=rep1&type=pdf. Accessed 16 June 2021.

Albright, Ann Cooper (2013), 'Feeling in and out', in G. Brandstetter, G. Egert and S. Zubarik (eds), *Touching and Being Touched: Kinesthesia and Empathy in Dance and Movement*, Berlin: De Gruyter, pp. 263–73.

Alderson, Evan (1997), 'Ballet as ideology', in J. Desmond (ed.), *Meaning in Motion*, Durham: Duke University Press, pp. 121–32.

Aldrich, Elizabeth (2008), 'Plunge not into the mire of worldly folly: Nineteenth-century and early twentieth-century religious objections to social dance in the United States', in N. Jackson and T. Shapiro-Phim (eds), *Dance, Human Rights, and Social Justice: Dignity in Motion*, Lanham: Scarecrow Press, pp. 20–33.

Alexander, Andrew (2011), 'American Dance Festival kicks off with long-time director Charles Reinhart at the helm for the last time', *Creative Loafing*, 17 June, https://americandancefestival.org/wp-content/uploads/2013/03/06_17_11_CL_ADFKicksOff.pdf. Accessed 14 June 2021.

Alexandre, Jane (2017), *Dance Leadership: Theory into Practice*, London: Palgrave Macmillan.

Allegranti, Beatrice (2011), 'Ethics and body politics: Interdisciplinary possibilities for embodied psychotherapeutic practice and research', *British Journal of Guidance & Counselling*, 39:5, pp. 487–500, https://doi-org.ezproxy1.lib.asu.edu/10.1080/03069885.2011.621712. Accessed 23 June 2021.

Allison, Evvie (2018), 'Do freelance dancers need a union?', *Dance Magazine*, 27 June, https://www.dancemagazine.com/freelance-dancers-union-2579158664.html. Accessed 23 June 2021.

Alter, Judith B. (1996), *Dance-Based Dance Theory: From Borrowed Models to Dance-Based Experience*, New York: Peter Lang.

Anderson, Jack (2014), 'Thoughts of a pluralist', *Dance Chronicle*, 37:2, pp. 156–62, https://doi.org/10.1080/01472526.2014.915462. Accessed 15 June 2021.

APAP Equitable Partnership Working Group (2020), 'Building ethical and equitable partner-ships in the performing arts', https://www.apap365.org/Portals/1/PDFs/Programs/APAP%20 BEEP%204.19.21.pdf. Accessed 27 June 2021.

APAP (n.d.), 'Statement of values and code of ethics', https://www.apap365.org/Portals/1/ PDFs/About/Statement%20of%20Values%20and%20Code%20of%20Ethics%202016. pdf. Accessed 27 June 2021.

Aprahamian, Serouj (2021), 'Going off! The untold story of breaking's birth', doctoral disser-tation, Toronto: York University.

Arnold, Matthew (1865), *Essays in Criticism*, Cambridge: Macmillan.

Artaud, Antonin and Morgan, James O. (1958), 'The theatre and cruelty', *The Tulane Drama Review*, 2:3, pp. 75–77, https://doi-org.ezproxy1.lib.asu.edu/10.1177/1532708612440254. Accessed 25 June 2021.

ASQ (American Society for Quality) (n.d.), 'What is change management', https://asq.org/ quality-resources/change-management. Accessed 26 June 2021.

Bales, Melanie and Nettl-Fiol, Rebecca (eds) (2008), *The Body Eclectic: Evolving Practices in Dance Training*, Urbana: University of Illinois Press.

Banks, Daniel (2015), 'Hip hop as pedagogy: Something from something', *Theatre Topics*, 25:3, pp. 243–59, http://login.ezproxy1.lib.asu.edu/login?url=https://www-proquest-com.ezproxy1.lib.asu.edu/scholarly-journals/hip-hop-as-pedagogy-something/ docview/1733454300/se-2?accountid=4485. Accessed 25 June 2021.

Banes, Sally (1994), 'On your fingertips: Writing dance criticism', *Writing Dancing in the Age of Postmodernism*, Hanover: UP of New England, pp. 24–43.

Bannon, Fiona (2018), *Considering Ethics in Dance, Theatre and Performance*, Cham: Springer International Publishing AG.

Barnett, Laura (2007), 'Portrait of the artist – Judith Jamison', *The Guardian*, 28 August, http:// www.guardian.co.uk/stage/2007/aug/28/dance. Accessed 12 June 2021.

Barnett, Robert (2010), telephone interview with author, 16 July.

Bartosik, Kimberly (2014), 'Foundations, funding and philanthropy', Report prepared for the Brooklyn Commune Project's research group, 'Philanthropy and funding within the perform-ing arts', January, https://brooklyncommune.org/the-bkcp-report/foundations-funding-and-philanthropy/. Accessed 27 June 2021.

'Basic Agreement Between American Guild of Musical Artists and San Francisco Ballet Association July 1, 2016 Through June 30, 2021' (2016–21).

Bass, Bernard M. and Riggio, Ronald (2014), *Transformational Leadership*, New York: Routledge.

Bauer, Claudia (2017), 'Krissy Keefer Dance Brigade: fierce, feminist and 40', *San Francisco Chronicle*, 15 January, https://www.sfchronicle.com/performance/article/Dance-Brigade-Fierce-feminist-and-40-10857947.php. Accessed 12 June 2021.

Beard, Katherine (2018), '8 Dance pros on the biggest mistakes new choreographers make', *Dance Spirit*, 21 June, https://www.dancespirit.com/mistakes-choreographers-make-2565625381. html. Accessed 12 June 2021.

Beardsley, Eleanor and Kheriji-Watts, Katie (2021), 'In France, performing artists are guaranteed unemployment income', *NPR All Things Considered*, 11 Jan, https://www.npr.org/2021/01/11/954994402/how-france-is-helping-its-artists-during-the-pandemic. Accessed 18 June 2021.

Becker, Carol (1990), *Social Responsibility and the Place of the Artist in Society*, Chicago: Lake View Press.

Becker, Carol (2002), *Surpassing the Spectacle: Global Transformations and the Changing Politics of Art*, Lanham: Rowman & Littlefield Publishers.

Behar, Ruth (1996), *The Vulnerable Observer: Anthropology That Breaks Your Heart*, Boston: Beacon Press.

Bennahum, Ninotchka (2017), 'Anna Halprin's radical body in motion', in N. Bennahum, W. Perron, B. Robertson and J. Rockwell (eds), *Radical Bodies: Anna Halprin, Simone Forti, and Yvonne Rainer in California and New York, 1955–1972*, Oakland: University of California Press, pp. 56–87.

Bennett, Arnold (1913), *Paris Nights, and Other Impressions of Places and People*, New York: G.H. Doran.

Bennett, Susan (1990), *Theatre Audiences: A Theory of Production and Reception*, London: Routledge.

Bermudez, Jose and Gardner, Sebastian (eds) (2006), *Art and Morality*, London: Routledge.

Biehl-Missal, Brigitte and Springborg, Claus (2015), 'Dance, organization, and leadership', *Organizational Aesthetics*, 5:1, pp. 1–10, https://oa.journals.publicknowledgeproject.org/index.php/oa/article/view/52. Accessed 26 June 2021.

Bing-Heidecker, Liora (2022), 'The Godseeker: Akim Volynsky and ballet as a Jewish quest', in N. M. Jackson, R. Pappas and T. Shapiro-Phim (eds), *The Oxford Handbook of Jewishness and Dance*, New York: Oxford University Press, pp. 311-336.

Bird, Dorothy and Greenberg, Joyce (1997), *Bird's Eye View: Dancing with Martha Graham and On Broadway*, Pittsburgh: University of Pittsburgh Press.

Blackwood, Michael (1988), *Retracing Steps: American Dance Since Postmodernism*, Michael Blackwood, Videocassette, New York: Michael Blackwood Productions.

Bocher, Barbara and Darius, Adam (2012), *The Cage: Dancing for Jerome Robbins and George Balanchine*, North Charleston: CreateSpace.

Bodensteiner, Kirsten A. (2000), 'Criticism refined: An analysis of selected dance criticism of Alan M. Kriegsman', Ph.D. thesis, Washington: American University.

Bolt, Barbara (2015), 'Beneficence and contemporary art: When aesthetic judgment meets ethical judgment', *Visual Methodologies*, 3:2, pp. 53–66, http://www.academia.edu/22587340/Beneficence_and_contemporary_art_when_aesthetic_judgment_meets_ethical_judgment. Accessed 25 June 2021.

Borrelli, Christopher (2013), 'Everybody's a curator', *Chicago Tribune*, 4 October, https://www.chicagotribune.com/entertainment/ct-xpm-2013-10-04-ct-ae-1006-borrelli-curation-20131004-story.html. Accessed 18 June 2021.

Borstel, John (n.d.), 'Liz Lerman dance exchange: An aesthetic of inquiry, an ethos of dialogue', *Animating Democracy*, https://animatingdemocracy.org/sites/default/files/documents/labs/dance_exchange_case_study.pdf. Accessed 15 June 2021.

Botham, Sho (2012), 'Ethical issues in the training and development of dance teachers in the private sector', doctoral dissertation, Brighton: University of Brighton.

Bowman, Wayne (2016), 'Artistry, ethics and citizenship', in D. J. Elliot, M. Silverman and W. D. Bowman (eds), *Artistic Citizenship: Artistry, Social Responsibility, and Ethical Praxis*, New York: Oxford University Press, pp. 59–80.

Boyer, Abel (1706), *The English Theophratus*, London: William Turner and John Chantry.

Brackenridge, Celia H. (2001), *Spoilsports: Understanding and Preventing Sexual Exploitation in Sport*, New York: Routledge.

Bresnahanm, Ali, Katan-Schmid, Einav and Houston, Sara (2020), 'Dance as Embodied Ethics', in L. Cull and A. Lagaay (eds), *The Routledge Companion to Performance Philosophy*, New York: Routledge, pp. 379–86.

Borzillo, Carrie (2011), 'Maksim Chmerkovskiy on "Dancing with the Stars," Blows Up at Len Goodman', *Entertainment Weekly*, 25 October, http://insidetv.ew.com/2011/10/25/dancing-with-the-stars-maks-chmerkovskiy-len-goodman/. Accessed 18 June 2021.

brown, adrienne maree (2017), *Emergent Strategy: Shaping Change, Changing Worlds*, Chico: AK Press.

Bryson, Norman (1997), 'Cultural studies and dance history', in J. Desmond (ed), *Meaning in Motion*, Durham: Duke University Press, pp. 55–78.

Buber, Martin (2020), *I and Thou*, New York: Clydesdale Press.

Buckle, Richard (1971), *Nijinsky*, New York: Simon and Schuster.

Buckroyd, Julia (n.d.), 'Ethics in dance: A debate yet to be held', *Ethics in Dance*, http://www.ethicsdance.co.uk/resources/downloads/ethics-in-dance---a-debate-yet-to-be-held.pdf. Accessed 16 June 2021.

Burns, James MacGregor (1978), *Leadership*, New York: HarperPerennial.

Calamoneri, Tanya, Dunagan, Colleen and McCarthy-Brown, Nyama (2020), 'Ethical dance pedagogy', *Journal of Dance Education*, 20:2, pp. 55–64, https://doi-org.ezproxy1.lib.asu.edu/10.1080/15290824.2019.1566607. Accessed 25 June 2021.

Candelario, Rosemary (2010), 'A manifesto for moving: Eiko & Koma's delicious movement workshops', *Theatre, Dance and Performance Training*, 1:1, pp. 88–100, https://doi.org/10.1080/19443920903432494. Accessed 25 June 2021.

Cappelle, Laura (2019), 'Five major dance critics stepped down last season. What does that mean for the future of the field?', *Dance Magazine*, 7 August, https://www.dancemagazine.com/5-major-dance-critics-put-down-the-pen/?rebelltitem=1#rebelltitem1. Accessed 18 June 2021.

CARE: Community Alliance for Research and Engagement (2009), *Principles and Guidelines for Community-University Research Partnerships*, New Haven: Yale University.

Carroll, Noël (2000), 'Art and ethical criticism: An overview of recent directions of research', *Ethics*, 110:2, pp. 350–87.

Castro, Yanira et al (2020), 'Creating new futures: Phase 1; working guidelines for ethics & equity in presenting dance & performance', 18 July, https://drive.google.com/drive/folders/1B6bbiFTBP1UAvt9qFchr7nLUndh7zorA. Accessed 27 June 2021.

Caute, David (2008), *The Dancer Defects: The Struggle for Cultural Supremacy During the Cold War*, Oxford: Oxford University Press.

Chan, Phil and Pazcoguin, Georgina (2019), 'A fresh cup of tea: How to make nutcracker more inclusive', *Dance Magazine*, 21 October, https://www.dancemagazine.com/chinese-nutcracker-2641019670.html?rebelltitem=3#rebelltitem3. Accessed 16 June 2021.

Cherbo, Joni Maya and Wyszomirski, Margaret J. (2000), *The Public Life of the Arts in America*, Piscataway: Rutgers University Press.

The Child's Bill of Rights in Dance (1998), 'NDEO', https://www.ndeo.org/content.aspx?page_id=22&club_id=893257&module_id=55658. Accessed 16 June 2021.

Chremos, Asimina and Catrambone, Kathy (2012), 'Working it', *Time Out Chicago*, 1 February, http://timeoutchicago.com/arts-culture/dance/37144/working-it. Accessed 16 June 2021.

Cochran, Mary (2010), personal communication, 16 June 2010 and 22 June 2010.

Cole, Babette (1999), *Bad Habits!* New York: Dial.

Congressional Record (1989), 'Comments on Andres Serrano by members of the United States Senate' (ed. Julie Van Camp), https://web.csulb.edu/~jvancamp/361_r7.html. Accessed 27 June 2021.

Conquet, Angela (2020), 'And then, do you remember, and now, what now … Farewell to an arts organ/isation', *Dancehouse Diary*, March.

Contra-Tiempo; Activist Dance Theater (n.d.), 'Mission & Values', *Contra-Tiempo*, https://www.contra-tiempo.org/what-we-do#mission. Accessed 21 June 2021.

Cramer, Franz Anton (2003), 'Dance criticism: Negotiating knowledge, taste, and power', *Sarma*, 2 March, http://sarma.be/docs/1037. Accessed 18 June 2021.

Crimmins, James E. (2021), 'Jeremy Bentham', in E. N. Zalta (ed.), *The Stanford Encyclopedia of Philosophy* (Summer Edition), https://plato.stanford.edu/archives/sum2021/entries/bentham/. Accessed 19 June 2021.

Croce, Arlene (1994), 'Discussing the undiscussable', *New Yorker*, 26 December, pp. 54–60.

Croft, Claire (2014), 'Feminist dance criticism and ballet', *Dance Chronicle*, 37:2, pp. 195–217.

Cunningham, Merce (1955), 'The impermanent art', 7 Arts No. 3, Colorado: Falcon's Wing Press, pp. 69–77, https://www.mercecunningham.org/the-work/writings/the-impermanent-art/. Accessed 21 June 2021.

Curran, Sean (2010), telephone interview with author, 19 July.

Daly, Ann (2002), *Critical Gestures: Writings on Dance and Culture*, Middletown: Wesleyan University Press.

Daly, Ann (2014), 'Applauding Isadora's Motto: Sans Limites', *Houston Woman Magazine*, May/June, p. 4.

Dance Magazine (2013), 'Burning question: Is *Nutcracker* racist?', *Dance Magazine*, 1 December, https://www.dancemagazine.com/burning_question_is_nutcracker_racist-2306921922.html. Accessed 26 June 2021.

Dance USA (2011), 'A critical change at The Village Voice', *Dance/USA*, 22 September, https://www.danceusa.org/ejournal/2011/09/22/a-change-at-the-village-voice. Accessed 2 July 2021.

Dance USA (2021), 'Equitable contracting', *Living document created by the The Dance/USA Joint Working Group*, https://www.danceusa.org/technical-and-standardization-documents. Accessed 27 June 2021.

Dancers Forum (2002), 'The dancers forum compact', *For a Working Artistic Relationship Between Dancers and Choreographers*, https://s3.amazonaws.com/NYFA_WebAssets/Pictures/1d633b67-07c1-403c-aa78-8132f0fe9825.pdf. Accessed 23 June 2021.

Daniel, Yvonne (2005), *Dancing Wisdom: Embodied Knowledge in Haitian Vodou, Cuban Yoruba, and Bahian Candomblé*, Chicago: University of Illinois Press.

Danto, Arthur (1964), 'The artworld', *The Journal of Philosophy*, 61:19, pp: 571–84.

Davida, Dena (2021), personal correspondence, 29 September 2021.

Davida, Dena, Gabriels, Jane, Hudon, Véronique and Pronovost, Marcel (eds) (2019), *Curating Live Arts: Critical Perspectives, Essays, and Conversations on Theory and Practice*, New York: Berghahn.

Dawkins, Gemma (2010), 'Dancing with risk: Risk-taking as a performance practice in contemporary dance', Honours thesis, Edith Cowan University, https://ro.ecu.edu.au/theses_hons/1177. Accessed 16 June 2021.

De Mille, Agnes (1992), *Martha: The Life and Work of Martha Graham*, London: Hutchinson.

DeFrantz, Thomas F. (2004), 'The black beat made visible: Hip hop dance and body power', in A. Lepecki (ed.), *Of the Presence of the Body: Essays on Dance and Performance Theory*, Middletown: Wesleyan University Press, pp. 64–81.

DeFrantz, Thomas F. (2005), 'African American dance – Philosophy, aesthetics, and "Beauty"', *Topoi*, 24:1, pp. 93–102, https://doi.org/10.1007/s11245-004-4165-7. Accessed 17 June 2021.

DeFrantz, Thomas F. and McGregor, Paloma (eds), Proceedings from the conference, 'Configurations in motion: Performance curation and communities of color', North Carolina: Duke University, June 27–28, 2015. Hosted by SLIPPAGE: Performance/Culture/Technology at Duke University.

Denby, Edwin (1998), *Dance Writings and Poetry*, New Haven: Yale University Press.

Desmond, Jane (1991), 'Dancing out the difference: Cultural imperialism and Ruth St. Denis's "Radha" of 1906', *Signs: Journal of Women in Culture and Society*, 17:1, pp. 28–49, https://www.jstor.org/stable/3174444. Accessed 25 June 2021.

Dorfman, David (2012), telephone conversation with the author, 21 July.

Drybrugh, Jamieson (2019), 'Location of possibilities: Exploring dance technique pedagogy through transformation and care', *Journal of Dance Education*, 19:3, pp. 89–97.

Duncan, Isadora (2013), *My Life*, New York: Liveright Publishing Corporation.

Durkin, Kieran (2014), 'Anti-humanism: A radical humanist defense', in *The Radical Humanism of Erich Fromm: Critical Political Theory and Radical Practice*, New York: Palgrave Macmillan, pp. 129–64.

Dyer, Becky and Löytönen, Teija (2012), 'Engaging dialogue: Co-creating communities of collaborative inquiry', *Research in Dance Education*, 13:1, April, pp. 121–47.

Eaton, Marcia Muelder (2001), *Merit, Aesthetic and Ethical*, Oxford: Oxford University Press.

Eddy, Martha (2009), 'A brief history of somatic practices and dance: Historical development of the field of somatic education and its relationship to dance', *Journal of Dance and Somatic Practices*, 1:1, pp. 5–27.

Engster, Daniel (2007), 'The nature of caring and the obligation to care', *The Heart of Justice: Care ethics and Political Theory*, Oxford University Press, 1 May, Oxford Scholarship Online, https://www.oxfordscholarship.com/view/10.1093/acprof:oso/9780199214358.001.0001/acprof-9780199214358-chapter-2. Accessed 28 May 2020.

Etchells, Tim (1999), 'Shirtology, texts and interviews', *RB Jerome Bel*, January, http://www.jeromebel.fr/index.php?p=5&lg=2&cid=187. Accessed 29 June 2021.

'Ethical Journalism' (n.d.), https://www.nytimes.com/editorial-standards/ethical-journalism.html#rulesForSpecializedDepartments. Accessed 18 June 2021.

Evans, Richard (2010), 'Entering upon novelty: Policy and funding issues for a new era in the arts', *GIA Reader*, 21:3 (Fall), http://www.giarts.org/article/entering-upon-novelty. Accessed 17 June 2021.

Fayette, James (2010), telephone interview with author, 8 July.

Fisher, Jennifer (1998), 'The annual *Nutcracker*: A participant-oriented, contextualized study of *The Nutcracker* ballet as it has evolved into a Christmas ritual in the United States and Canada', Ph.D. thesis, Riverside: University of California, Riverside.

Fisher, Jennifer (2003), '"Arabian coffee" in the land of the sweets', *Dance Research Journal*, 35, pp. 146–63.

Fisher, Jennifer (2011), personal correspondence with author, 17 July.

Fitzgerald, Mary (2008), 'Community dance: Dance Arizona Repertory Theatre as a vehicle of cultural emancipation', in N. M. Jackson and T. Shapiro-Phim (eds), *Dance, Human Rights, and Social Justice: Dignity in Motion*, Lanham: Scarecrow Press, pp. 256–69.

Flanders Today (2018), 'Twenty women accuse Jan Fabre of sexual harassment', *The Bulletin*, 14 September, https://www.thebulletin.be/twenty-women-accuse-jan-fabre-sexual-harassment. Accessed 23 June 2021.

Forsyth, Sondra (2018), 'BWW review: Juilliard Spring Dances 2018, as superb as ever following Larry Rhodes' retirement', *Broadway World*, 26 March, https://www.broadwayworld.com/bwwdance/article/BWW-Review-Juilliard-Spring-Dances-2018-as-Superb-as-Ever-Following-Larry-Rhodes-Retirement-20180326. Accessed 21 June 2021.

Fortin, Sylvie (2008), *Danse et Santé*, Quebec City: Presses de l'Universite du Quebec.

Foster, Kenneth (2010), 'Thriving in an uncertain world: Arts presenting change and the new realities', https://www.researchgate.net/publication/281557619_Thriving_in_an_Uncertain_Wo rld_Arts_Presenting_Change_and_the_New_realities. Accessed 27 December 2021.

Foster, Susan (2010), 'Dancing bodies', *Theater*, 40:1, Winter, pp. 24–29.

Foucault, Michel (1975), *Discipline and Punish: The Birth of the Prison*, New York: Random House.

Franko, Mark (2006), 'Dance and the political: States of exception', *Dance Research Journal*, 38:1&2, pp. 3–18.

Gan, Natalie Tin Yin and Oke, Emily Dundas (eds) (2020), *Configurations in Motion: Performance Curations and Communities of Colour*, 4th iteration. Booklet publication and online series sponsored on the Dance West Network, Canada, https://dancewest.net/projects/performance-curation-projects. Accessed 17 June 2021.

Garafola, Lynn (2010), 'Making dances: Process and practice in Diaghilev's Ballets Russes', in K. Fenbock and N. Haitzinger (eds), *Denkfiguren – Performatives zwischen Bewegen, Schreiben und Erfinden: Für Claudia Jeschke*, Munchen [Munich]: 300 Seitan, pp. 77–93.

Gere, David (ed.) (1995), *Looking Out: Perspectives on Dance and Criticism in a Multicultural World*, New York: Schirmer Books.

Ghekiere, Ilse (2020), '#Metoo, herstory in dance – On activism, solidarity and precision', *Kunstenpunt*, 31 March, https://www.kunsten.be/nu-in-de-kunsten/metoo-herstory-in-dance-on-activism-solidarity-and-precision/. Accessed 15 June 2021.

Giguere, Miriam (2019), 'Dance trends: Choreographic plagiarism: When does borrowing become stealing?', *Dance Education in Practice*, 5:1, pp. 29–32.

Gilligan, Carol (1993), *In a Different Voice: Psychological Theory and Women's Development*, Cambridge: Harvard University Press.

Gingrich, Newt (2001), 'Cutting cultural funding: A reply', *Time*, 24 June, http://content.time.com/time/magazine/article/0,9171,134577,00.html. Accessed 18 June 2021.

Giuliani, Massimo (2003), *Centaur in Auschwitz: Reflections on Primo Levi's Thinking*, Lanham: Lexington Books.

Glass, Aaron (2004), 'The thin edge of the wedge: Dancing around the potlatch ban, 1921–1951', in N. M. Jackson (ed.), *Right to Dance: Dancing for Rights*, Banff: The Banff Centre Press, pp. 51–82.

Glowacka, Dorota and Boos, Stephen (eds) (2002), *Between Ethics and Aesthetics: Crossing the Boundaries*, Albany: State University of New York Press.

Goad, Kimberly (1998), 'Culture beauties and the beast: The sex scandal that nearly destroyed the Fort Worth Dallas Ballet', *Culture Beauties and the Beast*, October, https://www.dmagazine.com/publications/d-magazine/1998/october/culture-beauties-and-the-beast/. Accessed 16 June 2021.

Goldman, Danielle (2010), *I Want to be Ready: Improvisation as a Practice of Freedom*, Ann Arbor: University of Michigan.

Gordon, Suzanne (1983), *Off Balance: The Real World of Ballet*, New York: Pantheon Books.

Gordon, Suzanne (2010), 'Starving for their art', *The Boston Globe*, 12 December, http://www.boston.com/bostonglobe/editorial_opinion/oped/articles/2010/12/12/starving_for_their_art/. Accessed 5 January 2021.

Gose, Rebecca and Siemietkowski, Grace (2018), 'A collaboration in care: Re-visioning teacher-student dialogue in dance education', *International Journal of Education and the Arts*, 19:14, pp. 1–36, http://www.ijea.org/v19n14/. Accessed 25 January 2022.

Gottschild, Brenda Dixon (2003), *The Black Dancing Body*, New York: Palgrave Macmillan.

Gottschild, Brenda Dixon (1998), *Digging the Africanist Presence in American Concert Dance*, Westport: Praeger.

Government of Canada (2018), 'Panel on research ethics, TCPS 2 – Chapter 10: Qualitative research', *Panel on Research Ethics*, https://ethics.gc.ca/eng/tcps2-eptc2_2018_chapter10-chapitre10.html. Accessed 25 June 2021.

Graves, James Bau (2004), *Cultural Democracy: The Arts, Community and the Public Purpose*, Champaign: University of Illinois Press.

Gray, John (2012), 'A point of view: Are tyrants good for art?', BBC, 10 August, https://www.bbc.com/news/magazine-19202527. Accessed 15 June 2021.

Green, Hank (2016), 'Crash course: Ethics', YouTube, 5 December, https://www.youtube.com/watch?v=PrvtOWEXDIQ. Accessed 21 June 2021.

Green, Jill (1993), 'Fostering creativity through movement and body awareness practices: A postpositivist investigation into the relationship between somatics and the creative process', doctoral dissertation, Columbus: The Ohio State University.

Green, Jill (2001), 'Socially constructed bodies in American dance classrooms', *Research in Dance Education*, 2:2, pp. 155–73, https://www-tandfonline-com.ezproxy1.lib.asu.edu/doi/abs/10.1080/14647890120100782.

Green, Jill (2004a), 'Docile bodies: A threat or a necessity in educating dancers', *Proceedings International Dance Conference, Ethics and Politics Embodied in Dance*, Theatre Academy Helsinki, 9–12 December, pp. 38–42, http://citeseerx.ist.psu.edu/viewdoc/download?doi=10.1.1.453.792&rep=rep1&type=pdf. Accessed 16 June 2021.

Green, Jill (2004b), 'Creativity and management in dance institutions: A moral dilemma', *Proceedings International Dance Conference, Ethics and Politics Embodied in Dance*, Theatre Academy Helsinki, pp. 43–48, http://citeseerx.ist.psu.edu/viewdoc/download?doi=10.1.1.453.792&rep=rep1&type=pdf. Accessed 16 June 2021.

Greene, Maxine (1978), *Landscapes of Learning*, New York: Teachers College Press.

Greene, Maxine (1988), *The Dialectic of Freedom*, New York: Teachers College Press.

Greenleaf, Robert (1973) *The Servant as Leader*, South Orange: Greenleaf Publishing Center.

Groover, D. L. (2010), 'Breath made visible', *Houston Press*, 1 July, https://www.houstonpress.com/arts/breath-made-visible-6578416. Accessed 18 June 2021.

Guilbert, Laure (2012), *Danser Avec le 3e Reich: Les Danseurs Modernes Sous le Nazisme*, Bruxelles: A. Versaille.

Gummow, Jodie (2014), 'Culturally impoverished: US NEA spends 1/40th of what Germany does out for arts per capita', *AlterNet*, 5 February, https://www.alternet.org/2014/02/culturally-impoverished-us-nea-spends-140th-what-germany-doles-out-arts-capita/. Accessed 18 June 2021.

Gutierrez, Miguel (2002), 'The perfect dance critic', *Movement Research Journal* #25, Fall, https://www.miguelgutierrez.org/writing/2019/6/20/the-perfect-dance-critic. Accessed 18 June 2021.

Hamera, Judith (2007), *Dancing Communities: Performance, Difference and Connection in the Global City*, New York: Palgrave Macmillan.

Hampson, Christopher (2018), 'Behavior in the ballet world: A statement from Scottish Ballet CEO/Artistic Director Christopher Hampson', *Scottish Ballet Website*, 5 March, https://www.scottishballet.co.uk/articles/behaviour-in-the-ballet-world. Accessed 22 June 2021.

Hanna, Judith Lynn (2012), *Naked Truth: Strip Clubs, Democracy and a Christian Right*, Austin: University of Texas Press.

Harari, Dror (2009), 'Risk in performance: Facing the future', *Theatre Research International*, 34:2, pp. 173–79.

Hardman, Alun and Jones, Carwyn (2011), *The Ethics of Sports Coaching*, London: Routledge.

Hargreaves, Andy (1994), *Changing Teachers, Changing Times: Teachers' Work and Culture in the Postmodern Age*, New York: Teachers College Press.

Hayden, Melissa (1981), *Dancer to Dancer: Advice for Today's Dancer*, Garden City: Anchor.

Hayes, John (2018), *The Theory and Practice of Change Management*, New York: Palgrave.

Heiber, Nora (2020), personal communication, 3 August.

Hess, Felix (2020), 'Injury in PopAction', *Streb*, 13 November, https://www.facebook.com/watch/?v=218832333004373. Accessed 25 June 2021.

Hirdman, Anja Maria (2011), 'Tears on the screen: Bodily emotionalism in reality-TV', *Observatorio*, 5:1, pp. 19–33.

Hirsch, David H. (1991), *The Deconstruction of Literature: Criticism after Auschwitz*, Providence: Brown University Press.

Hirsh, David (2018), *Contemporary Left Antisemitism*, London: Routledge.

Hisrich, Matthew (2018), 'An examination of change management strategies contributing to a work climate supportive of ethical employee behavior and decisions in US colleges', doctoral dissertation, Adelphi: University of Maryland University College.

Hitlin, Stephen (2008), *Moral Selves, Evil Selves: The Social Psychology of Conscience*, New York: Palgrave MacMillan.

Hodgins, Paul (2019), 'Hodgins: Is government spending for the arts the whole story?', *Voice of OC*, 25 July, https://voiceofoc.org/2019/07/is-government-spending-for-the-arts-the-whole-story/. Accessed 27 June 2021.

Horwitz, Andy (2011), 'Anne Teresa de Keersmaeker vs. Beyonce', *Culturebot*, 24 October, https://www.culturebot.org/2011/10/11496/anne-teresa-de-keersmaeker-vs-beyonce/. Accessed 16 June 2021.

Horwitz, Andy (2012), 'Talking about dance criticism and the changing world', *Culturebot*, 4 July, https://www.culturebot.org/2012/07/13868/talking-about-dance-criticism-and-the-changing-world/. Accessed 18 June 2021.

Horwitz, Andy (2014), 'Considering Alastair, questioning realness', 19 January, https://www.culturebot.org/2014/01/20493/considering-alastair-questioning-realness/. Accessed 27 June 2021.

Houston, Sarah (2004), 'Changing lives? Ethics in community dance practice', *Proceedings International Dance Conference, Ethics and Politics Embodied in Dance*, Theatre Academy Helsinki, p. 59, http://citeseerx.ist.psu.edu/viewdoc/download?doi=10.1.1.453.792&rep=rep1&type=pdf. Accessed 16 June 2021.

Hytone, David (2015), 'Episode 25', *The Makers Podcast*, 25 June, https://themakers.libsyn.com. Accessed 27 June 2021.

ICA/Boston (Institute of Contemporary Art/Boston) (2014), http://www.icaboston.org/programs/performance/trajal-harrell/. Accessed 15 March 2014.

Ingber, Judith Brin (2011), *Seeing Jewish and Israeli Dance*, Detroit: Wayne State University Press.

Jackson, George (2014), 'Pleasure examined', *Dance Chronicle*, 37:2, pp. 169–77.

Jackson, Naomi (ed.) (2004), *Right to Dance: Dancing for Rights*, Banff: Banff Centre for Press.

Jackson, Naomi (2014), 'Ecology, dance presenting, and social justice', in G. Cools and P. Gielen (eds), *The Ethics of Art: Ecological Turns in the Performing Arts*, Amsterdam: Valiz, pp. 197–226.

Jackson, Naomi (2016), 'Moving comfortably between continuity and disruption: Somatics and urban dance as embodied responses to civic responsibility', in D. Elliott, M. Silverman and W. Bowman (eds), *Artistic Citizenship: Artistry, Social Responsibility, and Ethical Praxis*, New York: Oxford University Press, pp. 163–88.

Jackson, Naomi (2019), 'Curatorial discourse and equity: Tensions in contemporary dance presenting in the United States', in D. Davida, M. Pronovost, V. Hudon and J. Gabriels (eds), *Curating Live Arts: Critical Perspectives, Essays, and Conversations on Theory and Practice*, New York: Berghahn Books, pp. 101–13.

Jackson, Naomi and Shapiro-Phim, Toni (eds) (2008), *Dance, Human Rights, and Social Justice: Dignity in Motion*, Lanham: Scarecrow Press.

Jamison, Judith (2007), 'To thine own self be true', *NPR*, This I Believe, 2 April, https://www.npr.org/templates/story/story.php?storyId=9249892#. Accessed 15 June 2021.

Järvinen, Hanna (2004), 'Dance technique and the natural genius', *Proceedings International Dance Conference, Ethics and Politics Embodied in Dance*, Theatre Academy Helsinki, pp. 66–85, http://citeseerx.ist.psu.edu/viewdoc/download?doi=10.1.1.453.792&rep=rep1&type=pdf. Accessed June 16 2021.

Jin, K. Gregory, Drozdenko, Ronald and DeLoughy, Sara (2013), 'The role of corporate value clusters in ethics, social responsibility, and performance: A study of financial professionals and implications for the financial meltdown', *Journal of Business Ethics*, 112:1, pp. 15–24.

Johnson, Elizabeth (2020), email exchange with author, 20 June.

Johnston, Jill (1998), *Marmalade Me*, Middletown: Wesleyan University Press.

Jones, Bill T. (2000), 'Graduation speech – Bill T. Jones', *Swathmore*, 29 May, https://www.swarthmore.edu/past-commencements/graduation-speech-bill-t-jones. Accessed 14 June 2021.

Jowitt, Deborah (2004), *Jerome Robbins: His Life, His Theater, His Dance*, New York: Simon & Schuster.

Jowitt, Deborah (2006), 'Getting it', *The Village Voice*, 21 February, https://www.villagevoice.com/2006/02/21/getting-it/. Accessed 18 June 2021.

Jowitt, Deborah (2011), personal correspondence, 1 July.

Jowitt, Deborah, Alston, Richard, Kain, Karen, Kylian, Jiri and Philp, Richard (2001), *Not Just Any Body: Advancing Health, Well-Being and Excellence in Dance and Dancers*, Owen Sound: Ginger Press.

Kackman, Michael, Binfield, Marnie, Thomas Payne, Matthew, Perlman, Allison and Sebok, Bryan (eds) (2010), *Flow TV: Television in the Age of Media Convergence*, New York: Routledge.

Kampeas, Ron (2020), 'American Jews: Are you white?', *The Jerusalem Post*, 8 April, https://www.jpost.com/diaspora/american-jews-are-you-white-624072. Accessed 18 June 2021.

Kant, Marion (2008), 'Practical imperative–German dance, dancers, and Nazi politics', in N. M. Jackson and T. Shapiro-Phim (eds), *Dance, Human Rights, and Social Justice: Dignity in Motion*, Lanham: Scarecrow Press, pp. 5–19.

Kant, Marion (2022), 'Then in what sense are you a Jewish artist? Conflicts of the "emancipated" self', in N. M. Jackson, R. Pappas and T. Shapiro-Phim (eds), *The Oxford Handbook of Jewishness and Dance*, New York: Oxford University Press, pp. 288–310.

Kant, Marion and Karina, Lilian (2004), *Hitler's Dancers: German Modern Dance and the Third Reich*, New York: Berghahn Books.

Katan-Schmid, Einav (2020), *The British Journal of Aesthetics*, 60:1, January, pp. 102–05.

Kaufmann, Sarah (2011), 'Beyonce: "Countdown" video and the art of stealing', *Washington Post*, 18 November, https://www.washingtonpost.com/lifestyle/style/beyonce-countdown-video-and-the-art-of-stealing/2011/11/15/gIQAj0WbYN_story.html. Accessed 16 June 2021.

Kaufmann, Sarah (2018), 'Why this is the moment for dancers to behave badly', *Washington Post*, 2 March, https://www.washingtonpost.com/entertainment/theater_danc/why-this-is-the-moment-for-dancers-to-behave-badly/2018/02/28/3ea4724a-1c23-11e8-8a2c-1a6665f59e95_story.html. Accessed 16 June 2021.

Kealiinohomoku, Joann W. (1981), 'Ethical considerations for choreographers, ethnologists and white knights', *Journal of the Association of Graduate Dance Ethnologists*, 5, pp. 10–23.

Kelley, Brandi Dawn (2019), 'Contesting bodies: Former competitive dancers' perceptions of their own bodies', Ph.D. thesis, Irvine: UC Irvine.

Kelly, Deirdre (2012), *Ballerina: Sex, Scandal, and Suffering Behind the Symbol of Perfection*, Greystone: Douglas & McIntyre.

Kelso, Paula T. (2003), 'Behind the curtain: The body, control, and ballet', *Edwardsville Journal of Sociology*, 3:2, pp. 1–11.

Kennett-Hensel, Pamela A. and Payne, Dinah M. (2018), 'Guiding principles for ethical change management', *Journal of Business and Management*, 24:2, pp. 19–45.

Kenny, Carolyn and Fraser, Tina Ngaroimata (eds) (2012), *Living Indigenous Leadership: Native Narratives on Building Strong Communities*, Vancouver: UBC Press.

Kim, Diana (2005), 'The literalists', *Fourth Wall*, Walker, 8 September, https://walkerart.org/magazine/the-literalists. Accessed 1 July 2021.

Kimitch, Benjamin Akio (2021), 'Commensurate with experience', *Movement Research Performance Journal*, 55, June, https://benjaminakio.medium.com/commensurate-with-experience-39a6e5c13d2a. Accessed 3 July 2021.

King, Alonzo (2016), 'The importance of dance education by Alonzo King', 5 June, https://www.npr.org/templates/story/story.php?storyId=9249892#. Accessed 15 June 2021.

King, Alonzo (2017), 'Art thought, by Alonzo King', 16 May, https://www.npr.org/templates/story/story.php?storyId=9249892#. Accessed 15 June 2021.

Kirby, Michael (1974), 'Criticism: Four faults', *The Drama Review: TDR*, pp. 59–68.

Klein, Shelley (2018), 'Eighty years ago, both Sigmund Freud and the "Degenerate" art exhibition came to Longon', *Frieze*, 30 August, https://frieze.com/article/eighty-years-ago-both-sigmund-freud-and-degenerate-art-exhibition-came-london. Accessed 15 June 2021.

Koff, Susan (2004), 'Ethics of being a dance educator', *Proceedings International Dance Conference, Ethics and Politics Embodied in Dance*, Theatre Academy Helsinki, pp. 86–90, http://citeseerx.ist.psu.edu/viewdoc/download?doi=10.1.1.453.792&rep=rep1&type=pdf. Accessed June 16 2021.

Kourlas, Gia (2012), 'Laurie Berg and Liliana Dirks-Goodman talk about AUNTS dance group', *TimeOut New York*, 15 July, https://www.timeout.com/newyork/dance/laurie-berg-and-liliana-dirks-goodman-talk-about-aunts-dance-group. Accessed 18 June 2021.

Kramer, Kenneth Paul (2003), *Martin Buber's I and Thou: Practicing Living Dialogue*, New York: Paulist Press.

Kraut, Anthea (2016), *Choreographing Copyright: Race, Gender, and Intellectual Property in American Dance*, New York: Oxford University Press.

Kriegsman, Alan M. (1982), 'Beyond stillness', *Washington Post*, 30 November, https://www.washingtonpost.com/archive/lifestyle/1982/11/30/beyond-stillness/8b4faf14-8f7e-46fb-8ced-3297940e7891/. Accessed 26 June 2021.

Kwan, SanSan (2017), 'When is contemporary dance?', *Dance Research Journal*, 49:3, pp. 38–52.

Lakes, Robin (2005), 'The messages behind the methods: The authoritarian pedagogical legacy in western concert dance technique training and rehearsals', *Arts Education Policy Review*, 106:5, pp. 3–20.

Lakes, Robin (2008), 'The hidden authoritarian roots in western concert dance', in N. Jackson and T. Shapiro-Phim (eds), *Dance, Human Rights, and Social Justice: Dignity in Motion*, Lanham: Scarecrow Press, pp. 109–30.

Latemore, Greg (2016), 'An ethical approach to teaching organizational change management', in K. Ogunyemi (ed.), *Teaching Ethics Across the Management Curriculum, Volume II: Principles and Applications*, New York: Business Expert Press, pp. 113–34.

Lawrence, D. H. (1995), *Women in Love*, New York: New American Library.

Lawrence, Greg (2001), *Dance with Demons: The Life of Jerome Robbins*, New York: G. P. Putnam.

Lepecki, A. (2007), 'Machines, faces, neurons: Towards an ethics of dance', *The Drama Review*, 51:3, pp. 118–23.

Lerman, Liz (1993), 'Toward a process for critical response', *High Performance*, 16:4, pp. 46–49, https://counterpulse.org/liz-lermans-critical-response/. Accessed 1 July 2021.

Lerman, Liz (2011a), *Hiking the Horizontal*, Middletown: Wesleyan University Press.

Lerman, Liz (2011b), interview with author, 14 July.

Lerman, Liz and Borstel, John (2003), *Liz Lerman's Critical Response Process: A Method For Getting Useful Feedback on Anything You Make, From Dance to Dessert*, Takoma Park: Liz Lerman Dance Exchange.

Levy, Clifford J. (2010), 'Young Americans embrace rigors of the Bolshoi', *The New York Times*, 31 May, https://www.nytimes.com/2010/06/01/arts/dance/01bolshoi.html. Accessed 15 June 2021.

Lewis, Jamal (2016), 'The ugly side of shade culture', *Fader*, 30 June, https://www.thefader.com/2016/06/30/the-ugly-side-of-shade-culture. Accessed 3 July 2021.

Livingston, Jennie (1990), *Paris Is Burning*, Off White Productions Inc.

Lockyer, Tonya (2015), Skype interview with author, 11 May.

Loney, Glenn (1983), 'The legacy of Jack Cole: Rebel with a cause, part nine', *Dance Magazine*, November, pp. 75–80.

Long, Suzanna and Spurlock, David G. (2008), 'Motivation and stakeholder acceptance in technology-driven change management: Implications for the engineering manager', *Engineering Management Journal*, 20:2, pp. 30–36.

Löytönen, Teija (2008), 'Emotions in the everyday life of a dance school: Articulating unspoken values', *Dance Research Journal*, 40:1, pp. 17–30.

Macaulay, Alastair (2010), 'Timeless alchemy, even when no one is dancing', *The New York Times*, 28 November, https://www.nytimes.com/2010/11/29/arts/dance/29nutcracker.html. Accessed 30 June 2021.

Macaulay, Alastair (2011), personal correspondence with author, 2 July.

Mainwaring, Madison (2015), 'The death of the American dance critic', *The Atlantic*, 6 August, https://www.theatlantic.com/entertainment/archive/2015/08/american-dance-critic/399908/. Accessed 19 June 2021.

Malnig, Julie, Nugent, Ann and Satin, Leslie (2009), 'Dialogues: Writing dance', *Dance Research Journal*, 42:2, Winter, pp. 89–95.

Malzacher, Florian, Tupajić, Tea and Zanki, Petra (eds) (2010), *Frakcija #55*, Special Issue: 'Curating Performing Arts'.

Mandala, Sumana (2020), 'Traditional challenges, challenging tradition: Helping students find agency in Bharata-Natyam at the junction of Ancient Indian thought, somatic practices & feminist pedagogy', *Journal of Dance Education*, 21:2, pp. 1–11.

Manning, Frankie and Millman, Cynthia R. (2007), *Frankie Manning: Ambassador of Lindy Hop*, Philadelphia: Temple University Press.

Manning, Susan (2006), *Modern Dance, Negro Dance: Race in Motion*, Minnesota: University of Minnesota Press.

Margalit, Avishai (1996), *The Decent Society* (trans. N. Goldblum), Boston: Harvard University Press.

Marshall, Alex (2020), 'Royal ballet suspends choreographer over sexual misconduct claims', *The New York Times*, 30 January, https://www.nytimes.com/2020/01/30/arts/dance/royal-ballet-liam-scarlett-suspended.html. Accessed 14 June 2021.

Noey, Christopher (2019), 'Martha@Mother', Vimeo, https://vimeo.com/260816061. Accessed 12 April 2022.

Mattingly, K. (2019), 'Digital dance criticism: Screens as choreographic apparatus', *The International Journal of Screendance*, 10, https://screendancejournal.org/article/view/6524/5225#fnref39. Accessed 1 July 2021.

Maynard, Olga (1959), *The American Ballet*, Philadelphia: Macrae Company.

McCarthy-Brown, Nyama (2017), *Dance Pedagogy for a Diverse World: Culturally Relevant Teaching in Theory, Research and Practice*, Jefferson: McFarland & Company, Inc., Publishers.

McDonagh, Don, Croce, Arlene and Dorris, George (1969), 'A conversation with Edwin Denby: Part 2', *Ballet Review*, 2:6, pp. 32–45.

McMains, Juliet (2021), 'Fostering a culture of consent in social dance communities', *Journal of Dance Education*, pp. 1–9, https://doi.org/10.1080/15290824.2020.1851693. Accessed 26 June 2021.

Mehra, Samantha (2010), 'Dance, culture and the printed word: A call for the cosmopolitan dance critic', *Forum for Modern Language Studies*, 46:4, pp. 431–40.

Miller, Alice (1990), *For Your Own Good: Hidden Cruelty in Child-Rearing and the Roots of Violence*, New York: Farrar, Straus and Giroux.

Miller, Sam (2012), personal interview with author, 7 August.

Miller Jr., Courtney and Stevenson, Tim (2010), *The Business of Dance: Everything You Need to Know About the Hollywood Dance Industry*, Miller/Stevenson Publishing.

Mission Statement (2022), TURBA, p. 2.

Money, Keith (1982), *Anna Pavlova: Her Life and Art*, New York: Alfred A. Knopf.

Monroe, Raquel L. (2011), '"I don't want to do African… What about my technique?": Transforming dancing places into spaces in the academy', *The Journal of Pan African Studies*, 4:6, pp. 38–55.

Moore, Darnell L. and Davis II, Wade (2013), 'Tongues untied: Shade culture – Throwing shade, reflecting light', *Huffpost*, 2 February, https://www.huffpost.com/entry/tongues-untied-shade-culture----throwing-shade-reflecting-light_b_2945321. Accessed 18 June 2021.

Morgan, Kathryn (2020), 'REAL TALK: My "Today Show" appearance | body image & mental health in ballet', YouTube, 29 February, https://www.youtube.com/watch?v=lD0xB8VNzSk. Accessed 20 June 2021.

Murphy, Jacqueline Shea (2007), *The People Have Never Stopped Dancing: Native American Modern Dance Histories*, Minneapolis: University of Minnesota Press.

NDEO (1998), 'The child's bill of rights in dance', National Dance Education Organization, https://www.ndeo.org/content.aspx?page_id=22&club_id=893257&module_id=55658. Accessed 22 June 2021.

NEA (2018), 'U.S. trends in arts attendance and literary reading: 2002–2017: A first look at results from the 2017 survey of public participation in the arts', September, Washington: NEA Office of Research & Analysis, https://www.arts.gov/sites/default/files/2017-sppapreviewREV-sept2018.pdf. Accessed 27 June 2021.

NEA Chronology (1993), *The Christian Science Monitor*, 6 August, https://www.csmonitor.com/1993/0806/06131.html. Accessed 27 June 2021.

Nelson, Robin (2013), *Practice as Research in the Arts: Principles, Protocols, Pedagogies, Resistances*, New York: Palgrave Macmillan.

NIH (2011), *Principles of Community Engagement, Second Edition*, June, https://www.atsdr.cdc.gov/communityengagement/index.html. Accessed 25 June 2021.

Noddings, Nel (2013), *Caring: A Relational Approach to Ethics and Moral Education*, Berkeley: University of California Press.

OED (Oxford English Dictionary) (2019), 'criticism, n.', December, https://www-oed-com.ezproxy1.lib.asu.edu/view/Entry/44598?redirectedFrom=Criticism#eid. Accessed 2 July 2021.

OED (Oxford English Dictionary) (2020), 'critic, n.1', June, https://www-oed-com.ezproxy1.lib.asu.edu/view/Entry/44587?rskey=R1j4v7&result=1#eid. Accessed 2 July 2021.

O'Toole, Sean (2016), 'My true country is my body', *Frieze*, 23 November, https://www.frieze.com/article/my-true-country-my-body. Accessed 16 June 2021.

Pakes, Anna (n.d.), 'Knowing through dance-making: Choreography, practical knowledge and practice-as-research', https://pure.roehampton.ac.uk/ws/portalfiles/portal/816200/Knowing_through_dance_making_revised_Mar_2016.pdf. Accessed 16 June 2021.

Papan-Matin, Firoozeh (2009), 'The case of Mohammad Khordadian, an Iranian male dancer', *Iranian Studies*, 42:1, pp. 127–38.

Paterson, Vincent (2021), email correspondence with author, 27 May.

Peek, Ella (n.d.), 'Ethical criticism of art', *Internet Encyclopedia of Philosophy*, https://iep.utm.edu/art-eth/. Accessed 1 July 2021.

Performa Magazine (2007), 'Why dance in the art world? Jérôme Bel and RoseLee Goldberg in Conversation', https://performamagazine.tumblr.com/post/31462096878/why-dance-in-the-artworld-j.r.me-bel-and-roselee. Accessed 29 June 2021.

Perlstein, Talia, Tabull, Reuven and Sagee, Rachel (2022), 'Believing body, dancing body: Dance and faith in the religious sector in Israel', in N. M. Jackson, R. Pappas and T. Shapiro-Phim (eds), *The Oxford Handbook of Jewishness and Dance*, New York: Oxford University Press, pp. 191–215.

Pethybridge, Ruth (2014), 'Relative proximity: Reaching towards an ethics of touch in cross-gen-erational dance practice', *Journal of Dance & Somatic Practices*, 6:2, pp. 175–87.

Plank, Tonya (2007), 'Don't listen to Alastair Macaulay! or, rather, do listen to him, but listen to everyone else as well!!!', *Tonya Plank Mad Hot Dance Romance*, 5 July, https://www.tonyaplank.com/2007/07/05/dont-listen-to-alastair-macaulay-or-rather-do-listen-to-him-but-listen-to-everyone-else-as-well/. Accessed 18 June 2021.

Pogrebin, Robin (2004), 'Exuding Balanchine's essence', *The New York Times*, 23 April, https://www.nytimes.com/2004/04/23/movies/exuding-balanchine-s-essence.html?scp=2&sq=Balanchine,%20messiah&st=cse&pagewanted=3. Accessed 21 June 2021.

Pogrebin, Robin (2018), 'Toning down Asian stereotypes to make "The Nutcracker" fit the times', *The New York Times*, 13 November, https://www.nytimes.com/2018/11/13/arts/dance/nutcracker-chinese-tea-stereotypes.html. Accessed 16 June 2021.

Pollard, Cheryl L. (2015), 'What is the right thing to do: Use of a relational ethic frame-work to guide clinical decision-making', *International Journal of Caring Sciences*, 8:2, pp. 362–68.

Purpel, David E. (1989), *The Moral & Spiritual Crisis in Education: A Curriculum for Justice and Compassion in Education*, Granby: Bergin & Garvey.

Quin, Edel, Rafferty, Sonia and Tomlinson, Charlotte (2015), *Safe Dance Practice*, Champaign: Human Kinetics.

Rachels, James and Rachels, Stuart (2007), *The Elements of Moral Philosophy*, New York: McGraw-Hill.

Read, Herbert (1967), *Art and Alienation: The Role of the Artist in Society*, New York: Horizon Press.

REDCAT (Roy and Edna Disney/Calarts Theater) (2014), http://www.redcat.org/event/antigone-srtwenty-looks-or-paris-burning-judson-church-l. Accessed 10 August 2014.

Reinhart, Charles (2012), telephone interview with author, 23 July.

Ridout, Nicholas (2009), *Theatre and Ethics*, New York: Palgrave Macmillan.

Risner, Doug (2002), 'Rehearsing heterosexuality: *Unspoken* truths in dance education', *Dance Research Journal*, 34:2 (Winter), pp. 63–78.

Risner, Doug (2008), 'Equity in dance education: Momentum for change', *Journal of Dance Education*, 8:3, pp. 75–78.

Risner, Doug and Stinson, Susan W. (2010), 'Moving social justice: Challenges, fears and possi-bilities in dance education', *International Journal of Education & the Arts*, 11:6, pp. 1–26, https://files.eric.ed.gov/fulltext/EJ881573.pdf. Accessed 24 June 2021.

Risner, Douglas S. and Schupp, Karen (2020), *Ethical Dilemmas in Dance Education: Case Studies on Humanizing Dance Pedagogy*, Jefferson: McFarland & Company.

Risse, Mathias (2000), 'The morally decent person', *Southern Journal of Philosophy*, 38, pp. 263–79.

Riva, Laura (2017), 'The dancer's bill of rights and obligations', *The Dancing Grapevine, Danceplace*, 2 February, https://danceplace.com/grapevine/the-dancers-bill-of-rights-and-obligations/. Accessed 16 June 2021.

Rolnick, Melissa (2020), personal correspondence with author, 18 July.

Rosenberg, Doug (2022), 'It was there all along: Theorizing a Jewish narrative of dance and (post-)modernism', in N. M. Jackson, R. Pappas and T. Shapiro-Phim (eds), *The Oxford Handbook of Jewishness and Dance*, New York: Oxford University Press, pp. 404–29.

Roses-Thema, Cynthia (2008), *Rhetorical Moves: Reclaiming the Dancer as Rhetor in a Dance Performance*, Saarbrückenm: VDM Publishing.

Rossen, Rebecca (2014), *Dancing Jewish: Jewish identity in American Modern and Postmodern Dance*, New York: Oxford University Press.

Rouhiainen, L. (2008), 'Somatic dance as a means of cultivating ethically embodied subjects', *Research in Dance Education*, 9:3, pp. 241–56.

Roy, Sanjoy (1998), 'Marmalade Me by Jill Johnston', *Dance Now*, Autumn, pp. 92–94.

Rubidge, Sarah (2004), 'Artists in the academy: Reflections on artistic practice as research', *Dance Rebooted: Initializing the Grid*, 1 July, https://ausdance.org.au/articles/details/artists-in-the-academy-reflections-on-artistic-practice-as-research. Accessed 25 June 2021.

Rubidge, Sarah (2000), 'Identity in flux: A theoretical and choreographic enquiry into the identity of the open dance work', doctoral dissertation, London: City University London.

Ryan, Richard M. and Deci, Edward L. (2006), 'Self-regulation and the problem of human autonomy: Does pscychology need choice, self-determinism, and will?', *Journal of Personality*, 74:6, pp. 1557–86.

Said, Edward Wadie (1978), *Orientalism*, New York: Pantheon Books.

Sandoval, Greg (2008), 'Globetrotting YouTube dancer shares his tech secrets', *c/net*, 10 July, https://www.cnet.com/news/globetrotting-youtube-dancer-shares-his-tech-secrets/. Accessed 1 June 2021.

Santiago, John (2008), 'Confucian ethics in the analects as virtue ethics', *Philosophical Ideas and Artistic Pursuits in the Traditions of Asia and the West: An NEH Faculty Humanities Workshop. Paper 8*, http://dc.cod.edu/nehscholarship/8. Accessed 15 June 2021.

Sarkis, Stephanie (2012), '65 Quotes on dancing', *Psychology Today*, 17 February, http://www.psychologytoday.com/blog/here-there-and-everywhere/201202/65-quotes-dancing. Accessed 7 May 2012.

Scanlon, Thomas (1998), *What We Owe to Each Other*, Cambridge, MA and London, England: The Belknap Press of Harvard University Press.

Schechter, Dave (2016), 'Are Jews white? It's complicated', *Atlanta Jewish Times*, 19 December, https://atlantajewishtimes.timesofisrael.com/jews-white-complicated/. Accessed 18 June 2021.

Schiller, Gretchen (2015), 'Grasping gestures. Practice based research', *Hermès, La Revue*, 2:72, pp. 98–102, https://www.cairn.info/revue-hermes-la-revue-2015-2-page-98.htm. Accessed 25 June 2021.

Schwadron, Hannah and Marks, Victoria (2022), 'I, you, we: Dancing interconnections and Jewish betweens', in N. M. Jackson, R. Pappas and T. Shapiro-Phim (eds), *The Oxford Handbook of Jewishness and Dance*, New York: Oxford University Press, pp. 277–87.

Schyns, Birgit and Schilling, Jan (2013), 'How bad are the effects of bad leaders? A meta-analysis of destructive leadership and its outcomes', *The Leadership Quarterly*, 24:1, pp. 138–58.

Scott, Walter (ed.) (1808), *The Works of John Dryden*, vol. 5, London: James Ballantyne and Co, https://www.gutenberg.org/files/16208/16208-h/16208-h.htm. Accessed 2 July 2021.

Senior, Jennifer (2002), 'Mark Morris', *New York*, 5 December, http://nymag.com/nymetro/arts/dance/n_8102/. Accessed 16 June 2021.

Severn, Margaret (1992), 'Scenes from a dancer's life, Part one: 1910–1919', *Dance Chronicle*, 15:3, pp. 253–90.

Shapiro, Sherry (1998), *Dance, Power, and Difference: Critical and Feminist Perspectives on Dance Education*, Champaign: Human Kinetics.

Sheehy, Brett (2009), 'Confessions of a gatekeeper', *Address to the Inaugural Currency House/Australia Business Arts Foundation*, 31 March, https://currencyhouse.org.au/sites/default/files/ConfessionsGatekeeper.pdf. Accessed 18 June 2021.

Sherman, Jane and Schlundt, Christena L. (1986), 'Who's St. Denis? What is she?', *Dance Chronicle*, 10:3, pp. 305–29.

Shiner, Larry (2003), *The Invention of Art: A Cultural History*, Chicago: University of Chicago Press.

Shusterman, Richard (2008), *Body Consciousness: A Philosophy of Mindfulness and Somaesthetics*, Cambridge: Cambridge University Press.

Siegel, Marcia B. (1977), *Watching the Dance Go By*, New York: Houghton Mifflin.

Siegel, Marcia B. (1998), 'Bridging the critical distance', in A. Carter (ed.), *The Routledge Dance Studies Reader*, New York: Routledge, pp. 91–97.

Siegel, Marcia B. (2001), 'Using lexicons for performance research: Three duets', in G. Berghaus (ed.), *New Approaches to Theatre Studies and Performance Analysis*, Berlin: De Gruyter, pp. 205–16.

Siegel, Marcia B. (2005), 'Critical Practice in the Age of Spin', *DCA News* Winter 2005, Dance Critics Association, p. 1.

Siegel, Marcia B. (2011), personal correspondence with author, 12 July.

Simon, Scott (2013), 'Fosse's genius: Working even as he was dying', *Interview with Sam Wasson*, Weekend Edition Saturday, 2 November, https://www.npr.org/2013/11/02/242536059/fosses-genius-working-even-as-he-was-dying. Accessed 17 June 2021.

Smith, Christian (2011), *What Is a Person?: Rethinking Humanity, Social Life, and the Moral Good from the Person Up*, Chicago: University of Chicago Press.

Smith, Ralph Alexander (2006), *Culture and the Arts in Education: Critical Essays on Shaping Human Experience*, New York: Teachers College Press.

Sontag, Susan (2001), *Against Interpretation and Other Essays*, New York: Picador.

Sparti, Barbara (1996), 'The function and status of dance in the 15th-century Italian courts', *Dance Research*, 14:1, pp. 42–61.

Spears, Larry (1996), 'Reflections on Robert K. Greenleaf and servant-leadership', *Leadership & Organization Development Journal*, 17:7, pp. 33–35, http://dx.doi.org.ezproxy1.lib.asu.edu/10.1108/01437739610148367.

Springer, Dawn (2006), 'The right to move: An examination of dance, Cabaret Laws, and social movements', *Proceedings of the Society of Dance History Scholars*, June, pp. 117–23.

Stahl, Jennifer (2018), 'Alastair Macaulay says goodbye: What it's been like as the controversial chief dance critic', *Dance Magazine*, 31 October, https://www.dancemagazine.com/alastair-macaulay-2615485861.html?rebelltitem=5#rebelltitem5. Accessed 18 June 2021.

'Statement of Values and Code of Ethics', APAP, https://www.apap365.org/Portals/1/PDFs/About/Statement%20of%20Values%20and%20Code%20of%20Ethics%202016.pdf. Accessed 18 June 2021.

Stauffer, David C. and Maxwell, Delois L. (2020), 'Transforming servant leadership, organizational culture, change, sustainability, and courageous leadership', *Journal of Leadership, Accountability and Ethics*, 17:1, pp. 105–16.

Steinwald, Michèle (2014), 'Noticing the feedback: A proposal to the contemporary dance field, and/or this revolution will be crowdsourced', Proceedings Envisioning the Practice: International Symposium on Performing Arts Curation, Montréal, 2012, pp. 22–38.

Stephens, E. J. (2011), 'Busby Berkeley: Chaos and Complexity', *Deadwrite's Dailies*, 14 March, https://deadwrite.wordpress.com/tag/busby-berkeley/. Accessed 19 June 2021.

Stinson, Susan (1984), *Reflections and Visions A Hermeneutic Study of Dangers and Possibilities in Dance Education*, Greensboro: University of North Carolina at Greensboro.

Stinson, Susan (1985a), 'An argument for social and moral arts curricula', in T. Barrett and J. Koroscik (eds), *Proceedings of the Annual Meeting of the American Educational Research Association, March 31–April 4, 1985: Arts and Learning SIG*, Washington, DC: American Educational Research Association, pp. 68–75.

Stinson, Susan (1985b), 'Curriculum and the morality of aesthetics', *Journal of Curriculum Theorizing*, 6:3, pp. 66–83.

Stinson, Susan (2004), 'Professional ethics and personal values: Intersections and decisions in dance education', *Proceedings International Dance Conference, Ethics and Politics Embodied in Dance, Theatre Academy Helsinki*, pp. 23–35, http://citeseerx.ist.psu.edu/viewdoc/download?doi=10.1.1.453.792&rep=rep1&type=pdf. Accessed 16 June 2021.

Stinson, Susan W., Blumenfeld-Jones, Donald and Dyke, Jan Van (1990), 'Voices of young women dance students: An interpretive study of meaning in dance', *Dance Research Journal*, 22:2, pp. 13–22.

Stone, Gregory A., Russell, Robert F. and Patterson, Kathleen (2004), 'Transformational versus servant leadership: A difference in leader focus', *Leadership & Organization Development Journal*, 25:4, pp. 349–61.

Swann, Carol, Leguizamann, Zea, Grant, Sam and Eddy, Martha (2021), 'Social Somatics', http://www.carolswann.net/social-somatics/. Accessed 17 June 2021.

Szilard, Paul (2002), *Under My Wings: My Life as an Impresario*, New York: Limelight Editions.

Szporer, Philip (2014), 'Criticism as a contested concept', *Dance Chronicle*, 37:2, pp. 189–94.

Tangen, Rulan (2015), 'Awardee Rulan Tangen', https://www.artheals.org/ahn-awardee/rulan-tangen-2015-ahn-awardee.html. Accessed 15 January. Note: The Arts & Healing Network officially closed in December 2015.

Taper, Bernard (1996), *Balanchine: A Biography*, Berkeley: University of California Press.

Taubert, Gottfried (2012), *The Compleat Dancing Master a Translation of Gottfried Taubert's Rechtschaffener Tantzmeister (1717)*, vols 1 and 2 (translated with introduction and annotation by T. Russell), New York: Peter Lang.

Thomas, J. D. (1969), 'The intentional strategy in Oscar Wilde's dialogues', *English Literature in Transition, 1880–1920*, 12:1, pp. 11–20.

Thomas, Robyn and Hardy, Cynthia (2011), 'Reframing resistance to organizational change', *Scandinavian Journal of Management*, 27:3, pp. 322–31.

Thompson, James and Fisher, Amanda Stuart (2020), *Performing Care: New Perspectives on Socially Engaged Performance*, Manchester: Manchester University Press.

The Today Show (2010), '"Fat" Ballerina: "I'm not overweight"', *Today Show*, NBC, 12 December, https://www.today.com/video/fat-ballerina-im-not-overweight-44652099714. Accessed 2 July 2021.

Tolstoy, Leo (1995), *What Is Art?*, New York: Penguin Books.

Torres, Leonardo Giron (2020), 'Injury + opportunity in PopAction', *Streb*, 28 August, https://www.facebook.com/watch/?v=355212142170971. Accessed 25 June 2021.

Tucker, Shawn R. (2015), *The Virtues and Vices in the Arts: A Sourcebook*, Eugene: Cascade Books.

United States. Congress. House. Committee on Un-American Activities (1953), *Investigation of Communist Activities in the New York City Area: Hearings, Parts 5-8*, Washington: U.S. Government.

United States, National Commission for the Protection of Human Subjects of Biomedical and Behavioral Research (1978), *The Belmont Report: Ethical Principles and Guidelines for the Protection of Human Subjects of Research*, Bethesda: The Commission, U.S. Government Print. Off.

US Bureau of Labor Statistics (2009), 'Occupational employment and wage statistics', https://www.bls.gov/oes/tables.htm. Accessed 29 June 2021.

U.S. Department of Health & Human Services (n.d.), 'The office of research integrity', https://ori.hhs.gov/content/chapter-3-The-Protection-of-Human-Subjects-Definitions. Accessed 25 June 2021.

Universal Declaration of Human Rights, United Nations, http://www.un.org/en/documents/udhr/. Accessed 7 May 2012.

USA Gymnastics Code of Ethical Conduct (2021), 'Code of Ethical Conduct', https://usagym.org/PDFs/AboutUSAGymnastics/code_ethical_conduct.pdf Accessed 28 December 2021.

Villarreal, Alexandra (2018), '"It's like a cult": How sexual misconduct permeates the World of Ballet', *The Guardian*, 2 November, https://www.theguardian.com/stage/2018/nov/02/ballet-stage-me-too-sexual-abuse-harassment. Accessed 22 June 2021.

Voarino, N., Couture, V., Mathieu-Chartier, S., St-Hilaire, E., Williams-Jones, B., Lapointe, F. J., Noury, C., Cloutier, M. and Gauthier, P. (2019), 'Mapping responsible conduct in the uncharted field of research-creation: A scoping review', *Accountability in Research*, 26:5, pp. 311–46.

von Bismarck, Beatrice (2013), 'Extra academy #17: Beatrice von Bismarck: capitalizing attitudes – Re-enacting exhibitions', *Extra City*, November, https://extracitykunsthal.be/en/events/extra-academy-17-beatrice-von-bismarck-2. Accessed 30 June 2021.

Walker, Margaret (2007a), 'The politics of transparency and the moral work of truth', in *Moral Understandings: A Feminist Study in Ethics*, 2nd ed., New York: Oxford University Press, pp. 211–34.

Walker, Margaret (2007b), *Moral Understandings: A Feminist Study in Ethics*, 2nd ed., New York: Oxford University Press.

Wagner, Ann (1997), *Adversaries of Dance: From the Puritans to the Present*, Urbana and Chicago: University of Illinois Press.

Warburton, Edward C. (2004), 'Who cares? Teaching and learning care in dance', *Journal of Dance Education*, 4:3, pp. 88–96, http://search.ebscohost.com.ezproxy1.lib.asu.edu/login.aspx?direct=true&db=s3h&AN=SPHS-958052&site=ehost-live&scope=site. Accessed 17 June 2021.

Wasik, Kathy (2012), 'Skin deep', *The Performance Club*, 9 November, https://theperformance-club.org/skin-deep/. Accessed 27 June 2021.

Wasson, Sam (2013), *Fosse*, Boston: Houghton Mifflin Harcourt.

Way, Brenda (2005), 'Brenda Way, artistic dance director, answers questions', *Grist*, 1 March, http://www.grist.org/article/way2. Accessed 15 June 2021.

Webster, Paul (2002), 'Little "rats" of Paris Opera suffer for their ballet fame', *The Observer*, 8 December, http://www.guardian.co.uk/world/2002/dec/08/france.arts. Accessed 2 January 2021.

Wetzel, Ralf and Renterghem, Nathalie Van (2015), 'How to access organizational informality: Using movement improvisation to address embodied organizational knowledge', *Organizational Aesthetics*, 5:1, pp. 47–63.

Whyte, Raewyn Joy (1989), 'Writing dancing: The scope and limits of contemporary modern dance criticism', MA thesis, Vancouver: Simon Fraser University.

Wilde, Oscar (1891), 'The soul of man under Socialism', https://www.marxists.org/reference/archive/wilde-oscar/soul-man/. Accessed 13 June 2021.

Wilde, Oscar (1905), *Intentions*, New York: Brentano's.

Wilkens, Steve (2011), *Beyond Bumper Sticker Ethics*, 2nd ed., Westmont: InterVarsity Press.

Willis, Tara Aisha (2017), 'Walking with UBW: An interview with Chanon Judson by Tara Aisha Willis', *Urban Bush Women Choreographic Center Initiative*, 4 January, http://www.urban-bushwomencenter.org/voicesfromthebush/?offset=1489505976967. Accessed 15 June 2021.

Wittkower, Rudolf and Wittkower, Margot (2007), *Born Under Saturn: The Character and Conduct of Artists: A Documented History from Antiquity to the French Revolution*, New York: New York Review of Books.

Wookey, Sara (2015), *Who Cares? Dance in the Gallery and Museum*, London: Siobhan Davis Dance.

Wookey, Sara (2011), 'Open letter to artists', *The Performance Club*, 23 November, https://theperformanceclub.org/open-letter-to-artists/. Accessed 23 June 2021.

Wozny, Nancy (2018), 'What these five choreographers actually think of their reviews', *Dance Magazine*, 11 July, https://www.dancemagazine.com/dance-reviews-2585511975.html. Accessed 18 June 2021.

Wozny, Nancy (2020), 'What do dance curators actually do?' *Dance Magazine*, 20 March, https://www.dancemagazine.com/dance-curators-2645501519.html?rebelltitem=2#rebelltitem2. Accessed 18 June 2021.

Wray, Ama (2017), 'Embodiology® What is it?', https://vimeo.com/231471427. Accessed 26 June 2021.

Wray, Ama (2014), '"Embodiology" by Dr. Sheron Wray, UC-Irvine; embodied knowledge: Sensory studies in the 21st Century', *University of Wisconsin-Madison*, 3 October, https://www.youtube.com/watch?v=ZtOgys79OUE. Accessed 26 June 2021.

Wright, Emily (2021), *Dancing to Transform: How Concert Dance Becomes Religious in American Christianity*, Bristol: Intellect.

Zeitner, David, Rowe, Nicholas and Jackson, Brad (2015), 'Embodied and embodiary leadership: Experiential learning in dance and leadership education', *Organizational Aesthetics*, 5:1, pp. 167–87.

Zoladz, Lindsay (2019), '"Fosse/Verdon" was at its best when it was doing what Bob Fosse couldn't do himself', *The Ringer*, 28 May, https://www.theringer.com/pop-culture/2019/5/28/18643234/fosse-verdon-finale-season-sam-rockwell-michelle-williams-fx. Accessed 15 June 2021.

Zollar, Jawole Willa Jo (2014), 'Jawole Willa Jo Zollar: Coming together to create', *Faith & Leadership*, 10 February, https://faithandleadership.com/jawole-willa-jo-zollar-coming-together-create. Accessed 15 June 2021.

Index

CPSIA information can be obtained
at www.ICGtesting.com
Printed in the USA
BVHW061711080922
646354BV00003B/18